Although he spends part of every summer in Norfolk, as an inveterate traveller, **ALEXANDER STEWART** (left), has walked, trekked and tramped in more than thirty countries around the world. Over the last fifteen years he has written guidebooks for several publishers including for Trailblazer: *New Zealand – The Great Walks*, *The Walker's Haute Route* and the original book on which this guide is based, *Peddars Way and Norfolk Coast Path*.

Author

Norfolk Coast Path and Peddars Way
First edition 2018

Publisher: Trailblazer Publications
The Old Manse, Tower Rd, Hindhead, Surrey, GU26 6SU, UK
info@trailblazer-guides.com ☐ trailblazer-guides.com

British Library Cataloguing in Publication Data
A catalogue record for this book is available from the British Library

ISBN 978-1-905864-98-0

© **Trailblazer 2018**: Text and maps

Series Editor: Anna Jacomb-Hood   **Editor and layout**: Anna Jacomb-Hood
Cartography: Nick Hill   **Proof-reading**: Clare Weldon   **Index**: Jane Thomas
Photographs: © Alexander Stewart (except flora & bird photos © Bryn Thomas)

The maps in this guide were prepared from out-of-Crown-
copyright Ordnance Survey maps amended and updated by Trailblazer.

Dedication

For Katie, Rory, Merryn and Esme, who love this place.

Acknowledgements

I'd like to thank the people all along the Peddars Way and Norfolk Coast Path who assist-
ed me with the research for this book, showed me such hospitality and took time to answer
my many, many queries. As ever, thanks to the team at Trailblazer as well: Bryn Thomas
for encouraging me to explore this stunning region and providing me with the opportunity
to write and travel; Anna Jacomb-Hood for diligently editing and tying the text together to
make this a better book; Nick Hill for interpreting my drawings and producing the maps,
Clare Weldon for proofreading and Jane Thomas for the index.
    Thank you, too, to all the Trailblazer readers who wrote in with comments and sugges-
tions; in particular, Keith Apps, Allison Bradnock, Carol Buxton, Matthew Chaddock,
Marlene Cousins, Alison Gibson, Maurice Humphries, Chris Layton and Tania Young.

A request

The author and publisher have tried to ensure that this guide is as accurate and up to date
as possible. Nevertheless things change. If you notice any changes or omissions that should
be included in the next edition of this book, please write to Trailblazer (address on p2 or
email us at info@trailblazer-guides.com. A free copy of the next edition will be sent to per-
sons making a significant contribution.

Warning: long distance walking can be dangerous

Please read the notes on when to go (pp13-16) and outdoor safety (pp83-6). Every effort
has been made by the author and publisher to ensure that the information contained herein
is as accurate and up to date as possible. However, they are unable to accept responsibility
for any inconvenience, loss or injury sustained by anyone as a result of the advice and information given in this guide.

Updated information will be available on: ☐ **www.trailblazer-guides.com**

Photos – This page: Tower Windmill, just outside Burnham Overy Staithe (see p151)
Front cover and previous page: Beach huts on Wells beach (p158)
Overleaf: Big skies over Holkham Beach (p154) © Alexander Stewart

Printed in China; print production by D'Print (☎ +65-6581 3832), Singapore

Norfolk
Coast Path &
PEDDARS WAY

KNETTISHALL HEATH – HUNSTANTON – HOPTON-ON-SEA

77 large-scale maps & guides to 45 towns and villages

PLANNING – PLACES TO STAY – PLACES TO EAT

ALEXANDER STEWART

TRAILBLAZER PUBLICATIONS

INTRODUCTION

PART 1: PLANNING YOUR WALK

PART 2: THE ENVIRONMENT & NATURE

PART 3: MINIMUM IMPACT WALKING & OUTDOOR SAFETY

Contents

PART 4: ROUTE GUIDE AND MAPS

Using this guide
Trail maps 87

APPENDICES

Contents

ABOUT THIS BOOK

This guidebook contains all the information you need. The hard work has been done for you so you can plan your trip from home without spending hours on the internet or perusing the usual pile of books, maps and guides.

When you're all packed and ready to go, there's comprehensive public transport information to get you to and from the trail and 64 detailed maps (1:20,000) and 13 town plans to help you find your way along it. The route guide section includes:

● All standards of accommodation with reviews of campsites, hostels, B&Bs, guesthouses and hotels
● Walking companies if you want an organised tour and baggage-transfer services if you just want your luggage carried
● Suggested itineraries for all types of walkers
● Answers to all your questions: when to go, degree of difficulty, what to pack, and how much the whole walking holiday will cost
● Walking times and GPS waypoints
● Cafés, pubs, tearooms, takeaways, restaurants and shops for buying supplies
● Rail, bus and taxi information for all places along the path
● Maps of the main towns and villages: Thetford, Castle Acre, Old Hunstanton, Hunstanton, Burnham Deepdale, Wells-next-the-Sea, Cley next the Sea, Sheringham, Cromer, Mundesley, Sea Palling and Great Yarmouth
● Historical, cultural and geographical background information

---

❏ MINIMUM IMPACT FOR MAXIMUM INSIGHT

Everybody needs a break; climb a mountain or jump in a lake.
Christy Moore, *Lisdoonvarna*

Why is walking in wild and solitary places so satisfying? Partly it is the sheer physical pleasure: sometimes pitting one's strength against the elements, sometimes relaxing on the springy turf or sand. The beauty and wonder of the natural world restore our sense of proportion, freeing us from the stresses and strains of everyday life.

All this the countryside gives us and the least we can do is to safeguard it by supporting rural economies, local businesses and environmentally sensitive forms of transport, and low-impact methods of farming and land use. In this book there is a detailed and illustrated chapter on the wildlife and conservation of Norfolk and a chapter on minimum impact walking with ideas on how to tread lightly in this fragile environment. By following these principles we can help to preserve our natural heritage for future generations.

About this book

INTRODUCTION

In that country of luminous landscapes and wide horizons where the wind runs in the reeds and the slow rivers flow to our cold sea, a man may still sense and live something of the older England which was uninhabited, free and natural.
Alan Savory, *Norfolk Fowler*

On the surface, the Peddars Way and Norfolk Coast Path seem unlikely companion routes. One is an ancient 'dry' route to the shoreline whilst the other is a more modern trail vulnerable to the vagaries of the North Sea. However, this marriage of convenience results in one of the most straightforward and enjoyable National Trails to walk.

> ... one of the most straightforward and enjoyable National Trails to walk

It was Noel Coward, in *Private Lives*, who labelled Norfolk 'very flat', dismissing at a stroke Britain's fifth largest county as being rather dull. True, this is a peaceful, undramatic countryside without mountain ranges, valleys or major towns, yet it is full of subtle charms, littered with picturesque villages and populated with

Above: Approaching Wells harbour from the beach.

secret spaces, wild shores and some spectacular scenery, all bathed in a very particular light created by the area's legendary wide skies.

Heading north on the Peddars Way there's time to ponder the bewildering notion that the Romans, who created the path, were far from the first to pass this way. Even then the route from Knettishall Heath to the coast, from the forested Suffolk–Norfolk border to the sea, was an ancient highway, a safe, dry chalk ridge above the treacherous mudflats, fens and marshes. There is a lazy roll to the fields and farmland, nothing too taxing for your lungs or legs, but enough to change the perspective thus concealing a windmill or church tower, hiding the remnants of Neolithic and Bronze Age civilisations, and delaying tantalising glimpses of the coast. This part of Norfolk has always had a raw deal and is rarely thought of in the same light as the more celebrated northern coast. As a result, it is quieter and emptier, but no less magical. The landscape around Little Cressingham, Castle Acre and Sedgeford is frequently underrated but if you are willing to forgo a few urban pleasures for a couple of days this timeless stretch of Norfolk is very rewarding.

The Romans, who created the path, were far from the first to pass this way.

Dog-legs in the notoriously straight Roman road near Ringstead lead to the sea, where there is an unassuming meeting of the two paths at Holme. Nothing prepares you for the scale and beauty of the North Norfolk coast. From here on the Coast Path bears both west to Hunstanton – the official start point of the

Norfolk Coast Path – and east towards Cromer and on to Hopton-on-Sea. The Coast Path combines brisk head-up walking over beach, bunker and boardwalk, through fragile dunes and past salt-marshes, crumbling cliffs, and creeks of fast-filling, fast-emptying tidal water. Along this stretch there is a constant blurring of sea, salt, sand and sky, but rather than making the area too similar the coastline has an ever-changing beauty.

The western half of the coast path enjoys vast expanses of beach and dunes with plenty of sand and space between amenities, while the central section is a little tamer and tidier, with the sand succumbing to shingle and traditional fishing communities giving way to the charms of faded Victorian seaside towns such as Wells, Sheringham and Cromer. Nonetheless there are still some unmissable villages such as Stiffkey, Morston, Blakeney and Cley containing little more than a glorious church and a cluster of cottages centred on a pub serving outstanding food and

Above: Many villages in Norfolk have colourful signs featuring their crests. **Below**: Holkham Hall (see p156) is three miles from the trail and can be visited.

local ale. There are also some of the best nature reserves and wildlife or bird-spotting sites in the country. Beyond the pier at Cromer the eastern end of the coast path leans to the right as it rounds the long shoulder of Norfolk and heads towards Suffolk, to finish south of Great Yarmouth. Given the lack of information on this section of the coast you'd be forgiven for thinking that there's nothing here. The reality is that there are vast sandy beaches at Waxham, Horsey and Winterton-on-Sea that are a match for the beautiful beaches on the north coast. There's a seal colony right on the shore that rivals the breeding grounds at Blakeney Point. A number of once fashionable, upmarket seaside destinations act as counterpoints to the pleasure beaches and kiss-me-quick charm of the larger towns like Great Yarmouth.

In its full form, this is a walk to saunter along and savour in every respect; the many gastro pubs and restaurants boast some of the finest, freshest ingredients that Britain has to offer. Ecclesiastical remains all along the route are indicative of the wealth and status the region once enjoyed; the churches built on the profits of a thriving medieval wool trade are almost always worth a visit as are the grand Palladian-style houses. Walk slowly with your eyes open and spend time exploring this landscape with its simple lines and succumb to its many and varied charms.

HISTORY

The route of the **Peddars Way** is a combination of the historic and the more modern, the old and the purposely created. First used by migrating animals and then the hunters who pursued them, the remnants of ancient travellers are visible as shards of worked flint and Bronze Age tumuli. The path as we now know it was developed around AD61, when the Romans established routes across East Anglia in the wake of the defeat of the Iceni (a Celtic tribe who inhabited areas covered by modern-day Norfolk between the 1st century BC and the 1st century AD) and Queen Boudica (also written as Boudicca and Boadicea). The military route that was to become the Peddars Way, established between the Roman garrison at Colchester and the heart of Iceni land, was meant to offer access to all areas of the region and allow troops to police the rebellious territory. As with most Roman roads it was built in a straight line and constructed from locally sourced material.

❏ **England Coast Path**

With a projected total length of 2795 miles, the England Coast Path will cover the country's entire seashore and in so doing, be one of the world's longest walking routes. The stretches of English coastline that do not yet have pedestrian rights of way are in various stages of negotiation to establish access for walkers, with the goal being to open the England Coast Path in 2020. Joining sections such as the South West Coast Path and substantial stretches of the coasts of Sussex, Kent, Essex and Northumbria, the extension between Cromer and the border of Norfolk and Suffolk was up and running – or walking – by 2017.

It wasn't until the 15th or 16th centuries though that it was dubbed the Peddars Way in respect to the pilgrims who would walk the route to the coast and the religious centre at Walsingham. In fact, it is just the best known of several 'Peddars Ways' which developed at this time, which may simply be a generic term or reference to a frequently walked path. Although the Romans had long since left, the Way remained as a landmark and defining feature of the landscape, used to mark boundaries, connect communities and transport goods.

Above: The wind has been a useful source of power in Norfolk for centuries, driving mills to grind corn or drain water. Many of Norfolk's once very numerous windmills still remain, though not all retain their sails. This example is at Mill Farm, north of Ringstead.

In contrast, the **Norfolk Coast Path** is a deliberately constructed route, made up from a series of existing footpaths and sections of trail created to link them. The two routes were connected to form a Long Distance Path, a title officially bestowed on them in 1986, when the route was opened by HRH The Prince of Wales in a ceremony on Holme beach. Five years later the Long Distance Paths became National Trails (see box p81), and the pair were duly accorded this status.

As part of an ambitious programme to complete the England Coast Path (see box opposite), a trail that connects the entire English coast with its countless inlets, estuaries and jagged bits, the Norfolk Coast Path was extended from Cromer right round to Hopton-on-Sea and the border with Suffolk.

HOW DIFFICULT ARE THE PATHS?

Neither of these is a technically demanding walk and most people with a reasonable level of fitness ought to be able to complete either or both without any problems. However, do not underestimate the distances, or Norfolk's seemingly flat landscape; there are still gradients to tackle and the path can stretch ahead interminably if you are not well prepared.

Most people with a reasonable level of fitness ought to be able to complete either or both paths without any problems

Although more isolated, the Peddars Way is more straightforward; the going on grassy tracks, green lanes (unsurfaced country ways often with hedges either side and sometimes quite old) and metalled roads is easy and the gradients gentle. However, the distances between villages are greater and there are extended sections without the opportunity to replenish supplies of water or food. Once on the coast, the gradients are more pronounced, the sand and shingle underfoot are more enervating, and the path is more exposed to the elements. Always be aware of the ever-present

Above: Both the Peddars Way and the Norfolk Coast Path are well signposted. Look for the acorn symbol which is used to designate all National Trails in England and Wales.

danger of cliff edges, especially on the section between Mundesley and Sea Palling, where the coast and crumbling cliffs are in a constant battle with erosion caused by the waves, one that they aren't winning. Cliff falls can occur all along the route though, such as on the section between Cromer and Overstrand, where a slip in February 2018 left the path only accessible at low tide. Take care too on the broad expanses of beach, especially as the tide turns. Be aware of steeply shelving beaches, treacherous currents and a strong undertow, especially at Cley and Weybourne. There are also sections of trail on the beaches of east Norfolk where you can't follow the official trail along the sands at high tide – look out for notices and if necessary take the alternative, inland route to stay safe. The marshes also pose a potential threat and should be approached with caution. Accidents often happen later in the day when people lose their footing or their bearings as fatigue sets in. Be aware of your level of ability and plan your day accordingly. Do not attempt to do too much in a single stretch, instead go slowly, relax and take in everything around you.

HOW LONG DO YOU NEED?

This depends on your fitness and level of ability. If you are new to multi-day trekking do not try to walk too far in one day. The Peddars Way is 46 miles (74km) long and the Norfolk Coast Path 85½ miles (137km). With the short

Most people comfortably complete the walk in around 10-13 days

section from the end of the Peddars Way at Holme to the official start of the Coast Path in Hunstanton, you will walk 134 miles (215km) if you cover the entire route described here. Although the National Trail can be completed in as little as seven days, most people comfortably complete the walk in around 10-13 days and still have time to explore the villages and towns along its length. If you want to enjoy the beaches, explore some of the historic churches

---

❏ **Peddars Way and Norfolk Coast Path certificate**
National Trails offer completion certificates to walkers who finish any of the designated routes, including either the Peddars Way, Norfolk Coast Path, or indeed the whole trail. Visit the website (🖥 shop.nationaltrail.co.uk/collections/certificates-badges) and click on 'Completion certificates' to fill in your details. If you buy a certificate (from £5), you also get free entry to their Hall of Fame. As a memento of your trip you can also buy woven cloth badges (from £3.50).

and houses or loiter in the seaside towns longer, allow closer to two weeks. Similarly, if you wish to make side trips or build in excursions to see the seals on Blakeney Point (see box p170) or the birds, particularly along the coast, factor in a couple more days.

If you are camping don't underestimate how much longer it will take you to carry a full pack and all your gear the same distance. Rather than yomping across the countryside, consider travelling more slowly; by taking it easy more of the area's subtle delights and secrets will become apparent. On pp31-3 there are some suggested itineraries for people walking at different speeds. If you only have a long weekend or a couple of days concentrate on the best bits; there is a list of recommended day and weekend walks in the box on pp34-5.

See pp31-3 for some suggested itineraries covering different walking speeds

INTRODUCTION

When to go

SEASONS

In general, Norfolk is dry in comparison to the rest of the UK, with Breckland (see p56) on the Norfolk–Suffolk border actually the driest part of the country.

However, Norfolk is exposed to the full force of the weather sweeping in from the North Sea so expect conditions to be changeable and be prepared for rain or a strong wind at any time of year. Equally, the area enjoys a high percentage of clear, sunny days when temperatures can soar. Although there are no obvious best times to go, the main walking season is from Easter to the end of September.

The main walking season is from Easter to the end of September

Spring
The fresh spring days can be particularly pleasant on the Peddars Way; as the weather warms up and the days grow longer the surrounding countryside begins to come to life, wild flowers start to bloom and crops in the cultivated fields begin to grow. Animals start to establish territories and look for a mate while in March birds begin to migrate to their summer breeding grounds. You can still be caught by a cold snap or icy wind well into May though, so be prepared for changeable conditions.

Summer
The popular tourist towns along the North Norfolk coast can get particularly busy during the school holidays in July and August as the weather is at its warmest. Wildlife is also at its most visible, with juvenile animals beginning to appear and chicks that have left the nest starting to search for their own food. By the end of the season birds become quieter as they moult their worn feathers, so head to the heathland or woodland to see the diverse flora instead.

Autumn

An attractive time of year with leaves changing colours and fruits, berries and nuts beginning to adorn the hedgerows. Birds begin to gather in preparation for their migration and animals start to look for suitable hibernation sites. By the end of the season, in October, summer migrant birds are replaced by winter migrants arriving from Scandinavia, Germany and Russia. This is also the rutting season for red and fallow deer, which fight to protect their territories and breeding females.

❑ FESTIVALS AND ANNUAL EVENTS

January to April

● **New Year's Day swim** – Takes place in a number of the coastal locations but most famously in the sea off Hunstanton.

● **University of East Anglia (UEA) Literary Festival** (🖳 uea.ac.uk/litfest) – A bi-annual literary festival in Norwich, showcasing work by many of Britain's finest writers and poets. Talks taking place throughout the spring, and also in the autumn.

● **Deepdale Hygge** (🖳 deepdalebackpackers.co.uk/hygge) A celebration of the North Norfolk Coast in late March; it is held at Burnham Deepdale (see p148).

● **Spring Craft Fair** – Craft exhibition and sale typically held on the last Saturday of April in the Queens Hall in Watton (see p100).

May/June

● **Poetry-next-the-Sea** – Small poetry and literary festival based in Wells-next-the-Sea on the second weekend in May, with poets from around the world giving readings.

● **Crab and Lobster Festival** (🖳 crabandlobsterfestival.co.uk) – Sheringham and Cromer. A two-day celebration of community and heritage in late May. Includes concerts, cookery demonstrations, the World Pier Crabbing Championship and a RNLI demonstration.

● **Houghton International Horse Trials** (🖳 musketeer.co.uk, click on Events) – Four-day event in the last week of May at Houghton Hall (see p120) with the world's leading riders competing. Plus falconry displays and other events for non-equestrians.

● **North Norfolk Country Fair** – Traditional fair held outside Weybourne on the last weekend in May, featuring stalls and craft sales as well as dog and bird displays.

● **Hunstanton & District Festival of Arts** (🖳 hdfa.org.uk) – Various events including music recitals held throughout the month, mostly at Princess Theatre (see p134).

● **Hunstanton Carnival** (🖳 hunstantoncarnival.co.uk) – Street entertainment, music, games and activities on the Green in Hunstanton, on the last Sunday of the month.

July

● **Holkham Country Fair** (🖳 holkhamcountryfair.co.uk) – Spectacular large-scale event with trade stands and performances celebrating the countryside, its traditions and its conservation, held every other year (odd-numbered years) in the grounds of Holkham Hall (see box p156) in mid-July.

● **Potty Morris & Folk Festival** (🖳 pottyfestival.com) – Around 20 teams of folk and morris dancers perform their traditional steps on the first weekend of July in Sheringham, using the Lobster Pub as the headquarters for the event.

● **Holt Festival** (🖳 holtfestival.org) – A celebration of the arts, featuring music, theatre, comedy, literature, fine art and spoken word performances on the streets and in venues in Holt during the last week of July.

Winter

Many locals claim that this is their favourite time of year, with the crowds of visitors dispersed yet the weather cold and crisp enough to still crunch along a shingle beach or stroll through a nature reserve where the trees are bare so you stand a better chance of spotting secretive birds. The weather can vary from crisp bright days to snow, rain or hail.

Throughout November thousands of geese arrive from their breeding grounds and seal pups are born.

July (cont'd)
● **British Superbike Championship** (🖳 britishsuperbike.com) – The UK road-racing superbike championship descends on the Snetterton Circuit north-east of Thetford (see p89) in mid-July for a round of high-speed racing.
● **British Touring Car Championship** (🖳 btcc.net/calendar/snetterton) – the Snetterton Circuit (see p89) plays host to a round of touring-car racing in late July.

August
● **Wells Carnival** (🖳 wellscarnival.co.uk) – A traditional summer carnival in the first week of August – processions, floats, fancy dress, competitions and activities for all.
● **Hunstanton Kite Festival and Classic Car Rally** (🖳 hunstanton-rotary.org.uk) – Displays of flying and acrobatics as well as other practical activities during the third week of August with some glorious classic cars also on display.
● **Cromer Carnival** (🖳 cromercarnival.co.uk) – One of the largest carnivals in the county, takes place in the third week of August with parades, competitions, fireworks and fancy dress.

September to December
● **North Norfolk Food & Drink Festival** (🖳 northnorfolkfoodfestival.co.uk) – Food stalls, cookery demonstrations and tasting sessions as well as other village-fête fare taking place over the first weekend of the month, in the walled garden at Holkham Hall (see p156).
● **Wells Pirate Festival** (🖳 wellsmaltings.org.uk/wells-pirate-festival) – A rollicking weekend of family fun around the quay and on the water that includes a smugglers ball, boat trips and historical recreations.
● **1940s' Weekend** – A popular event in Sheringham and Holt organised by North Norfolk Railway (see p182) that sees people dress up in uniform or 1940s' civilian dress for a weekend of music, food, vintage cars and veteran bicycles.
● **Deepdale Festival** (🖳 deepdalebackpackers.co.uk/festival) A small music festival in late September in Burnham Deepdale.
● **Norwich Beer Festival** (🖳 norwichcamra.org.uk) – Week-long festival in Norwich's St Andrew's and Blackfriars' Hall at the end of September, featuring more than 200 real ales from Britain's best independent breweries as well as a selection of bottled beers and ciders.
● **University of East Anglia (UEA) Literary Festival** – Autumn event of this literary festival; see UEA Literary Festival p14.
● **Norfolk Restaurant Week** (🖳 norfolkrestaurantweek.co.uk) – Make the most of almost 50 unmissably priced menus at some of the region's best restaurants in Norfolk's largest dining event, a culinary celebration of the vibrant food scene here late October/early November.

Average max/min temperatures (Norfolk)

Average rainfall (Norfolk)

Hours of daylight (Norwich)

TEMPERATURE

Norfolk sits at the crossroads of four wind patterns, with easterlies coming off the continent, southerlies carrying warmer air, westerlies bringing temperate conditions and northerlies channelling colder winds. Generally though, the Norfolk climate is temperate and even in winter the air temperature is relatively mild. Consequently, temperatures are generally quite comfortable at any time of year and on rare occasions the summer can actually get too hot for walking.

RAINFALL

Norfolk is relatively dry for the UK but can still occasionally feel the force of the violent weather systems that sweep in from the North Sea. Most rainfall occurs from late summer and into winter, with spring being a drier period.

DAYLIGHT HOURS

If walking in autumn (particularly after the clocks have changed; see box opposite), winter or early spring, you must take account of how far you can walk in the available light.

Colour photos (following pages)

● **C1 (opposite)**: Castle Acre (see p112) is said to have some of the finest village earthworks (**top**) in England. Also interesting are the ruins of the Cluniac Priory here (**middle**), founded in 1089. **Bottom**: The distinctive striped cliffs of Hunstanton.

● **C2 Left, top**: Brightly coloured beach huts on Wells beach; **bottom**: All Saints' Church, Thornham. **Right, top**: Approaching Thornham on the path along the sea defence wall; **Bottom**: Old fishing hull beached above a channel in the marshes, beneath big blue skies.

● **C3** The vast skies and wide sands of Holkham Beach (see p154).

● **C4 Left, top**: Lighthouse at Happisburgh (see p205). **Left, middle**: WW2 pillbox at Horsey Gap (p211). **Left, bottom**: Bridge over mudflats, Siffkey. **Right, top**: Boats moored in the channels by Morston harbour; **Bottom**: Eroded cliffs beyond Overstrand.

● **C5 Left, top**: Blakeney Point; samphire (**middle**, see p23) is perfect with most fish dishes; Blakeney's twin-towered church (**bottom**). **Right**: Boats moored at Blakeney Quay.

● **C6 Top left**: Cromer (see p189) and its famous pier.

HAPPISBURGH

PLANNING YOUR WALK

Practical information for the walker

ROUTE FINDING

This should be straightforward since the entire path is clearly visible, well-trodden and marked with clear signage. Finger-posts marked with an acorn symbol show the direction of the path at most junctions. The Peddars Way is perfectly straight in many places and can be seen arrowing across the countryside, while the Norfolk Coast Path largely follows the North Norfolk shoreline, occasionally detouring inland. Where you have to cross Great Yarmouth to conclude the trek, look for stickers showing the National Trail acorn symbol on lampposts instead of the traditional finger signposts.

GPS

While modern Wainwrights will scoff, more open-minded walkers will accept that GPS technology can be an inexpensive, well-established if non-essential navigational aid. In no time at all a GPS receiver with a clear view of the sky will establish your position and altitude in a variety of formats, including the British OS grid system, to within a few metres. However, a GPS is not a replacement for a map and compass. Although modern units are robust and durable, it only takes a flat battery to render them useless. You should view the two systems as compatible and use both older and newer technologies together. A GPS will prevent you from making exaggerated errors when navigating and will reduce the time it takes to correct mistakes if you do stray off the path.

Using GPS with this book is an option. Without it you could end up ambling confidently along the wrong path. With it you can quickly establish your position and work out how to return to your last known position on the trail.

Using GPS with this book

It is not expected that you will walk along checking off the GPS waypoints found throughout the book, since the detailed maps and route

---

(Opposite) The windmill at Cley next the Sea is now a B&B (see p174).

descriptions are more than sufficient for finding your way on the Peddars Way and Norfolk Coast Path most of the time. Only when you are unsure of your position or need reassurance as to which way to go might you feel the need to reach for your GPS for confirmation.

The maps in the route guide include numbered waypoints; these correlate to the list on pp229-31, which gives the latitude/longitude position in a decimal minute format as well as a description. Where the path is vague, or there are several alternatives, you will find more waypoints. Typically landmarks or other significant features are also waymarked. Waypoints are less common in towns or villages but can still be found to help you pin down the path ahead or identify a junction.

You can manually key the nearest presumed waypoint from the list into your GPS as and when the need arises. Alternatively, with less room for error when inputting the co-ordinates, download the complete list for free as a GPS-readable file (that doesn't include the text descriptions) from the Trailblazer website. You'll need the correct cable and adequate memory in your unit (typically the ability to store 500 waypoints or more). The file as well as instructions on how to interpret an OS grid reference can be found on the Trailblazer website: 🖳 trailblazer-guides.com.

It's also possible to buy state-of-the-art digital mapping to import into your GPS unit, assuming that you have sufficient memory capacity, but it's not the most reliable way of navigating and the small screen on your pocket-sized unit will invariably fail to put places into context or give you the 'big picture'. This is also a far more expensive option than buying the traditional OS paper maps which, whilst bulkier, are always preferable.

Bear in mind that the vast majority of people who tackle the Peddars Way and Norfolk Coast Path do so perfectly successfully **without** a GPS unit. Instead of rushing out to invest in one, consider putting the money towards good-quality waterproofs or footwear instead. That said, a GPS unit may assist in the odd dicey decision, and if used correctly in tandem with this book's waypoints might just see you safely to the next pub or overnight stop that much more quickly.

ACCOMMODATION

Accommodation is available along the length of the Peddars Way and Norfolk Coast Path. However, there is not a lot of choice along the Peddars Way, which passes through a thinly populated part of the county, and on occasions there are just one or two options each night. In these instances you may find it difficult to pick and choose something appropriate for your budget so may opt to detour from the path to one of the larger nearby villages or towns, where you will generally find a wider range of places to stay.

Once you arrive on the coast there is generally more choice, from campsites to luxury hotels, although as you head round the coast from Cromer towards Hopton-on-Sea there is substantially less than on the more popular North Norfolk Coast. The route guide (Part 4) includes a full selection of places to stay both on the trail and in the nearby villages.

Book all accommodation in advance (see box p20), especially during the high season (Easter to September). Pre-planning is crucial, particularly for barren areas such as the start of the Peddars Way.

Also take into account the fact that although there are fewer people on the trail outside the summer season there are, however, fewer beds as some establishments shut down over the winter months.

Camping

Camping is an excellent way of immersing yourself in a landscape and there is a great deal of satisfaction to be gained from spending both the day and night in the great outdoors. Technically **wild camping** (see p80) is not permitted anywhere along the Peddars Way or Norfolk Coast Path although a friendly farmer or landowner may allow you to pitch a tent in a field. However, there are several official campsites, with basic facilities such as shower and toilet blocks, charging £5-18 per person, making this the most economical way of walking the path.

You may need to use B&B-style accommodation not only on the Peddars Way and on the Coast Path between Cromer and Hopton-on-Sea, but also if you are planning short days as the campsites are not spaced evenly along the path. Equally at certain times of year you may find them closed, so will have to make alternative arrangements.

Hostels

Hostels (both YHA and independent) are good places to meet like-minded fellow walkers and allow you to travel on a budget without having to carry camping gear. Rates (including bedding) are £10-20.50pp per night. However, there aren't any hostels on the Peddars Way, nor are there any along the Coast Path beyond Sheringham, so you will need to find alternative accommodation.

There are two comfortable, modern YHA hostels in Wells-next-the-Sea and Sheringham, and an independently run hostel at Hunstanton, that is affiliated to the YHA. In addition to traditional dorm rooms the hostels offer private rooms. Washing facilities are generally shared but increasingly en suite facilities are available. All have well-equipped kitchens (but Sheringham and Hunstanton also provide meals for an extra charge), a lounge and communal area as well as a drying room for wet gear. Credit cards are accepted and wi-fi/internet access is available. Booked beds are usually saved until 6pm on the day, so it's worth phoning ahead if you are unlikely to arrive before this time. See also box below.

The **independent hostel** at Burnham Deepdale has the same advantages as a YHA hostel in that it offers affordable accommodation in dormitory or private rooms (some with en suite facilities), provides bed linen and has a fully equipped

❏ **Youth Hostels Association**
You can join the Youth Hostels Association (**YHA**) of England and Wales (☎ 0800-019 1700 or ☎ 01629-592700, 🖥 yha.org.uk) at either of the hostels on the route, or over the phone or online; see their website for details. Despite their name YHA hostels are for anyone of any age. If you aren't a member you can still stay at the hostels but you must pay a £3 supplement for each night's stay.

(side margin) PLANNING YOUR WALK

kitchen, but it is more informal and has fewer regulations. The Old Red Lion (see p114) in Castle Acre effectively operates as an independent hostel.

The only **bunkhouse** accommodation is at Courtyard Farm, just outside Ringstead. Although it is more basic, the barn is full of character and well worth visiting, if only for one night. Good value at just £15pp, the drawback is that you will need to bring your own bedding and cooking equipment.

Bed and Breakfasts (B&Bs)

B&Bs are a great British tradition, and Norfolk boasts some excellent examples of this type of accommodation. They vary greatly in terms of style and quality, and also in price, but usually consist of a bed in someone's house and a substantial cooked breakfast to start the day. For visitors from outside the UK it can provide an insight into the daily routines and workings of a family home.

What to expect Most walkers are after a hot bath and a comfortable bed after a day on the trail. The B&Bs featured in this guide are selected because of their proximity to the path and therefore their usefulness to the walker.

Places vary but in general few have **single rooms (S)** so if you are walking on your own you are likely to have to pay a single occupancy supplement to stay in a twin or double room.

Twin (T) and **double (D) rooms** are often confused, but a twin usually contains two single beds whilst a double has just the one double bed. **Triple/quad rooms** sleep up to three/four people but most of these have a double bed and one/two single beds or bunk beds; thus two people in a group of three or four, may have to share the double bed. The room can also be used as a double or twin. Rooms are often en suite, but some have separate private or shared facilities; these tend to be slightly cheaper.

❑ Booking accommodation

You should always book your accommodation. In summer there can be a lot of competition for beds and in winter some of the properties shut. However, in the peak season many places have a **minimum stay policy** of at least two nights for advance bookings, though nearer the time if they have a vacancy most will accept a single-night stay.

YHA hostels can be booked through the centralised reservation system over the phone or online (see box p19), or through 🖥 hihostels.com. B&Bs, guesthouses, hotels and pubs can also often be booked online via their website or by email, but some places prefer people to call. Almost always you will get the best rate by booking direct rather than through an online booking agency.

Usually you will have to pay a **deposit** or the full charge at the time of booking. If you are unable to keep your reservation make sure you let the establishment know so they can offer it to someone else instead.

Apart from hostels many accommodation options are happy to accept dogs (this is noted in the text) and/or (young) children, but check in advance as not all do.

Some tourist information centres (see p46) offer a bed-booking service. They charge a £3 fee plus 10% of the first night's accommodation; the latter is deducted from the final bill paid to the proprietor. Alternatively, they can give you all the relevant contact details for places to stay.

Tariffs B&Bs vary in price from £25pp for two sharing for the most rudimentary accommodation to £110pp (or more) in rather more luxurious establishments. Most charge around £30-40pp for two sharing. Single occupancy of a double or twin room is usually available for a supplement, though in many cases in the peak season you will need to expect to pay the room rate. Rates are often lower during the winter months and you can cut costs further by asking for a room only rate.

Note that a lot of places to stay now apply flexible pricing, which means rates can vary from those quoted here.

Guesthouses, hotels, pubs and inns

One step up from B&Bs, **guesthouses** tend to be smarter and more sophisticated, with evening meals, a communal lounge and a bar for guests. Rates at guesthouses generally range from £30 to £50pp for two sharing.

Pubs and inns generally offer B&B-style accommodation, again with a bar within easy stumbling distance. Most along the route are high quality and relatively restrained, but you may find that noisy, tipsy neighbours are a problem if you are after an early night. Rates also range from £30 to £50pp for two sharing.

Hotels are usually less well equipped for walkers and the higher rates (from £100pp for two sharing) may put off the cash-conscious traveller. However, there are some good-value places to stay and you may well want to treat yourself in the course of your trip, particularly since there are some wonderful hostelries along the route.

Holiday cottages

If you are part of a small group or are considering basing yourself in one place for an extended period of time, consider a holiday cottage. This can be an effective way of exploring a section of the Norfolk Coast Path for instance using public transport (see pp51-4), travelling to and from a start and finish point each day. A good base for this type of trip would be one of the attractive villages along the coast as there is a good bus service.

Prices for cottages start around £150pp for a week based on 4-6 sharing, but vary considerably according to season, size of property and location. Cottages haven't been included in this book; contact the tourist information centre (see box p46) in the area for details of what's available. The Landmark Trust (⌨ landmarktrust.org.uk) also has a few properties in Norfolk.

Airbnb

The rise and rise of Airbnb (⌨ airbnb.co.uk) has seen private homes and apartments opened up to overnight travellers on an informal basis. While accommodation is primarily based in cities, the concept is spreading to tourist hotspots in more rural areas, but do check thoroughly what you are getting and the precise location. While the first couple of options listed may be in the area you're after, others may be far too far afield for walkers. At its best, this is a great way to meet local people in a relatively unstructured environment, but do be aware that these places are not registered B&Bs, so standards may vary, yet prices may not necessarily be any lower than the norm.

FOOD AND DRINK

Breakfast and lunch

If staying in B&B-style accommodation **breakfast** tends to be a hearty, substantial cooked meal with many ingredients sourced from local produce. The amount of food may be more than you are used to or indeed want; ask for a lighter continental or vegetarian version if you'd rather. Alternatively, if you want an early start, or prefer no breakfast, ask for a packed lunch instead.

A number of places offering B&B-style accommodation can also provide a packed **lunch** if given enough notice and for an additional fee. This is particularly useful on the Peddars Way where some stages pass though sections of countryside without access to places at which to buy food en route; check the route guide in Part 4 to make sure that you don't inadvertently go hungry. Alternatively, along much of the path there are bakeries or small shops where you can buy the ingredients to make your own. Cafés and pubs also often offer lunches, be it sandwiches or more substantial dishes.

Evening meals

Hotels and guesthouses usually offer an evening meal but most other accommodation options, other than pubs, don't. Most B&Bs are close enough to pubs or restaurants for you to have some choice in the evening. The proprietors of those that aren't may offer to run you to and from the nearest pub for supper.

The North Norfolk region is blessed with some outstanding **pubs** and inns, which will provide just the motivation for you to complete each daily section. Most offer both lunch and evening meals; some even open early to provide breakfast. The standard varies from hearty pub grub to be eaten in the bar to very high quality à la carte meals served in tasteful dining rooms. Although you might be happy with whatever is put in front of you after a hard day's walk, you'd do well to treat yourself occasionally to the best the region has to offer.

In many of the towns there are also excellent **restaurants**, with seasonal menus often influenced by the proximity of the sea and the local farmland. The larger seaside towns also have **takeaway** joints and cheap fast-food options as well as the ubiquitous fish & chips vans. Open later than most restaurants, often till after 11pm, they can come in handy if you finish your day late.

Buying camping supplies

If you are camping, food, fuel and outdoor equipment become important considerations. There aren't many equipment shops along the route so come prepared with whatever you think you'll need. During the summer you can usually buy fuel from campsite shops as well as general stores in the larger towns. Remember though that these may be shut during the winter months or only open for a limited number of hours. Check the services details in Part 4 for more information. The Peddars Way is particularly barren when it comes to trying to source supplies of any kind.

Drinking water

The exposed North Norfolk countryside and wide-open beaches can get very hot during the summer months, therefore you may need to drink as much as 2-4 litres

❏ Local food

Norfolk has a strong tradition of farming and walkers will soon see the benefits when sampling the local produce. Being stuck out of the way has meant that Norfolk eateries have also had to strive to attract attention. The result is that the region is now known for its fantastic local produce and there are scores of good-quality restaurants, pubs and delis, making it an ideal destination for foodies.

● **Seafood** Drawing on the bountiful reserves right on its doorstep, each of the coastal villages has developed a seafood speciality: Brancaster its mussels, Stiffkey its cockles (see p166), Wells its whelks, Sheringham its lobsters and Cromer its crabs. Head to the Smokehouse in Cley (see p174) to pick up umpteen delicious varieties of seafood, such as North Norfolk kippers, preserved using a traditional process.

The main **seasons** are: **mussels** – best in 'ber' months ie September to December; **crabs** – late March to early October; **lobsters** – July to October; **cockles** – January to April; **whelks** – June to September.

● **Game, meat & poultry** The grain fields and coastal marshes shelter a mass of game: partridge, quail, woodcock, wild duck and pheasant. The area is also known for its Norfolk Black turkeys, famous for their distinctive, gamey flavour. Hare also frequently appears on menus, as does rare-breed pork, organic lamb and naturally reared beef. Venison from the grounds of Houghton Hall is also available in butchers and restaurants.

The main **seasons** are; **partridge** – September to February; **quail** – year-round but best June to September; **woodcock** – October to January; **wild duck** – September to January; **pheasant** – October to February.

● **Cheese** Cheese-making is another skill associated with the area. Catherine Temple, of Mrs Temple's Cheeses close to Wells, makes the finest in East Anglia; you can pick up her wares in delis in towns and villages throughout North Norfolk. Try the simple Wighton; mature, crumbly, Cheshire-style Walsingham; or the creamy, semi-soft Binham Blue. Elsewhere look for: Norfolk Dapple, a hard cheddar-style cheese with a distinctive dappled rind; Norfolk Tawny, which is bathed in Norfolk strong dark ale; and Norfolk White Lady, a soft, slightly sharp sheep's milk cheese.

● **Mustard** The fields around Norwich are also full of brilliant yellow mustard seed, used to produce hot English mustard. The name **Colman** is synonymous with the stuff. Originally a flour miller, Jeremiah Colman began to mill mustard seed in 1814 and the Colman factory still produces mustard to this day.

● **Samphire** Samphire (see also p74), sometimes referred to as 'glasswort' or more colloquially as 'poor man's asparagus', is a wild, succulent sea vegetable that can be harvested all along the coast. The season starts in June and lasts until about August; samphire can be cooked like French beans or pickled, as was popular in Victorian times. During the season bundles are often for sale from stalls outside houses in the villages adjacent to the sea. Delicious organic vegetables are widely available as well.

● **Treacle tart** Norfolk is as famous for its **treacle tart** as the North East, although both versions differ slightly; the Norfolk tart is sometimes referred to as Norfolk treacle custard tart but actually it's just a lighter version, with a subtle hint of lemon.

❏ **LOCAL BEERS AND CIDERS**

The fields of barley seen during the summer also fuel the region's burgeoning micro-brewery business. In fact, there are more than 30 breweries in the county, making it the second most prolific in terms of production. Each produces distinctive ales and distributes them to pubs and restaurants in the area.

While walking the path though, try the following to pick up a flavour of the area.

Beers

● **Woodforde's** (🖥 woodfordes.co.uk) Woodforde's, based in Drayton, are the county's leading brewer and produce award-winning bitters. Their signature beer, **Woodforde's Wherry** (3.8%) is fresh and zesty and widely available. Also worth trying are: **Nelson's Revenge** (4.5%), an amber-coloured rich bitter that's slightly sweet and citrusy; **Admiral's Reserve** (5%), a strong copper-coloured, fruit-flavoured beer that's dangerously drinkable; and **Sundew** (4.1%), a subtle, golden beer that's lighter and more refreshing. Alternatively, try **Mardler's** (3.5%), a nut-brown mild, or **Norfolk Nog** (4.6%), a smooth, rich, ruby-red ale with a velvety texture. The more adventurous might want to consider Woodforde's barley wines; the aptly named **Headcracker** (7%) is pale but strong and full-bodied, while **Norfolk Nip** (8%) is a dark mahogany drink with an intense flavour.

● **Brancaster Brewery** (🖥 brancasterbrewery.co.uk) Competition comes from Brancaster, a five-barrel brewery yards from the Jolly Sailors pub in Brancaster Staithe (see p146). Try their **Brancaster Best** (3.8%), a refreshing, hoppy pale ale; **Oyster Catcher** (4.2%), a fuller-bodied beer with a distinct flavour; **Malthouse Bitter** (4.4%), a pale amber ale; or a pint of **The Wreck** (4.9%), a malty, coffee-flavoured beer named after the wreck of the *SS Vina* which lies just off Brancaster Beach.

● **Tipple's** (🖥 tipplesbrewery.com) A relatively recent addition to the local brew world, Tipples have gained a good reputation for their classic English ales: **Redhead** (4.2%), an amber-coloured bitter with a slightly nutty flavour and **Hanged Monk** (3.8%), a deep-coloured, sweeter mild, are both worth keeping an eye out for.

Ciders

Cider drinkers should look out for **Whin Hill Norfolk Cider** (🖥 whinhillnorfolk cider.co.uk); the apples and pears for their ciders, perrys and apple juices are grown on their own orchards 10 miles south-west of Wells and then pressed using equipment housed in old 18th-century barns and outbuildings adjacent to the main car park in town. There is also a shop in Wells (see p159) selling their produce.

of water a day. If you're feeling lethargic it may be that you are dehydrated, so force yourself to consume some water, even if you don't feel thirsty. Avoid drinking directly from streams and waterways that run alongside or cross the path; the water tends to have flowed across farmland and is unlikely to be safe to drink.

Drinking-water taps and water fountains are marked on the maps in the route guide. Where they are sparse you could ask a shopkeeper or pub landlord for a glass of water or to fill your bottle from their tap.

MONEY

On some sections of the path, particularly the Peddars Way, there is a distinct lack of **banks** and **ATMs**. Although some local convenience stores and other independent shops offer '**cashback**', where they advance you a sum of money against a debit or credit card; a minimum spend may be required. Some Link ATMs are also 'pay to use'; the charges for withdrawing money are clearly posted on the machine.

With this in mind, it is a good idea to take plenty of **cash**, discretely stashed in a moneybelt for security. Although pubs, restaurants and hotels may allow you to pay by debit or credit card, smaller shops, B&Bs and campsites often insist on cash. Some hostels accept debit/credit cards but cash is always safest.

See also p43 and the town and village facilities table on pp36-9.

Using the post office for banking

Several British banks have agreements with the Post Office to allow customers to make cash withdrawals using a chip-and-pin debit card over the counter at post offices throughout the country. Some post offices also have a free-to-use ATM. Although there are only a few post offices along the trail, they are a useful substitute for the walker. Visit 🖳 postoffice.co.uk and look under 'Products & Services' then 'Branch and banking services' for a full explanation of the service and use 'Branch Finder' for a full list of post office branches and their respective services.

OTHER SERVICES

Towns have at least one **supermarket** and most villages have a **grocery** or **convenience store**. Some villages and towns have a **post office** from where, in addition to getting cash (see above) you can mail back unnecessary items if your pack is too heavy. Thanks to the rise of smartphones, internet cafés are a rarer sight, but you'll still find **public internet access** in the libraries. Most libraries as well as pubs, cafés and B&Bs have **free wi-fi** for customers who have their own devices. Most towns have lost their **public telephones** – in the smaller villages, particularly in rural areas along the Peddars Way, the traditional red telephone boxes remain as heritage symbols, but have long since been disconnected.

In Part 4 special mention is made of services relevant to the walker such as banks, ATMs, outdoor equipment shops, launderettes, pharmacies and tourist information centres; the latter can be used for finding and booking accommodation amongst other things.

WALKING COMPANIES

For people looking to make their trip as straightforward and hassle free as possible, there are some specialist companies who offer a range of services from accommodation booking to self-guided tours.

At the time of writing no company provides a group/guided walking tour for this national trail.

Baggage transfer

HikeHelp (☎ 07879-495734, 🖳 hikehelp.co.uk; based in Hales) The only specialist bag courier service for these paths. They will collect your luggage just after breakfast and deliver it to your next overnight stop; they aim to ensure it arrives before you do. They cover the Norfolk Coast Path from Hunstanton to Hopton, and Peddars Way from Knettishall to Holme. They charge £12 per bag per day and the maximum weight per bag is 18kg.

Taxi firms can also provide a baggage-transfer service within a local area. Additionally, some **B&Bs** offer a similar service; where relevant, details are given in the route guide.

❏ **Information for foreign visitors**

● **Currency** The British pound (£) comes in notes of £100, £50, £20, £10 and £5, and coins of £2 and £1. The pound is divided into 100 pence (usually referred to as 'p', pronounced 'pee') which comes in silver coins of 50p, 20p, 10p and 5p, and copper coins of 2p and 1p.

● **Money** Up-to-date **rates of exchange** can be found on 🖳 xe.com/currencyconverter, at some post offices, or at any bank or travel agent.

● **Business hours** Most **village shops** are open Monday to Friday 9am-5pm and Saturday 9am-12.30pm, though some open as early as 7.30/8am; many also open on Sundays but not usually for the whole day. Occasionally you'll come across a local shop that closes at lunchtime on one day during the week, usually a Wednesday or Thursday; this is a throwback to the days when all towns and villages had an 'early closing day'. **Supermarkets** are open Monday to Saturday 8am-8pm (often longer) and on Sunday from about 9am to 5 or 6pm, though main branches of supermarkets generally open 10am-4pm or 11am-5pm.

Main **post offices** generally open Monday to Friday 9am-5pm and Saturday 9am-12.30pm though where the branch is in a shop PO services are sometimes available whenever the shop is open; **banks** typically open at 9.30/10am Monday to Friday and close at 3.30/4pm, though in some places both post offices and banks may open only two or three days a week and/or in the morning, or limited hours, only. **ATMs (cash machines)** located outside a bank, shop, post office or petrol station are open all the time, but any that are inside will be accessible only when that place is open. However, ones that charge, such as Link machines, may not accept foreign-issued cards.

Pub hours are less predictable as each pub may have different opening hours. However, most pubs on the Norfolk Coast Path and Peddars Way continue to follow the traditional Monday to Saturday 11am to 11pm, Sunday to 10.30pm, but some still close in the afternoon, especially during the winter months.

The last entry time to most **museums and galleries** is usually half an hour, or an hour, before the official closing time.

● **National (Bank) holidays** Most businesses in Norfolk (and the UK) are shut on 1st January, Good Friday and Easter Monday (March/April), the first and last Monday in May, the last Monday in August, 25th December and 26th December.

● **School holidays** State-school holidays in England are generally as follows: a one-week break late October, two weeks over Christmas and the New Year, a week mid February, two weeks around Easter, one week at the end of May/early June (to coincide with the bank holiday at the end of May) and five to six weeks from late July to early September. Private-school holidays fall at the same time, but tend to be slightly longer.

● **Documents** If you are a member of a National Trust organisation in your country bring your membership card as you should be entitled to free entry to National Trust properties and sites in the UK (see p61).

● **Travel/medical insurance** Although Britain's National Health Service (NHS) is free at the point of use, that is only the case for residents. All visitors to Britain should

Self-guided holidays

These are generally all-in packages which usually include detailed route advice, notes on itineraries, maps, accommodation booking, baggage transfer and transport to and from the start and finish of the walk. Most companies listed on p28 can also tailor-make a holiday. At the time of writing some companies offering the Norfolk Coast Path still finish at the original end point of Cromer, but it would be worth checking if this is still the case when you contact them.

be properly insured, including comprehensive health coverage. The **European Health Insurance Card (EHIC)** entitles EU nationals (on production of the EHIC card so ensure you bring it with you) to necessary medical treatment under the NHS while on a temporary visit here (probably until Brexit is complete, that is). For details, contact your national social security institution. However, this is not a substitute for proper medical cover on your travel insurance for unforeseen bills and for getting you home should that be necessary.

Also consider cover for loss and theft of personal belongings, especially if you are camping or staying in hostels, as there may be times when you'll have to leave your luggage unattended.

● **Weights and measures** In Britain milk is sold in pints (1 pint = 568ml), as is beer in pubs, though most other liquid including petrol (gasoline) and diesel is sold in litres. Distances on road and path signs are given in miles (1 mile = 1.6km) rather than kilometres, and yards (1yd = 0.9m) rather than metres. The population remains divided between those who still use inches (1 inch = 2.5cm), feet (1ft = 0.3m) and yards and those who are happy with millimetres, centimetres and metres; you'll often be told that 'it's only a hundred yards or so' to somewhere, rather than a hundred metres or so. Most food is sold in metric weights (g and kg) but the imperial weights of pounds (lb: 1lb = 453g) and ounces (oz: 1oz = 28g) are frequently displayed too. The weather – a frequent topic of conversation – is also an issue: while most forecasts predict temperatures in Celsius (C), many people continue to think in terms of Fahrenheit (F; see the temperature chart on p16 for conversions).

● **Time** During the winter the whole of Britain is on Greenwich Mean Time (GMT). The clocks move one hour forward on the last Sunday in March, remaining on British Summer Time (BST) until the last Sunday in October.

● **Smoking** Smoking in enclosed public places is banned. The ban relates not only to pubs and restaurants, but also to B&Bs, hostels and hotels. These latter have the right to designate one or more bedrooms where the occupants can smoke, but the ban is in force in all enclosed areas open to the public – even in a private home such as a B&B. Should you be foolhardy enough to light up in a no-smoking area, which includes pretty well any indoor public place, you could be fined, but it's the owners of the premises who suffer most if they fail to stop you, with a potential fine of £2500.

● **Telephones, internet access and wi-fi** From outside Britain the international country access code for Britain is ☎ 44 followed by the area code minus the first 0, and then the number you require. Within Britain, to call a landline number with the same code as the landline phone you are calling from, the code can be omitted: dial the number only. It's cheaper to phone at weekends and after 7pm and before 7am on weekdays. If you're using a **mobile (cell) phone** that is registered overseas, consider buying a local SIM card to keep costs down. See also p25.

● **Emergency services** For police, ambulance, fire brigade and coastguard dial ☎ 999 (or the EU standard number ☎ 112).

● **Absolute Escapes** (☎ 0131-240120, 🖳 absoluteescapes.com; Edinburgh) Offer seven itineraries in all for walking both paths together and separate trips for each one.

● **British and Irish Walks** (☎ 01242-254353, 🖳 britishandirishwalks.com; Cheltenham, Glos) Runs 6-day trips on both the Peddars Way and Norfolk Coast Path or the two can be combined; they can also tailor-make walks.

● **Celtic Trails** (☎ 01291-689774, 🖳 celtictrailswalkingholidays.co.uk; Chepstow) Itineraries on the Peddars Way (3-4 days), Norfolk Coast Path (3-5 days) and 6-10 days combining the two from Knettishall Heath to Cromer.

● **Contours Walking Holidays** (☎ 01629-821900, 🖳 contours.co.uk; Derbyshire) Offers 6- to 9-day trips as well as Peddars Way (3-4 days), Norfolk Coast Path (3-5 days) and a 2-day 'Taster' break (Brancaster to Blakeney).

● **Explore Norfolk** (☎ 07765 668188, 🖳 explorenorfolkuk.co.uk; King's Lynn, Norfolk) Offers walks along both paths and can tailor-make trips according to choice. They also publish a beach guide and walks with dogs (see p45).

● **Footpath Holidays** (☎ 01985-840049, 🖳 footpath-holidays.co.uk; Wilts) Provides a variety of itineraries along both paths and can tailor make as required; also offer a single-centred holiday of the highlights of the coast path.

● **Freedom Walking Holidays** (☎ 0773 388 5390, 🖳 freedomwalkingholidays .co.uk; Berks) Offers both paths and can adapt according to requirements.

● **HF Holidays** (☎ 0345 470 7558, 🖳 hfholidays.co.uk; Herts) Provides 7-day trips along Norfolk Coast Path from Hunstanton to Cromer.

● **Lets Go Walking** (☎ 020-7193 1252, 🖳 letsgowalking.com; Devon) Provides a variety of itineraries along Norfolk Coast Path and Peddars Way and can tailor make as required.

● **MarGins Walking and Glamping Holidays** (☎ 07787 534809, 🖳 walkand glamp.co.uk; Norfolk) Offers the Norfolk Coast Path (late Apr to end Sep) with accommodation in fully equipped, glamping tents which are set up for you.

● **Mickledore** (☎ 017687-72335, 🖳 mickledore.co.uk; Cumbria) Offers walks along both Norfolk Coast Path and Peddars Way either individually (3-4 days), or combined (6-9 days).

● **Responsible Travel** (☎ 01273-823700, 🖳 responsibletravel.com; Brighton) Walk the Norfolk Coast Path with their 5 days' walking/6 nights' itinerary.

● **The Walking Holiday Company** (☎ 01600-718219, 🖳 thewalkingholiday company.co.uk; Monmouthshire) A variety of itineraries lasting 3-10 days for either or both paths and can be tailored to your needs.

Guided holidays

● **RWH Travel** (☎ 01707-331133, 🖳 www.ramblersholidays.co.uk; Herts) Offer a 5-night 'Coast and Country Houses of Norfolk' holiday that focuses on gentle walking combined with sightseeing stately homes and country houses.

TAKING DOGS ON THE PEDDARS WAY & NORFOLK COAST PATH

Dogs and dog walkers are welcome on the Peddars Way and Norfolk Coast Path. Dogs are allowed on many of the beaches, and pubs or places to stay are often accommodating of them. There are though some areas where dogs are banned or must be kept on a lead at certain times of the year, most usually to minimise disturbance of wildlife such as little terns and ringed plovers that nest in the open and are very sensitive to dog disturbance. For more information, see pp231-3.

DISABLED ACCESS

Given Norfolk's reputation as a flat landscape it may come as no surprise to learn that sections of the Peddars Way and Coast Path are accessible by wheelchair. There are several sections where you can gain equal access to enjoy the countryside and coast although it's worth noting that the trail is frequently unsurfaced; along the sea walls at Sheringham and Cromer there is easy parking and a tarmac surface on which to explore. Elsewhere there are metalled surfaces and access to sections of board walk which may not be totally even but should be negotiable nonetheless. In this way it's possible to enjoy the saltmarsh and sea views at Holkham, Thornham and Blakeney. Between Old Hunstanton and Holme is a stretch of path that is alternately surfaced and unsurfaced but generally level and accessible.

The unsurfaced path between Holkham Gap and Pinewoods to the north of Wells is also readily accessible at either end, and even enough to tackle. To the east of Weybourne the cliff paths would provide spectacular views and several miles of accessible track, although there is a short section of compacted shingle to negotiate before joining the unsurfaced path. Both Snettisham Bird Reserve and Cley Marshes Reserve have hides with wheelchair access.

Sheringham Park on the outskirts of Sheringham has wheelchair-friendly waymarked paths leading to parkland views. Beyond Cromer there are large sections of path that make their way along the beaches. In places there's a promenade at the back of the beach that is accessible by wheelchair but often the only option is the sand, which is not.

Budgeting

The amount of money that you spend completing the walk will depend on the standard of accommodation you use and the quality of meals you enjoy. If you carry a tent, camp and cook your own meals you can expect to get by cheaply with minimal expenses. However, most people prefer some sort of night out and even the hardy camper may be tempted to swap their canvas for something more substantial when the rain is falling.

CAMPING

If you use the cheapest sites and prepare all your own meals from staple ingredients, you can survive on as little as £20-30 per person (pp) per day. However, if you want to factor in a meal out, a pint at the end of each day and a few unforeseen expenses along the route, it's more realistic to expect to spend £30-40pp per day.

HOSTELS AND BUNKHOUSES

Hostels/bunkhouse accommodation on the Norfolk Coast Path costs between £10 and £22.50pp. With the exception of the bunkhouse at Courtyard Farm, each has their own self-catering kitchen so you can save money by preparing meals using locally bought produce.

Occasionally you will need or want to eat out, which will increase your expenditure. Around £40-50pp should cover accommodation and the odd meal and post-walk ale. If you're going to eat out more nights than not, you ought to increase your budget to £60pp per day.

B&Bs, INNS, GUESTHOUSES AND HOTELS

B&B prices can be as little as £25pp per night (based on two sharing) but are often two to three times as much, especially if walking on your own as most establishments will levy a single occupancy supplement. The rate includes breakfast though. Incorporate a packed lunch, pint, pub meal and other expenses to your budget and you'll spend around £50-70pp per day.

If staying in a guesthouse or hotel, rates are likely to be higher; expect to pay £80-100pp per day. There are also opportunities along the route to stay in smart boutique accommodation that costs more than £100pp per night, and fine dining or Michelin-starred restaurants where you can blow the budget as well.

EXTRAS

Any number of forgotten items or last-minute expenses can eat into your budget so factor in a contingency fund for buses, ice-creams, beer, souvenirs, postcards and stamps; it all adds up!

Itineraries

The route guide in this book has not been split into rigid daily stages. Rather, it has been structured to provide you with accessible information in order to plan your own itinerary. The Peddars Way and Norfolk Coast Path can be tackled in various ways, the most challenging of which is to do it all in one go; this requires around 10-12 days.

Some people choose to complete the walk in three stages: The Peddars Way and coast path from Holme to Hunstanton; the coast path from Hunstanton to Cromer; and the remainder of the route from Cromer to Hopton-on-Sea. Alternatively, people tackle the trek as a series of short walks, returning year after year to do the next section. Others just pick and choose the best bits, skipping those areas that don't interest them as much. Still others go on linear day walks along the coast, using public transport to return to their base.

To help you plan your walk see the planning map (opposite the inside back cover) and the table of village and town facilities on pp36-9; the latter provides a full rundown of the essential information you will need regarding accommodation, eating options and services.

SUGGESTED ITINERARIES

The suggested itineraries in the boxes below, on p32 and on p33 may also be helpful; they are based on different accommodation types – camping, hostels and B&Bs – with each one then broken down into three alternatives according to how quickly you walk. These are only suggestions though; feel free to adapt them to your needs. You will need to factor in your travelling time before and after the walk too.

PLANNING YOUR WALK

CAMPING								
Relaxed			**Medium**			**Fast**		
Place	Approx Distance		Place	Approx Distance		Place	Approx Distance	
Night	miles	km		miles	km		miles	km
Peddars Way								
0 Knettishall Heath*			Knettishall Heath*			Knettishall Heath*		
1 (Merton)*	14	22.5	(Merton)*	14	22.5	S Pickenham	17½	28
2 S Pickenham	6¼	10	S Pickenham	6¼	10	Castle Acre	9½	15
3 (Swaffham)	6¼	10	Castle Acre*	9½	15	Holme*	20	32
4 Castle Acre*	6¾	11	(Sedgeford)*	14	22.5	(Hunstanton* 2½		4)
5 (Gt Bircham)	12½	20	Holme*	6	9			
6 Ringstead	6¼	10	(Hunstanton* 2½		4)			
7 Holme*	3	4.5						
(Hunstanton*	2½	4)						
Norfolk Coast Path								
Hunstanton*			Hunstanton*			Hunstanton*		
8 Burnham Deepdale	12	19	Burnham Deepdale	12	19	Burnham Deepdale	12	19
9 Wells	10½	17	Wells	10½	17	Blakeney	18	29
10 Blakeney	8	13	Cley*	10½	17	Cromer*	17	27.5
11 Sheringham*	10½	17	Cromer*	14	22.5			
12 Cromer*	5	8						

Notes:
- Places in brackets are a short walk off the official Peddars Way/Norfolk Coast Path
- * Alternative to specified accommodation option
- Beyond Cromer the only camping option is at **Waxham** (see p211), just after Sea Palling, so some 19 miles on from Cromer and around 19 miles from Hopton. This could be used for the fast-pace timetable but is not relevant for the slower ones, where walkers will have to switch to B&B-style accommodation (as there are also no hostels).

Once you have worked out a schedule turn to Part 4 for detailed information on accommodation, places to eat and other services in each village and town both on the route and close to it. In Part 4 there are also summaries of the route to accompany the detailed trail maps.

WHICH DIRECTION?

Traditionally the Peddars Way is tackled south to north and then the Norfolk Coast Path west to east. This way you are drawn towards the sea and then able to explore the salt-marshes and nature reserves strung along the coast.

Some may choose to walk in the opposite direction. The maps in Part 4 give timings and since these are relevant in either direction the guide can easily be used in reverse or simply for day trips.

SIDE TRIPS

The Peddars Way and Norfolk Coast Path give a fairly thorough impression of what the region has to offer. However, there are some sections and highlights that are worth spending more time on, if you have additional days to spare.

STAYING IN HOSTELS/BUNKHOUSES

	Relaxed			Medium			Fast		
Place	**Approx Distance**		**Place**	**Approx Distance**		**Place**	**Approx Distance**	
Night	miles	km		miles	km		miles	km
Peddars Way								
0 Knettishall Heath*			Knettishall Heath*			Knettishall Heath*		
1 (Thompson)*	10½	17	L Cressingham*	14½	23.5	L Cressingham*	14½	23.5
2 L Cressingham*	5½	9	Castle Acre	11½	18.5	Castle Acre	11½	18.5
3 Castle Acre	11½	18.5	Ringstead	17	27.5	Holme*	20	32
4 (Gt Bircham)*	12½	20	Holme*	3	4.5	(Hunstanton 2½		4)
5 Ringstead	6¼	10	(Hunstanton	2½	4)			
6 Holme*	3	4.5						
(Hunstanton	2½	4)						
Norfolk Coast Path								
Hunstanton			Hunstanton			Hunstanton		
7 Burnham	12	19	Burnham	12	19	Wells-next-	22½	36
Deepdale			Deepdale			the-Sea		
8 Wells	10½	17	Wells	10½	17	Cromer*	24½	39
9 Blakeney*	8	13	Sheringham	19	30.5			
10 Sheringham	10½	17	Cromer*	5	8			
11 Cromer*	5	8						

Notes
● Places in brackets are a short walk off the official Peddars Way/Norfolk Coast Path
● * Alternative to specified accommodation option available
● Between Cromer and Hopton there is no hostel or bunkhouse-style place and there is only one campsite (see p211) so walkers will have to use B&B-style accommodation

PLANNING YOUR WALK

STAYING IN B&B-STYLE ACCOMMODATION

	Relaxed			Medium			Fast	
Place	**Approx Distance**		**Place**	**Approx Distance**		**Place**	**Approx Distance**	
Night	miles	km		miles	km		miles	km
Peddars Way								
0 Knettishall Heath*			Knettishall Heath*			Knettishall Heath*		
1 (Thompson)	10½	17	L Cressingham	14½	23.5	L Cressingham	14½	23.5
2 L Cressingham	5½	9	Castle Acre	11½	18.5	Castle Acre	11½	18.5
3 Castle Acre	11½	18.5	Ringstead	17	27.5	Holme	20	32
4 (Gt Bircham)	12½	20	Holme	3	4.5	*(Hunstanton*	*2½*	*4)*
5 Ringstead	6¼	10	*(Hunstanton*	*2½*	*4)*			
6 Holme	3	4.5						
(Hunstanton	*2½*	*4)*						
Norfolk Coast Path								
Hunstanton			Hunstanton			Hunstanton		
7 Brancaster	9½	15	Burnham O S	12	19	Wells	22½	36
8 Burnham O S	6¼	10	Wells	10½	17	Cromer	24½	39
9 Wells	6¾	11	Cley	10½	17	Sea Palling	18	29
10 Blakeney	8	13	Cromer	14	22.5	Hopton*	20½	33
11 Sheringham	11½	18.5	Happisburgh	14	22.5			
12 Cromer	6¼	10	Winterton	10½	17			
13 Mundesley	8	12.75	Hopton*	14	22			
14 Sea Palling	10	16						
15 Winterton	6½	10.5				**NB** Places in brackets are a		
16 Great Yarmouth	7¾	12.5				short walk off the official		
17 Hopton*	6¼	10				Peddars Way/Norfolk Coast Path		

* The closest accommodation to Knettishall Heath is in Thetford (see p91) and the closest to Hopton is in Gorleston (see p226)

The Great Eastern Pingo Trail (8 miles/13km) is on the eastern edge of the Brecks; the trail starts and finishes in Stow Beddon, just to the east of Thompson (see p97), and takes in Thompson Common, Thompson Water and the village itself. Much of the walk goes through wooded countryside and wetlands and incorporates a section of the Peddars Way.

Blakeney Circular Walk (4½ miles/7.25km) is a fantastic walk along the sea defences from Blakeney to Cley, past the marshes and bird reserves, that returns to the start point via Wiveton and Blakeney Rd. Both Blakeney and Cley are stops on Sanders No 4 bus route; see p54.

The **boat trips** to Blakeney Point (see box p170) make a relaxing change to walking and provide an excellent excursion on a day off. A trip to Scolt Head Island (see p150) is also worth doing. If you are interested in wildlife an additional day or two spent exploring the **salt-marshes** and **wildlife reserves** anywhere along the coast will not go amiss.

EXTENDING YOUR WALK

The Greater Ridgeway

If you want to extend the Peddars Way, consider starting your walk earlier on the Greater Ridgeway, which runs from Lyme Regis, on the west Dorset coast, all the way to Hunstanton.

From Lyme Regis, the **Wessex Ridgeway** goes to Marlborough, Wilts, from where it is an easy walk to join **The Ridgeway** (see p240) from Overton Hill to Ivinghoe Beacon; a series of green lanes, farm and forestry tracks and

❑ THE BEST DAY AND WEEKEND WALKS

The old mill near Burnham Overy.

If you don't have time to walk the entire trail the following day and weekend walks highlight some of the best sections of the Peddars Way and Norfolk Coast Path.

The Coast Path from Hunstanton to Mundesley is particularly good for short walks as it is well served by Lynx's Coastliner 36 and Sanders No 4 bus services (see box p54); unless specified, both ends of the routes described below are stops on, or very near, a bus route (see pp51-4). Beyond Mundesley public transport is much more limited and you should bear this in mind when planning a day walk.

Day walks

● **Ringstead to Old Hunstanton** – 4 miles/6.5km (see pp129-32) A chance to enjoy the transition from the county's wide open spaces to its coast at Holme, finishing with a gentle stroll along the dunes to an attractive town. This can be a circular route (approx 7 miles/11.5km) if you walk back along the narrow road running north-west/south-east between Ringstead and Old Hunstanton but the second half doesn't provide as much interest. Note, this route is only possible with a car as there's no public transport to Ringstead.

● **Holme to Thornham** – 3¼ miles/5.25km (see p132 & p139) A wonderful introduction to the coast and the bird reserves that can be found amidst the beaches and marshes.

● **Brancaster to Burnham Deepdale** – 2¼ miles/3.5km (see pp144-8) A gentle linear walk along the edge of the salt-marshes that takes in the Roman fort at Branodunum and finishes in Burnham Deepdale where there is an excellent pub overlooking the marshes in which to relax.

● **Brancaster to Holkham Gap** – 10 miles/16km (see pp144-53) A longer walk that takes you from the salt-marshes onto the spectacular sands at Holkham Gap where you can explore the pine-backed beach before accessing the main road and picking up the Coastliner bus. For a shorter version consider the 4-mile/6.5km section of path between Burnham Overy Staithe and Holkham Gap instead.

● **Holkham Gap to Wells** – 3 miles/4.75km (see pp153-8) A short stroll that starts on Holkham Beach and means you have time to explore this superb stretch of sand paths collectively known as the **Icknield Way** run along the chalk spine from Ivinghoe Beacon in the Chilterns to Knettishall Heath in Suffolk, passing through Baldock, Royston, Great Chesterford and Icklingham, to meet the Peddars Way and thus reach the coast at Hunstanton.

Other possibilities
For the similarly adventurous there is the 226-mile (363km) **Around Norfolk Walk** which connects the Nar Valley Way, Peddars Way, Norfolk Coast Path, Weavers' Way and Angles Way. *(cont'd on p38)*

before a pleasant and easy walk through an attractive forested stretch via the beach to the north of Wells and the causeway that leads to the town itself. Holkham Gap is three-quarters of a mile from Holkham which is a stop on the Coastliner bus route.

● **Stiffkey to Cley** – 7 miles/11.25km (see pp164-73) A chance to meander along some of the most spectacular and scenic salt-marsh sections of the trail, past the best bird reserves in the region, with Blakeney Point dominating the horizon.

● **Sheringham to Cromer** – 5½ miles/8.75km (see pp180-9) A chance to climb inland from the coast enjoying spectacular views from Beeston Bump before exploring the forested slopes surrounding the National Trust property at Roman Camp then looking back to the coast from Norfolk's highest point before finally descending once again to finish in a bustling town. You can complete a circuit by walking back along the beach to turn this into a 9-mile/14.5km loop.

● **Cromer to Mundesley** – 8 miles/12.5km (see pp194-9) A chance to move from the hustle and bustle of Cromer down the beach past the attractive outposts of Overstrand and Trimingham to arrive at the time-trapped Victorian resort of Mundesley. Both ends are stops on Sanders No 5 bus route.

● **Happisburgh to Sea Palling** – 4 miles/6.5km (see pp204-9) A gentle stroll from the pretty village of Happisburgh with its classic red and white ringed lighthouse down the beach to Sea Palling, past small bays and areas where little terns nest. Both ends are on Sanders limited No 34 service.

● **Sea Palling to Winterton-on-Sea** – 6½ miles/10.5km (see pp209-14) A wild and empty section of coast that you will often have to yourself, with the bonus of a seal colony at Horsey, right on the shoreline, where you can watch the seals close up. Sea Palling is a stop on Sanders No 34 bus service and Winterton on First's 1/1A.

Weekend walks
Much of the Norfolk Coast can be connected in 2-day walks, taking in a variety of landscapes, villages and larger coastal resorts. For ideas, consider combining some of the day trips outlined here.

● **Brancaster to Cley** – 23 miles/36.75km (see pp144-73) An outstanding stretch that showcases the best of the coastal scenery and wildlife reserves and allows you to overnight in Wells.

You'll find a good range of local seafood on most menus.

PLANNING YOUR WALK

Place name (Places in brackets are a short walk off the Peddars Way/ Norfolk Coast Path)	Distance from previous place approx miles	km	Cash Machine (ATM)/Bank (CB = cashback only)	Post Office	VILLAGE AND Tourist Information Centre (TIC)/ Point (TIP)/
PEDDARS WAY					
Thetford			✔		TIC
Knettishall Heath					
Stonebridge/East Wretham	6½	10.5			
(Thompson)	4	6.5	✔	✔	
(Watton)	3	4.5	✔	✔	TIP
		(6¾ / 10.75 from Stonebridge)			
Little Cressingham	3	5 (8 / 13 from Stonebridge)			
(Great Cressingham)	2½	4			
South Pickenham	2½	4 (3 / 4.5 from Little Cressingham)			
(Swaffham)	3¾	6 (5¾ / 9 from South Pickenham)			TIC
(Sporle)	3½	5.5 (5½ / 8.75 from South Pickenham)			
Castle Acre	4½	7.25	CB	✔	
		(9 / 14.5 from South Pickenham)			
(Great Massingham)	6¼	10		✔	
(Harpley)	4	6.5 (7½ / 12 from Castle Acre)			
(Great Bircham)	6¼	10 (12½ / 20 from Castle Acre)			
(Snettisham)	6¼	10 (15½ / 25 from Castle Acre)			
(Sedgeford)	3	4.5 (15½ / 25 from Castle Acre)			
Ringstead	3	4.5 (17 / 27 from Castle Acre) CB			
Holme-next-the-Sea	3	4.5 (plus 2½ / 4 to Hunstanton)			
NORFOLK COAST PATH					
Hunstanton	1¼	2	✔	✔	TIC
Old Hunstanton	1½	2.5		✔	
Thornham	5¼	8.5			
Brancaster	4	6.25			
Brancaster Staithe	1½	2.5			
Burnham Deepdale	½	1	CB		TIP
(Burnham Market)	1¾	2.75 (2¾ / 4.5 from Burnham Deepdale)			
Burnham Overy Staithe	3¾	6			
(Holkham)	4½	7.25 (3¾ / 6 from Burnham Overy Staithe)			
Wells-next-the-Sea	3¾	6	✔	✔	TIC
		(6¼ / 10 from Burnham Overy Staithe)			
Stiffkey	3¾	6			
Morston	3	4.5		✔	
Blakeney	1½	2.5	✔	✔	
Cley next the Sea	2½	4			
(Weybourne)	5½	9 (5½ / 9 from Cley)		✔	
Sheringham	3½	5.5 (8½ / 13.5 from Cley) ✔	✔	TIC	
(West Runton)	1¾	2.75		✔	
East Runton	1¼	2			
Cromer	4½	7.25 (5 / 8 from Sheringham) ✔	✔	TIC	
Overstrand	2	3.25	✔	✔	
Mundesley	6	9.5	✔	✔	
(cont'd on p38)					

(cont'd on p38)

TOWN FACILITIES

Eating Place	Food Store	Campsite	Hostels YHA/ H (IndHostel)/ B (Bunkhouse)	B&B-style accommodation	Place name (Places in brackets are a short walk off Peddars Way/ Norfolk Coast Path)
✔ = one ✔✔ = two ✔✔✔ = three +				✔ = one; ✔✔ = two ✔✔✔ = three+	
					PEDDARS WAY
✔✔✔	✔			✔✔✔	**Thetford**
					Knettishall Heath
✔				✔	**Stonebridge/E Wretham**
✔				✔✔✔	**(Thompson)**
✔✔✔				✔✔✔	**(Watton)**
				✔	**Little Cressingham**
✔				✔	**(Great Cressingham)**
		✔*			**South Pickenham**
✔✔✔		✔		✔✔	**(Swaffham)**
✔	✔				**(Sporle)**
✔✔	✔		H	✔✔	**Castle Acre**
✔	✔	✔*		✔✔	**(Great Massingham)**
				✔	**(Harpley)**
✔✔✔	✔	✔		✔	**(Great Bircham)**
✔				✔	**(Snettisham)**
✔				✔✔	**(Sedgeford)**
✔	✔	✔	B	✔✔	**Ringstead**
✔				✔	**Holme-next-the-Sea**
					NORFOLK COAST PATH
✔✔✔	✔		H	✔✔✔	**Hunstanton**
✔✔✔	✔			✔✔✔	**Old Hunstanton**
✔✔✔	✔			✔✔✔	**Thornham**
✔				✔	**Brancaster**
✔					**Brancaster Staithe**
✔✔	✔	✔	H	✔	**Burnham Deepdale**
				✔	**(Burnham Market)**
✔				✔	**Burnham Overy Staithe**
✔				✔	**(Holkham)**
✔✔✔	✔	✔*	YHA	✔✔✔	**Wells-next-the-Sea**
✔✔	✔	✔		✔	**Stiffkey**
✔✔				✔✔	**Morston**
✔✔✔	✔	✔*		✔✔✔	**Blakeney**
✔✔✔	✔			✔✔✔	**Cley next the Sea**
✔✔	✔	✔		✔	**(Weybourne)**
✔✔✔	✔		YHA	✔✔	**Sheringham**
✔✔		✔		✔	**(West Runton)**
✔		✔*			**East Runton**
✔✔✔	✔			✔✔✔	**Cromer**
✔✔✔				✔✔	**Overstrand**
✔✔✔	✔			✔✔✔	**Mundesley**
					* campsite is a short walk away (cont'd on p39)

					VILLAGE AND
Place name (Places in brackets are a short walk off the Peddars Way/ Norfolk Coast Path)	**Distance from previous place** approx **miles km**	**Cash Machine (ATM)/Bank** (CB = cashback only	**Post Office**	**Tourist Information Centre (TIC)/ Point (TIP)/**	
NORFOLK COAST PATH *(cont'd from p36)*					
Walcott	4	6.5	✔	✔	
Happisburgh	2	3.25			
Sea Palling	4	6.5	✔	✔	
Winterton-on-Sea	6½	10.5	✔		
Great Yarmouth	7¾	12.5	✔	✔	TIC
Gorleston	3¾	6			
Hopton-on-Sea	2½	4			

TOTAL DISTANCE: Peddars Way and Norfolk Coast Path 131½ miles (211km)

Peddars Way: Knettishall to Holme – 46 miles (74 km)
Holme to Hunstanton – 2½ miles (4km)

(cont'd from p35) The 34-mile (54km) **Nar Valley Way**, which starts in King's Lynn, runs through the watershed of the River Nar to cross the Peddars Way at Castle Acre, although it continues to its finish point at Gressenhall. At Cromer, you can continue to Great Yarmouth by tackling the 56-mile (90km) **Weavers' Way** which combines footpaths, disused railway lines and some sections of minor road to travel inland from the farmland and woodland of the north to the grazing marshes of the Broadland river valleys.

❏ **Cycling or horse-riding – alternatives to walking**

If you want to explore the region but don't fancy doing so on foot, it is possible to access sections of the **Peddars Way** on bike and horseback.

● **Cycling** The route is easily accessed via the SUSTRANS cycle network, which intersects the trail at various stages and can be used to link Thetford (Route 13) and King's Lynn (Route 1) railway stations with the Peddars Way. Most of the Peddars Way can be cycled as the route is largely classified as a bridleway, marked with blue arrows, or unsurfaced country road.

Although there are short sections of public footpath, for instance between Knettishall Heath and the A11 trunk road, immediately prior to North Pickenham, from Fring to just south of Ringstead and on the final approach to Holme-next-the-Sea, there are alternative road links to bypass them, indicated on the maps in Part 4. There are also a few places where the trail is classified as a footpath, but here it simply runs parallel to a tarmac road, usually on the grass verge; cyclists must use the road at these points. The result is an attractive 50-mile cycle trail between Thetford and Holme-next-the-Sea.

There is, however, no right to cycle on the Norfolk Coast Path. Instead, there is a specifically created cycleway (**The Norfolk Coast Cycleway**) which runs just inland from the coast between King's Lynn and Cromer, using National Cycle Network

TOWN FACILITIES

Eating Place	Food Store	Campsite	Hostels YHA/ H (IndHostel)/ B (Bunkhouse)	B&B-style accommodation	Place name (Places in brackets are a short walk off Peddars Way/ Norfolk Coast Path)
✔= one				✔ = one;	
✔✔= two				✔✔= two	
✔✔✔= three +				✔✔✔= three+	

NORFOLK COAST PATH *(cont'd from p37)*

✔✔	✔				**Walcott**
✔✔				✔	**Happisburgh**
✔✔✔		✔*		✔✔	**Sea Palling**
✔✔✔	✔			✔✔✔	**Winterton-on-Sea**
✔✔✔	✔			✔✔✔	**Great Yarmouth**
✔✔				✔	**Gorleston**
					Hopton-on-Sea

* campsite is a short walk away

Norfolk Coast Path: Hunstanton to Hopton-on-Sea 85½ miles (137km)

The **Angles Way** is a 77½-mile (125km) route linking the Broads to the Brecks, connecting Great Yarmouth with the Peddars Way at Knettishall Heath. Alternatively, if you prefer a circuit to a linear walk, consider the **Iceni Way**, an 80-mile (129km) path which connects Knettishall Heath to Hunstanton via Thetford, Brandon, King's Lynn, Sandringham and Snettisham. By linking this and the Peddars Way it is possible to create an attractive circular loop.

Route 1 between King's Lynn and Wighton to the south-east of Wells and Regional Route 30 from here to Cromer and beyond to Great Yarmouth. A map (£2) is available from tourist information centres in the area.

Bike hire, which usually includes suggested routes and specific maps, is possible from the following: **Black Bikes** (see map p183; ☎ 01263-822255, 🖳 black-bikes.co .uk; 28 Beeston Rd, Sheringham) offers mountain bikes for half-day, 1-day, 3-day or week-long hire; booking in advance (available online) is recommended between June and August; **On Yer Bike Cycle Hire** (☎ 07584-308120, 🖳 norfolkcyclehire.co.uk; Nutwood Farm, Binham Rd, Wighton) offers mountain bikes, tandems and tricycles for half-day or 1- to 5-day hire; they will also arrange delivery to and collection from your accommodation, subject to distance. Deepdale Backpackers and Campsite, in Burnham Deepdale, also offers cycle hire; see p148 for details.

If planning to cycle in Norfolk consider getting *Norfolk Cycle Map* published by CycleCity.

● **Horse-riding** It is also possible to ride much of the Peddars Way on horseback although again you cannot follow the path where it is designated a public footpath, and must use alternative detours or stick to the tarmac road. Again, there is no right to ride on the Norfolk Coast Path.

PLANNING YOUR WALK

What to take

Deciding how much to take with you can be difficult. Experienced walkers know that you should take only the bare essentials but at the same time you must ensure you have all the equipment necessary to make the trip safe and comfortable.

KEEP YOUR LUGGAGE LIGHT

Carrying a heavy rucksack really can ruin your enjoyment of a good walk and can also slow you down, turning an easy 7-mile day into an interminable slog. Be ruthless when you pack and leave behind all those little home comforts that you tell yourself don't weigh that much really. This advice is even more pertinent to campers who have added weight to carry.

HOW TO CARRY IT

The **size** of your **rucksack** depends on where you plan to stay and how you plan to eat. If you are camping and self-catering you will probably need a 65- to 75-litre rucksack which can hold the tent, sleeping bag, cooking equipment and food. Hostellers should find a 40- to 60-litre rucksack sufficient. If you have gone for the B&B option you will find a 30- to 40-litre day pack is more than enough to carry what you need.

Make sure your rucksack has a stiffened back and can be adjusted to fit your own back comfortably. This will make carrying the weight much easier. Also ensure the hip belt and chest strap (if there is one) are fastened tightly as this helps distribute the weight with most of it being carried on the hips. Rucksacks are decorated with seemingly pointless straps but if you adjust them correctly it can make a big difference to your personal comfort while walking.

When **packing** the rucksack make sure you have all the things you are likely to need during the day near the top or in the side pockets, especially if you don't have a bum bag or daypack. This includes water bottle, snacks, waterproofs, your camera and this guidebook (of course). A good habit to get into is to always put things in the same place and memorise where they are.

It's also a good idea to keep everything in **canoe bags**, **waterproof rucksack liners** or strong plastic bags. If you don't it's bound to rain.

Consider taking a small **bum bag** or **daypack** for your camera, guidebook and other essentials for when you go sightseeing or for a day walk.

FOOTWEAR

Boots

Your boots are the single most important item of gear that can affect the enjoyment of your trek. In summer you could get by with a light pair of trail shoes if you're only carrying a small pack, although this is an invitation for wet, cold feet if there is any rain and they don't offer much support for your ankles. Some of the terrain can be quite rough so a good pair of walking boots is a safer bet. They must fit well and be properly broken in. It is no good discovering that your boots are slowly murdering your feet three days into a week-long trek. See p85 for more blister-avoidance advice.

Socks
The traditional wearing of a thin liner sock under a thicker wool sock is no longer necessary if you choose a high-quality sock specially designed for walking. A high proportion of natural fibres makes them much more comfortable. Three pairs are ample.

Extra footwear
Some walkers have a second pair of shoes to wear when they are not on the trail. Trainers, sport sandals or flip flops are all suitable as long as they are light.

CLOTHES

Experienced walkers will know the importance of wearing the right clothes. Don't underestimate the weather: Norfolk juts out into the North Sea so it's important to protect yourself from the elements. The weather can be quite hot in the summer but spectacularly bad at any time of the year. Modern hi-tech outdoor clothes can seem baffling but it basically comes down to a base layer to transport sweat from your skin; a mid-layer or two to keep you warm; and an outer layer or 'shell' to protect you from the wind and rain.

Base layer
Cotton absorbs sweat, trapping it next to the skin and chilling you rapidly when you stop exercising. A thin lightweight **thermal top** of a synthetic material is better as it draws moisture away keeping you dry. It will be cool if worn on its own in hot weather and warm when worn under other clothes in the cold. A spare would be sensible. You may also like to bring a **shirt** for wearing in the evening.

Mid-layers
In the summer a woollen jumper or mid-weight polyester **fleece** will suffice. For the rest of the year you will need an extra layer to keep you warm. Both wool and fleece, unlike cotton, have the ability to stay reasonably warm when wet.

Outer layer
A **waterproof jacket** is essential year-round and will be much more comfortable (but also more expensive) if it's also 'breathable' to prevent the build up of condensation on the inside. This layer can also be worn to keep the wind off.

Leg wear
Whatever you wear on your legs it should be light, quick-drying and not restricting. Many British walkers find polyester tracksuit bottoms comfortable. Poly-cotton or microfibre trousers are excellent. Denim jeans should never be worn; if they get wet they become heavy and cold, and bind to your legs.

A pair of **shorts** is nice to have on sunny days. Thermal **longjohns** or thick tights are cosy if you're camping but are probably unnecessary even in winter. **Waterproof trousers** are necessary most of the year. In summer a pair of wind-proof and quick-drying trousers is useful in showery weather. **Gaiters** are not really necessary but you may appreciate then when the vegetation around your legs is wet.

Underwear

Three changes of what you normally wear is fine. Women may find a **sports bra** more comfortable because pack straps can cause bra straps to dig painfully into your shoulders.

Other clothes

A **warm hat** and **gloves** should always be kept in your rucksack; you never know when you might need them. In summer you should also carry a **sun hat** with you, preferably one which also covers the back of your neck. Another useful piece of summer equipment is a **swimsuit**; some of the beaches are irresistible on a hot day. Also consider a lightweight super-absorbent microfibre travel **towel**, especially if you are camping or staying in hostels.

TOILETRIES

Only take the minimum: a small bar of **soap** in a plastic container (unless staying in B&B-style accommodation) which can also be used instead of shaving cream and for washing clothes; a tiny tube of **toothpaste** and a **toothbrush**; and one roll of **loo paper** in a plastic bag. If you are planning to defecate outdoors you will also need a lightweight **trowel** for burying the evidence (see pp79-80 for further tips). In addition a **razor**; **deodorant**; **tampons/sanitary towels** and a high-factor **sun screen** should cover all your needs.

FIRST-AID KIT

Medical facilities in Britain are excellent so you only need a small kit to cover common problems and emergencies; pack it in a waterproof container. A basic kit should contain: **aspirin** or **paracetamol** for treating mild to moderate pain and fever; **plasters/Band Aids** for minor cuts; **Moleskin**, **Compeed**, or **Second Skin** for blisters; a **bandage** for holding dressings, splints or limbs in place and for supporting a sprained ankle; elastic knee support (tubigrip) for a weak knee; a small selection of different-sized **sterile dressings** for wounds; **porous adhesive tape**; **antiseptic wipes**; **antiseptic cream**; **safety pins**; **tweezers** and **scissors**.

GENERAL ITEMS

Essential

The following should be in everyone's rucksack: a one-litre **water bottle or pouch**; a **torch** (flashlight) with spare bulb and batteries in case you end up walking after dark; **emergency food** (see p83) which your body can quickly convert into energy; a **penknife**; a **watch** with an alarm, although a smart-

PLANNING YOUR WALK

phone will also perform this function; and a **plastic bag** for packing out any rubbish you accumulate. A **whistle** is also worth taking; although you are very unlikely to need it you may be grateful of it in the unlikely event of an emergency (see p83).

Useful

Many would list a **camera** as essential but it can be liberating to travel without one once in a while; a **notebook** can be a more accurate way of recording your impressions. Other things you may find useful include a **book** to pass the time on train and bus journeys; a pair of **sunglasses**, particularly in summer; **binoculars** for observing wildlife; a **mobile phone** (though reception is patchy, particularly on the Peddars Way); a **walking stick** or pole to take the shock off your knees and a **vacuum flask** for carrying hot drinks. Although the path is easy to follow, a 'Silva' type **compass** and the knowledge of how to use it is a good idea in case you do lose your way.

CAMPING GEAR

Campers will need a decent **tent** (or bivvy bag if you enjoy travelling light) able to withstand wet and windy weather; a **sleeping mat**; a **stove** and **fuel** (there is special mention in Part 4 of which shops stock fuel); a **pan** with frying pan that can double as a lid/plate is fine for two people; a **pan handle**; a **mug**; a **spoon**; and a wire/plastic **scrubber** for washing up.

Campers should find that a 2- to 3-season **sleeping bag** will cope but obviously in winter a warmer bag is a good idea.

MONEY

There are not many banks or ATMs along the Peddars Way in particular so you will have to carry most of your money as **cash**. A **debit card** is the easiest way to withdraw money from banks or ATMs and a **credit card** can be used to pay in larger shops, restaurants and hotels.

A **cheque book** is very useful for walkers with accounts in British banks as a cheque may be accepted where a card is not, particularly at a B&B. However, you may have to have a debit card to act as a guarantee.

MAPS

The hand-drawn maps in this book cover the trail at a scale of 1:20,000; plenty of detail and information to keep you on the right track.

For those after a traditional paper map, you will need six Ordnance Survey maps (🖳 ordnancesurvey.co.uk) to cover the entire route.

The OS Explorer maps (with an orange cover) you'll need are: No 229 (Thetford Forest in the Brecks); 236 (King's Lynn, Downham Market & Swaffham); 250 (Norfolk Coast West – King's Lynn & Hunstanton); 251 (Norfolk Coast Central – Wells-next-the-Sea & Fakenham); 252 (Norfolk Coast East – Cromer & North Walsham) and OL40 (The Broads – Great Yarmouth &

❏ **Digital mapping**
There are several software packages available on the market today that provide Ordnance Survey maps for a PC or smartphone. The two best known are Memory Map and Anquet, but more suppliers join the list every year. Maps are supplied not in traditional paper format, but electronically, on DVD or USB media, or by direct download over the internet. The maps are then loaded into an application, also available by download, from where you can view them, print them and create routes on them. Additionally, the route can be viewed directly on a smartphone or uploaded to a GPS device. If your smartphone has a GPS chip, you will be able to see your position overlaid onto the digital map on your phone.

Many websites now have free routes you can download for the more popular digital mapping products. Anything from day walks to complete Long Distance Paths. It is important to ensure any digital mapping software on your smartphone uses pre-downloaded maps, stored on your device, and doesn't need to download them on-the-fly, as this may be expensive and will be impossible without a signal.

Smartphones and GPS devices should complement, not replace, the traditional method of navigation (a map and compass) as any electronic device is susceptible to failure and, if nothing else, battery failure. Remember that battery life will be significantly reduced, compared to normal usage, when you are using the built-in GPS and running the screen for long periods. **Stuart Greig**

Lowestoft), all at a scale of 1:25,000. Laminated, waterproof Active Map editions are also available.

Enthusiastic map buyers can reduce the cost of purchasing a full set: members of the Backpackers' Club (see box p46) can purchase maps at a significant discount through their map service. Alternatively, members of the Ramblers (see box p46) can borrow up to 10 maps from their library for a period of four weeks at 50p per map (£1 for weatherproof maps) plus post and packing. If you're a member of a public library in Britain you can often borrow OS maps from your local library as well.

Norfolk Coast Path Peddars Way AZ for walkers, part of the AZ Adventure Series (🖳 az.co.uk), is a booklet containing the relevant part of the OS maps, each to a scale of 1:25,000, for the whole walk and there is also an index.

You can also travel along the Peddars Way and Norfolk Coast Path virtually, as both have been street viewed by Google. Walkers carrying the Google Trekker camera, itself made up of 15 camera lenses, trek the trails and record them so that you can explore them from the comfort of your home with literal, ground-level views of what to expect.

RECOMMENDED READING AND VIEWING

Most of the following books can be found in the tourist information centres in Norfolk as well as good bookshops elsewhere in Britain.

General guidebooks
There are two guides to the architecture of the region in the Pevsner Architectural Guides series currently published by Yale University Press:

Volume 1 covers *Norwich and North-East Norfolk*, while the more immediately relevant Volume 2 deals with *North-West and South Norfolk*.

Norfolk Beaches Handbook by Suzy Watson is published by Explore Norfolk. It is a comprehensive guide to 28 beaches and their varied appeal with a focus on access, attractions and whether they're appropriate for children, dogs, etc.

Walking guidebooks
Pub Walks along the Peddars Way & Norfolk Coast Path and *Pub Walks in Norfolk*, both by Liz Moynihan, published by Countryside Books, contain 20 circular walks varying in length from three to eight miles. Suzy Watson (see above) has also written *Dog walks around the Norfolk Coast*, published by Explore Norfolk, a handy little book detailing 16 coastal dog walks.

General reading
There isn't a great deal of writing on the part of the country the Peddars Way and Norfolk Coast Path pass through. In 1883 Clement Scott wrote an article for the *Daily Telegraph* newspaper entitled 'Poppyland' that described the North Norfolk Coast and was responsible for bringing the region to the attention of the London literati. For a flavour though look out Paul Theroux's *Kingdom by the Sea*, in which the caustic travel writer travelled clockwise around the coast of Britain in the early 1980s to see what the country and its inhabitants were really like. Robert Macfarlane's beautiful eulogy, *The Wild Places,* contains a description of Blakeney Point and a night spent sleeping rough on the shingle.

The naturalist Richard Mabey grew up on the coast at Cley and there are references to Norfolk in many of his books, including *Beechcombings*. Mark Cocker's *Crow Country* is a detailed examination of the rooks and jackdaws that flock around the author's home in remote Norfolk.

For a fictional idea of the area, Arthur Conan Doyle's *The Hound of the Baskervilles* is based on the legend of Black Shuck, a ghost dog who terrorises the marshes off the North Norfolk coast, and Baskerville Hall was reputed to be inspired by a visit to Cromer Hall, a country house located a mile south of Cromer on Hall Rd. The present Grade II listed building was built in 1829 by architect William Donthorne in the Gothic style after the original structure burnt down. The hall is not open to the public but can be seen clearly from Hall Rd.

Film and TV
In addition to the literary titles that have come out of Norfolk, a great many films and television series have been shot in the area, taking advantage of its scenery and photogenic appearance. For instance, the beach at Holkham starred in the final scenes of *Shakespeare in Love*, while farmland at Burnham Deepdale was transformed into a North Korean paddy field for the James Bond film, *Die Another Day*.

The films *A Cock and Bull Story*, *The Eagles have Landed*, *Great Expectations* and *The Duchess* all feature Norfolk, as did the television series *Dad's Army* and *Kingdom*, the fictional central town of which is a composite of Swaffham and the quayside in Wells. *The Go-Between* by LP Hartley featured a central character who spent the summer of 1900 in Norfolk. The film

❑ **SOURCES OF FURTHER INFORMATION**

Trail information The Peddars Way and Norfolk Coast Path National Trail website (🖥 nationaltrail.co.uk/peddars-way-and-norfolk-coast-path) has a wealth of useful information about the trails and the area in general.

When actually on the trail look out for copies of the free *Norfolk Coast Guardian* (🖥 norfolkcoastguardian.co.uk) newspaper, which contains news and features about the Norfolk coast of interest to both tourists and locals as well as an events calendar. It is distributed in many of the shops, places of interest and tourist information centres along the trail. For general information on footpaths, bridleways and byways for walkers, cyclists and horse riders visit 🖥 www.norfolk.gov.uk/out-and-about-in-norfolk/norfolk-trails.

Tourist information
● **Tourist information centres (TICs)** TICs are based in towns throughout Britain and can provide all manner of locally specific information as well as an accommodation-booking service (see box p20). The TICs relevant to this route are in **Thetford** (p89), **Swaffham** (p108), **Hunstanton** (p135), **Wells-next-the-Sea** (p159), **Sheringham** (p182), **Cromer** (p192) and **Great Yarmouth** (p222).

There is also a well-equipped information service at Deepdale Backpackers in **Burnham Deepdale** (p148) which fulfils a similar function. In addition, there are information points in **Watton** (p100) and **Mundesley** (p199). These are generally staffed by volunteers and don't have the full range of services.

For further information visit 🖥 visitnorthnorfolk.com to see what's available to do, where you can stay, where you can eat out and for information on everything you need to put together a holiday itinerary.

Organisations for walkers
● **The Backpackers' Club** (🖥 backpackersclub.co.uk) A club aimed at people who are involved or interested in lightweight camping through walking, cycling, skiing, canoeing, etc. They produce a quarterly magazine, provide members with a comprehensive advisory and information service on all aspects of backpacking, organise weekend trips and also publish a farm-pitch directory. Membership costs £15/20/8.50 per year for an individual/family/anyone under 18 or over 65.
● **The Long Distance Walkers' Association** (LDWA; 🖥 ldwa.org.uk) An association of people with the common interest of long-distance walking. Membership includes a journal, *Strider*, three times per year giving details of challenge events and local group walks as well as articles on the subject. Individual membership is £13 a year whilst family membership for two adults and all children under 18 is £19.50.
● **Ramblers** (formerly Ramblers' Association; 🖥 ramblers.org.uk) Looks after the interests of walkers throughout Britain. They publish a large amount of useful information including their quarterly *Walk* magazine and monthly e-newsletters. Membership costs £35/46.50 individual/joint.

adaptation by Harold Pinter was filmed at Melton Constable and Heydon both of which are close to the Norfolk Coast path.

Flora and fauna field guides
To get the best of Norfolk's birdwatching pick up a guide to the avifauna of the area. *Where to Watch Birds in East Anglia* (Helm), by Peter Clarke, is a comprehensive guide to where to go to see the different species that visit the region.

It also contains site accounts, plans, maps, lists of birds and advice on planning birdwatching trips. *Birds of Norfolk* (Helm) written by a team of experts, provides detailed species' accounts and overviews of each of the birds to be found here. The *Best Birdwatching Sites in Norfolk* (Buckingham Press) by Neil Glenn is a light, readable guide to a range of sites that also includes forecasts as to which birds can be seen during which season. For a good general identification book look out the *Collins Birds Guide* by Lars Svensson, Killian Mullarney, Dan Zetterstrom and Peter Grant.

Getting to and from the Peddars Way and Norfolk Coast Path

A quick look at a map of Britain will show that Norfolk is relatively accessible and well connected to the rest of the country. The fact that it is within a fairly short hop of London and all the transport options available there means that sections of the county at least have become popular weekend retreats for city folk. In reality, although there are good road and rail links with the region, the start of the Peddars Way is poorly serviced.

Public transport, in the form of trains and coaches will get you to Thetford or Bury St Edmunds easily enough, but there is no public transport service to Knettishall Heath where the trail actually starts. Despite this the options available

---

❏ **Getting to Britain**

● **By air** Most international airlines serve London Heathrow and London Gatwick. In addition a number of budget airlines fly from many of Europe's major cities to the other London terminals at Stansted and Luton. Norwich International Airport (🖳 norwichairport.co.uk) is four miles north of Norwich city centre and has connections to a number of European destinations, often via Amsterdam. There are frequent bus services to the city centre. Alternatively, it is a short taxi ride.

● **From Europe by train (with or without a car)** Eurostar (🖳 eurostar.com) operate a high-speed passenger service via the Channel Tunnel between Paris/Brussels/Amsterdam and London. Trains arrive at and depart from St Pancras International Terminal, which also has good underground links to other railway stations. For more information about rail services between Europe and Britain contact your national rail operator or Railteam (🖳 railteam.eu). **Eurotunnel** (🖳 eurotunnel com) operates 'le shuttle', a train service for vehicles via the Channel Tunnel between Calais and Folkestone taking 35 minutes to cross between the two.

● **From Europe by ferry (with or without a car)** Numerous ferry companies operate routes between the major North Sea and Channel ports of mainland Europe and the ports on Britain's eastern and southern coasts as well as from Ireland to ports both in Wales and England. For further information see websites such as 🖳 directferries.co.uk.

● **From Europe by coach (bus)** Eurolines (🖳 eurolines.com) have a huge network of services connecting over 500 cities in 25 European countries to London.

(see p90) are better than driving to the start of the trail. The end of the Norfolk Coast Path at Hopton-on-Sea is similarly poorly connected so you will probably have to go back to Great Yarmouth as that has regular rail and National Express coach services.

NATIONAL TRANSPORT

By rail

For those walking the entire trail, the closest railway stations are at Thetford (15 miles from the start of the Peddars Way at Knettishall Heath; see p90) and Great Yarmouth just before the point where the Norfolk Coast Path concludes. King's Lynn is the closest railway station to Hunstanton for the start of the Norfolk Coast Path.

There are also stations at Sheringham, West Runton and Cromer, the mid-way point on the Coast Path; these are stops on the **Bittern Line** (part of Greater Anglia, see below; 🖳 bitternline.com). The Bittern Line offers a regular service, with good-value fares. The Bittern Ranger (adults £9, seniors £6, family £20) offers one day's unlimited train travel between Norwich and Sheringham and

PLANNING YOUR WALK

❏ **Rail services**
Note: not all stops are listed

Greater Anglia (🖳 greateranglia.co.uk)
● London Liverpool St to Cambridge, daily 2/hr
● London Liverpool St to Stansted Airport, daily 2-3/hr
● London Liverpool St to Norwich via Ipswich, Mon-Fri 2/hr
● London Liverpool St to King's Lynn, direct services Mon-Fri 2/day early morning and 3/day evening
● Cambridge to Norwich via Ely, Brandon, **Thetford**, Attleborough & Wymondham, daily 1/hr
● Ely to Norwich via **Thetford**, daily 1/hr
● **(Bittern Line)** Norwich to **Sheringham** via Hoveton & Wroxham, North Walsham, **Cromer** & **West Runton**, Mon-Sat approx 1/hr, Sun approx 1/hr but 7/day to West Runton
● **(Wherry Line)** Norwich to Great Yarmouth, daily 1/hr
● **(Wherry Line)** Norwich to Lowestoft, Mon-Sat 1/hr, Sun 7/day
● Ipswich to Lowestoft via Saxmundham & Beccles, Mon-Sat 1/hr, Sun 8/day
● Ipswich to Cambridge via Bury St Edmunds, Mon-Sat 1/hr, Sun 7/day
● Ipswich to Peterborough via Bury St Edmunds, Mon-Sat 8/day, Sun 5/day

Great Northern (🖳 greatnorthernrail.com)
● London King's Cross to Cambridge, daily 2/hr
● London King's Cross to King's Lynn via Cambridge & Ely, daily 1/hr

East Midlands Trains (🖳 eastmidlandstrains.co.uk)
● Liverpool Lime Street to Norwich via Nottingham, Peterborough, Ely & **Thetford**, Mon-Sat 11-12/day, Sun 5/day

Cross Country (🖳 crosscountrytrains.co.uk)
● Birmingham New St to Stansted Airport via Peterborough, Ely & Cambridge, daily approx 1/hr

includes bus travel on the Coastliner 36 bus service (see p50 and box p54) between Sheringham and Hunstanton. Tickets are available from the conductor on Bittern Line trains. The **Wherry Line** (🖳 wherryline.org.uk) runs between Norwich and Great Yarmouth/Lowestoft.

All timetable and fare information for the services can be found at National Rail Enquiries (☎ 03457-484950, 🖳 nationalrail.co.uk). Tickets can be booked online through the relevant rail operators (see box opposite), or through 🖳 thetrainline.com. For the best fares book as early as possible.

> ❏ **Steam train journeys**
> Two other options for travel by train in Norfolk are the services geared to sightseers: **North Norfolk Railway/Poppy Line** (see p182) is a full-size steam and diesel railway which runs between Sheringham and Holt, and **Wells and Walsingham Light Railway** (see p158), which is the longest 10½-inch gauge steam railway in the world.

By coach

National Express (☎ 0871-781 8178, lines open daily 10am-6pm but calls cost at least 13p a minute, 🖳 national express.com) is the main coach (long-distance bus) operator in Britain. Tickets can also be booked through the North Norfolk tourist information centres (see box p46). Coach travel is generally cheaper (non-refundable 'fun-fares' are available online for as little as £5 one way but expect to pay closer to £15 one way if you want more flexibility), but takes longer than travel by train. At the time of research there were no National Express services to Hunstanton and the service that used to run to Cromer had been suspended indefinitely. **Megabus** (🖳 uk.megabus.com), part of Stagecoach but providing low-cost coach travel, operates services to Norwich.

> ❏ **National Express coach services**
> **NX250** Heathrow Airport to Ipswich via Stansted Airport, daily 9/day
> **NX375** Bangor to Great Yarmouth via Norwich, Swaffham, King's Lynn, Birmingham & Liverpool, 1/day
> **NX490** London Victoria to Norwich via Thetford, daily 7/day
> **NX491** London Victoria to Great Yarmouth via Norwich, 2/day, 1/day continues to Gorleston & Lowestoft
> **NX498** London Victoria to Bury St Edmunds via Cambridge, 1/day

By car

Norfolk has good links to the national road network; the A17 runs into Norfolk from Lincolnshire whilst the A47 links Norfolk with Peterborough and Leicester, providing straightforward routes from the A1 and M1. The M11 and A12 provide links to London and the south-east. Thetford can be reached via the A11, which joins the M11 just south of Cambridge, or the A134 which links Bury St Edmunds to King's Lynn.

From Thetford it is a five-mile drive east on the A1066 (Rushford to Knettishall) road. There is a car park immediately opposite the start point of the

Peddars Way. However, it is not secure and you shouldn't leave your car here for an extended period – and particularly not for the time it takes to complete the trek.

The end of the Coast Path at Hopton-on-Sea is reached by following the A47 from Norwich, via Great Yarmouth and Gorleston, or by following the A146 and A143. The A149 links King's Lynn to Great Yarmouth and snakes along the coast connecting the small towns and villages rather than taking a more direct route inland.

LOCAL TRANSPORT

Local transport along the lengths of the Peddars Way and Norfolk Coast Path is of varied quality. The Peddars Way is very poorly served and a number of the smaller, more out-of-the-way villages are entirely unconnected to other towns or, at best, have one service a week. This is a problem if you are looking to do linear walks in the area or if you simply want to give your feet a rest and skip ahead. Once you arrive on the North Norfolk coast though the story improves, with a service (see below) designed to help tired coastal walkers and day trippers access the villages and towns along the route. However, the quality of service deteriorates again for the last sections of the walk.

The public transport map on pp52-3 shows the most useful bus and train routes and the box on p51 and p54 gives details of the frequency of services and whom you should contact for timetable information.

Coastal bus service

At the time of writing the excellent Coasthopper service was being taken over (from Stagecoach) by Lynx (36 Coastliner) and Sanders (Coasthopper Nos 4 & 5); see box p54. The new timetables weren't finalised, but it is expected that the service will continue to operate year-round along the North Norfolk coast and will be improved because services will continue to Mundesley rather than just to Cromer. Timetables will be available on both companies' websites but also at tourist information centres, hostels, cafés and other information outlets on and around the route. However, it is essential to check before travel as details can change.

Lynx will operate services from King's Lynn to Wells (and Walsingham), and Sanders from Wells to Mundesley. A variety of tickets are available (single, two-trip ie return, weekly, 10-trip and monthly) and tickets will be valid on both companies' (No 36 and No 4) services. However, if you expect to use the bus quite a bit it would be worth buying a **Coast** ticket (1-day £10, 3-day £21, or 7-day £36; reduced fares for children and family groups) for unlimited travel in the period of validity on Coastliner buses.

The services have a number of set pick-up and drop-off points but also operate on a hail-and-ride basis as long as they can stop in a safe place.

Almost all buses are step-free making them accessible to pushchairs and wheelchairs. Dogs are allowed on the buses but bicycles aren't.

❑ Public transport services

The following list is not completely comprehensive but does cover the most important services. Unless specified otherwise services operate year-round, though some may be less frequent in winter. For full and up-to-date details of bus services and timetables contact the individual companies or visit their websites. Alternatively, for an overview of public transport in the region and to plan your journey visit traveline's website (🖳 travelineeastanglia.co.uk), or call them (☎ 0871-200 2233) but be aware that calls costs at least 12p a minute.

   Note that not all stops are listed.

Bus services
Coach Services (☎ 01842-821509, 🖳 coachservicesltd.com)
40 King's Lynn to Thetford, Mon-Fri 2/day, Sat 1/day
81 Thetford to Watton, Mon-Fri 4/day
84 Bury St Edmunds to Thetford, Mon-Fri 9/day, Sat 6/day
86 Brandon to Bury St Edmunds via Thetford, Mon-Sat 5/day plus Mon-Fri 2/day, Sun 4/day
200/201 Mildenhall to Thetford via Brandon, Mon-Fri 6/day plus Sat 4/day
332 Bury St Edmunds to Thetford via Honington, Mon-Sat 3/day (evening only)

Suffolk Links Brecks Area Bus (BB; ☎ 01638-664304, 🖳 suffolkonboard.com)
Brecks Bus Thetford (bus or railway station) to Knettishall Heath; a Demand Responsive Transport (DRT) service (dial-a-ride), in the Brecks area, that operates Monday (except bank holidays) to Saturday between 7am and 7pm but must be booked (call Mon to Fri between 8am and 3.45pm); bookings can be made up to a fortnight in advance and in the peak season it is recommended you do book at least a week in advance.

Flexibus (☎ 0300-123 1145, 🖳 norfolk.gov.uk/flexibus)
This is another dial-and-ride service covering a number of the smaller towns and villages across the county. Call to arrange your travel destination, date and time at least 24hrs in advance; and on a Friday if you want to travel on a Monday.
Harling Flexibus (term time Mon-Fri 9am-2.30pm; school holidays Mon-Fri 8am-4pm) covers Attleborough, Diss & Thetford;
Swaffham Flexibus covers Sporle and Castle Acre (Mon-Fri 7am-7pm, Saturday service available);
Wayland Flexibus (term time Mon-Fri 9am-2.30pm; school holidays Mon-Fri 8am-4pm) travels between Attleborough and Watton.

Simonds (☎ 01379-647300, 🖳 simonds.co.uk)
338 Bury St Edmunds to Diss via Coney Weston, Mon-Fri 4/day, Sat 3/day

West Norfolk Community Transport (☎ 01553-776971, 🖳 wnct.co.uk)
12 North Pickenham to Swaffham, Mon-Fri 2-3/day, Sat 1-2/day
22 King's Lynn to Fakenham via Great Massingham, Harpley & Kiptons Wood, Mon-Fri 2/day plus 1/day from Great Massingham and 1/day to Kiptons Wood, Sat 1-2/day to Kiptons Wood only

(cont'd on p54)

PLANNING YOUR WALK

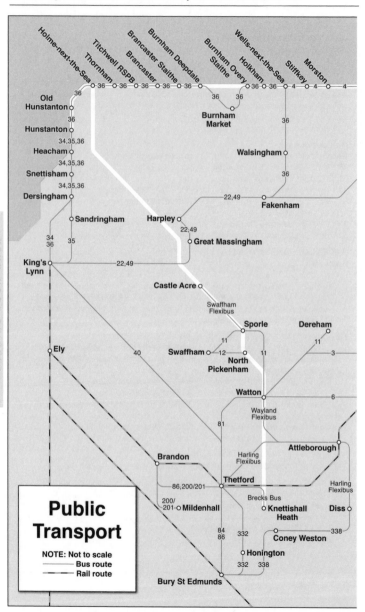

Holme-next-the-Sea
Thornham
Titchwell RSPB
Brancaster
Brancaster Staithe
Burnham Deepdale
Burnham Overy Staithe
Holkham
Wells-next-the-Sea
Stiffkey
Morston

36 — 36 — 36 — 36 — 36 — 36 — 36 — 36 — 4 — 4 — 4

Old Hunstanton
36

Hunstanton
36

Heacham
34,35,36

Snettisham
34,35,36

Dersingham
34,35,36

Sandringham
Harpley
Great Massingham

Burnham Market
36
36

Walsingham
36

22,49
Fakenham

22,49

King's Lynn
34 36
35
22,49

Castle Acre

Swaffham Flexibus

Sporle
Dereham

Swaffham
11
12
11

North Pickenham

11

Ely
40

Watton
6

Wayland Flexibus

81

Brandon
86,200/201
Thetford

Harling Flexibus

Attleborough

Harling Flexibus

200/201
Mildenhall

Brecks Bus

Knettishall Heath
Diss

84 86
332
332
338
Coney Weston

Honington

Bury St Edmunds

Public Transport

NOTE: Not to scale
—— Bus route
– · – Rail route

PLANNING YOUR WALK

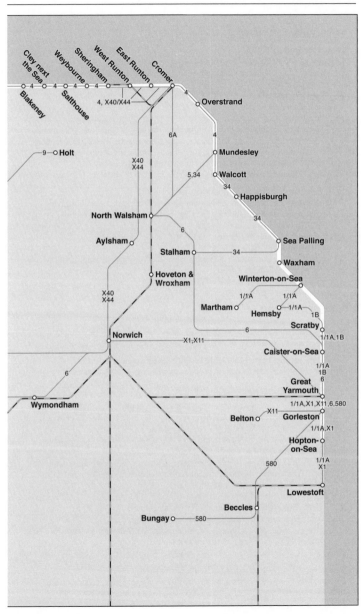

PLANNING YOUR WALK

Public transport services (*cont'd from p51*)

Bus services

Lynx (☎ 01553-611955, 💻 lynxbus.co.uk)
34 King's Lynn to Hunstanton via Dersingham, Snettisham & Heacham, Mon-Sat 2/hr, Sun 1/hr
35 King's Lynn to Hunstanton via Sandringham, Dersingham, Snettisham & Heacham, daily 1/hr
36 **Coastliner** King's Lynn to Fakenham via Dersingham, Snettisham, Heacham, Hunstanton, Old Hunstanton, Holme-next-the-Sea, Thornham, Titchwell RSPB Turn, Brancaster, Brancaster Staithe, Burnham Deepdale, Burnham Market, Burnham Overy Staithe, Holkham, Wells-next-the-Sea, Walsingham, daily 1/hr (2/hr from Hunstanton at peak times)
49 King's Lynn to Fakenham via Great Massingham & Harpley, Mon-Sat 5-6/day

First Norfolk & Suffolk (💻 firstgroup.com)
1/1A Lowestoft to Martham via Hopton-on-Sea, Gorleston, Great Yarmouth, Caister-on-Sea, Ormesby, Scratby, Hemsby & Winterton-on-Sea, Mon-Sat 1-2/hr, Sun 1/hr
1B Great Yarmouth to Hemsby via Caister-on-Sea & Scratby, Mon-Sat 2/hr, Sun 1/hr
X1 Norwich to Lowestoft via Great Yarmouth, Gorleston & Hopton-on-Sea, Mon-Sat 2/hr, Sun 1/hr
X11 Norwich to Belton via Great Yarmouth & Gorleston-on-Sea, Mon-Sat 2/hr, Sun 1/hr

Konectbus (☎ 03300-539358, 💻 konectbus.co.uk)
3 Norwich to Watton, Mon-Sat 1/hr, Sun 4/day
6 Norwich to Watton via Wymondham, Mon-Sat 1/hr
11 Dereham to Swaffham via Watton & Sporle, Mon-Fri 7/day, Sat 4/day

Sanders Coaches Limited (☎ 01263-712800, 💻 sanderscoaches.com)
Note: at the time of research these services were being revised so the details were not certain
4 **Coasthopper** Wells to Mundesley via Sheringham via Stiffkey, Morston, Blakeney, Cley-next-the-Sea, Salthouse, Weybourne, Sheringham, West Runton & East Runton. Cromer, Trimingham, Sidestrand & Overstrand, daily 2/hr
5 **Coasthopper** North Walsham to Holt, Mon-Sat 1-2/hr
5 **Coasthopper** North Walsham to Cromer, Sun 8/day
5A Norwich to North Walsham, Sun 7/day
6 Great Yarmouth to North Walsham via Caister & Stalham, Mon-Sat 8/day plus 3/day from Gorleston (term-time only)
6A North Walsham to Cromer via Thorpe Market, Mon-Fri 6/day, Sat 7/day
9 Holt to Fakenham, Mon-Sat 6-8/day (connects with No 5 at Holt)
34 North Walsham to Stalham via Mundesley (2/day), Bacton, Walcott, Happisburgh & Sea Palling, Mon-Fri 3/day, Sat 2/day (at Stalham change to the X10/X11 for services to Norwich)
X40/X44 Norwich to Sheringham via Aylsham, Cromer, East Runton, West Runton & Beeston Regis, Mon-Sat 1-2/hr

Border Bus (☎ 01502-714565, 💻 border-bus.co.uk)
580 Bungay to Great Yarmouth via Beccles & Gorleston, Mon-Sat 7/day

THE ENVIRONMENT & NATURE

2

The environment and conservation

To the uninitiated, the Peddars Way and Norfolk Coast Path don't seem all that distinctive. They lack many of the recognisable features of other national trails in England. Yet on closer examination it is possible to determine a wide variety of contrasting terrains and habitats from one end of the trail to the other: grasslands, heath, woodlands, forests, sand dunes, salt-marshes, wide beaches and vast stretches of coast. These varied environments are home to an equally diverse selection of flora and fauna. The following is not designed to be a comprehensive guide to all the animals, birds and plants you might encounter, but rather serves as an introduction to what you're likely to see.

By making an effort to look out for wildlife and plants as you walk the route you will garner a broader appreciation of the landscape and region you are passing through. You will begin to understand how the species you encounter interact with one another and will learn a little about the conservation issues that are so pertinent today.

LANDSCAPES

Norfolk has been moulded by a series of glaciations. The land has been shaped, smoothed and stripped by the passage of ice. The chalk ridge running through north-west Norfolk was rounded while wide swathes of clay and gravel were deposited on top of older rocks. Intriguing features such as the pingo ponds around Thompson Water (see box p97) remain as evidence of these successive ice ages. As the coast and cliffs have been subjected to erosion so they have given up a series of secrets. The bones and teeth of hippo, hyena and deer have been found while the 85%-complete fossil skeleton of a 15ft tall, 650,000-year-old elephant was unearthed in 1990 in the cliffs between East and West Runton, indicative of a time when the landscape looked very different indeed.

Within the Norfolk Coast AONB (see pp58-9) there are eight distinguishable landscape types. The **coastal region** with its open, remote and wild panorama of wide skies and long views to the sea is the most typical of the area and the one that conjures the most ready images. Characteristic features include marshes, sand dunes and shingle ridges as well as small coastal settlements comprising flint buildings, significant churches and windmills. In the east there are pollarded willows (heavily pruned each year to encourage a close, rounded head of branches) alongside long straight roads. In the west, rectilinear fields are defined by ditches, sparse hedges and occasional stands of trees.

Inland a varied, undulating landscape of rolling hills and large stretches of heathland dominates. Village estates are typified by buildings of attractive carrstone (coarse, grained, granular sandstone, usually yellowish brown).

In all, it is a region of wide and varied interest that is in a state of constant flux, being shaped and re-shaped by the elements and the tides.

Breckland Breckland is a fairly recent term for an internationally important landscape, coined to describe a much older setting identifiable from its surrounds by its terrain, land-use and distinctive wildlife. Broadly speaking, Breckland comprises a gently undulating, low plateau underlain by a bedrock of Cretaceous chalk, covered by thin deposits of sand and flint. What started as deciduous woodland was slowly razed by early Neolithic man in pursuit of flint (see box below), which was dug out of the ground here. The open heath was then grazed extensively by sheep and rabbits, removing the vegetation, exhausting the soil and turning it into a sea of loose, shifting sands, which meant that villages contracted and people moved out of the region or retreated to the river valleys. During the 18th and 19th centuries Scots pines were planted to try and bind the soil together and stabilise the land for cultivation, whilst in the 20th century land was given over to conifer plantations. The result is a modern landscape of open areas and flint-filled fields, dotted with stands of deliberately planted trees.

The greatest extent of remaining heathlands are centred on the Stanford Training Area and Brettenham Heath (see p96). The Brecks/Breckland are particularly cherished for this remaining heathland and the mosaics of grass-heath which support populations of invertebrates and ground-nesting birds. Traditionally they are areas of heather and grass although more recently they have been invaded by bracken and scrub. The area is significant for a wide range of flora and fauna dependent on open ground, arable margins and disturbed soil. Unique landforms such as pingo ponds are also important for insects. For more information see 🖳 brecks.org.

❏ Flint
Flint is a mineral found in bands within chalk and has played a big part in the history of the landscape across which the Peddars Way and Norfolk Coast Path travel. When man first found the ability to make tools, the people who lived in the region began to make arrowheads and knives from flakes of flint. It was also found to be useful in starting fires. Flint can still be seen in local village architecture as it is a very versatile building brick. The traditional fishermen's cottages all along the coast wouldn't look like they do today if it weren't for flint, and the atmosphere and the character of the area would be markedly different.

Norfolk Coast The North Norfolk coast is one of the best examples of an unspoilt coastline in England. The coast is separated from adjacent areas by a combination of light soils, climate, relief and land use. The area is drained by the rivers Wensum and Bure which flow south-eastwards into Broadland and by a number of smaller waterways such as the Glaven and Stiffkey that flow northwards, whilst the Nar drains westwards to The Wash. The gravels and sands left behind after the last Ice Age still determine the vegetation patterns. Habitats range from heaths and mires to woodlands and highly fertile soils that end in gently eroding sea cliffs. The coastal habitats themselves are constantly changing, with weather and waves responsible for shaping the shifting shingle ridges, sandflats, spits and dunes as well as filling the salt creeks and marshes that lie behind them. The result is that the coastline today is very different from the coastline in the past, and indeed the way it will look in the future; thriving ports are already landlocked or increasingly only accessible by small channels and rivulets as silt deposits choke access routes to the sea.

The significance and variety of habitats in the area means that it has been conserved as a series of connected nature reserves that run all the way from Holme to Weybourne. They are amongst the best examples of coastal environments in Britain and also feature biological and geomorphological sites of interest such as the barrier island at Scolt Head (see p150) and the shingle spit at Blakeney Point (see box p170).

CONSERVING THE PEDDARS WAY AND NORFOLK COAST PATH

As with much of the British Isles, the English countryside has had to cope with a great deal of pressure from the activities of an increasingly industrialised world. Even in Norfolk, which was largely by-passed by the industrial revolution and early developments, there are significant changes to land use and the way in which we live.

Almost every acre of land has been altered in some way by man; the need to feed an increasingly large population led to the landscape being cleared of trees and ploughed for crops. Agricultural intensification and decades of chemical farming have drained swathes of the countryside of much of its wildlife. The result of this is the landscape we see today. Ironically the verdant green colour we associate most with the English landscape is the one that best conveys its decimation – green without relief or shading is unnatural. Mark Cocker notes in *Crow Country* (see p45) that '… in Norfolk the obduracy of water has been the saving grace for the wildly beautiful north coast…' Nonetheless, what remains today are fragments of semi-natural woodland and hedgerows stretched across farmland. The chopping and changing of this landscape has had a negative impact on its biodiversity and a number of species have been lost whilst others are severely depleted.

There is a positive note though. There are still pockets of enormous beauty and the resulting habitat is, in parts, a rare one that provides an essential niche for endangered species.

GOVERNMENT AGENCIES AND SCHEMES

Natural England

Primary responsibility for countryside affairs in England rests with Natural England (🖳 gov.uk/government/organisations/natural-england); this organisation is responsible for enhancing biodiversity, landscape and wildlife in rural, urban, coastal and marine areas; promoting access, recreation and public wellbeing; and contributing to the way natural resources are managed. One of its roles is to designate national trails, national parks, areas of outstanding natural beauty, national nature reserves and sites of special scientific interest, and to enforce regulations relating to all these sites.

The top level of protection is afforded to **National Parks**, a designation that recognises the national importance of an area in terms of landscape, biodiversity and as a recreational source. This title does not imply national ownership though and they are not necessarily uninhabited wildernesses, meaning that the conservation of these areas is a juggling act between protecting the environment and ensuring the rights and livelihoods of those living within the park. There are 15 National Parks in the UK, including the Norfolk and Suffolk Broads which was granted the status in 1989, but no part of the Peddars Way or Norfolk Coast Path falls inside the boundary.

The area the two paths pass through is afforded a degree of protection though, with much of the route designated an **Area of Outstanding Natural Beauty** (AONB; National Association for Areas of Outstanding Natural Beauty 🖳 landscapesforlife.org.uk), the second highest level of protection. Norfolk Coast Path falls entirely within **Norfolk Coast AONB**, an area of largely undeveloped coastal land accorded protection in 1968. The AONB comprises three separate areas of coast, including the inter-tidal area and hinterland that backs it – in places the boundary for the strip of land classified as an AONB extends up to 6km inland, and in total 450 square kilometres of land are protected. The bulk of the AONB is a long section of coast from Old Hunstanton in the west to Bacton in the east. Within this area, Sheringham and Cromer, as well as the stretch of coast between them, are excluded because development work was already underway when the regulations were established.

The majority of the AONB includes the wild and remote coastal marshes of the North Norfolk Heritage Coast, a mixture of sand and mud flats, dunes, shingle, salt-marsh, reed-beds and grazing marsh. It also includes the glacial sand and gravel cliffs east of Weybourne as well as the rolling farmland, estates and woodland of the coastal hinterland and areas of heath that back the coast. In addition, there are two small outlying designated areas: in the west an area north of King's Lynn that includes Sandringham Estate and The Wash's mudflats, and in the east the sand dunes between Sea Palling and Winterton, where there is a small overlap with land designated part of the Norfolk and Suffolk Broads National Park.

Because the Norfolk Coast AONB is a large area and crosses some administrative boundaries, a wide number of groups and organisations are involved in managing it, and work in tandem with **Norfolk Coast Partnership** (NCP; see box below) to ensure its preservation. The NCP is funded by Natural England, Norfolk County Council, North Norfolk District Council, the Borough Council of King's Lynn and West Norfolk, and Great Yarmouth Borough Council.

The National Trails Officer (see box p46) works closely with the above organisations and councils to keep the Peddars Way and Norfolk Coast Path in good condition, although work on the ground may sometimes by undertaken by local authorities.

The next level of protection includes National Nature Reserves and Sites of Scientific Interest. There are over 220 **National Nature Reserves (NNRs)** in England, where wildlife comes first. This doesn't mean that they are no-go areas for people, just that visitors have to be careful not to damage the fragile ecosystems and wildlife within these places. Those in Norfolk include: Brettenham Heath (see p96) just before the A11 on leaving Knettishall Heath; Holme Dunes (see p129); Holkham (see p153); Scolt Head Island (see p150) off Burnham Overy Staithe; Blakeney (see box p170); and Winterton Dunes (see p213). Thetford Heath, south west of Thetford, in Suffolk, is also a National Nature Reserve although the Peddars Way actually starts north-east of here.

There are over 4000 **Sites of Special Scientific Interest (SSSIs)** in England, covering some 7% of the country's land area. These range in size from little pockets protecting wild flower meadows, important nesting sites or special geological features, to vast swathes of upland, moorland and wetland. SSSIs are a particularly important designation as they have some legal standing; they are managed in accordance with the landowners and occupiers who must give notice before starting any work likely to damage the site, and they must not proceed without written consent from Natural England.

There are more than 160 SSSIs in Norfolk although they are not given a high profile and deliberately little attention is drawn to them. Those along the Peddars Way and Norfolk Coast Path include: Breckland Forest and Farmland, Thompson Water, the River Nar, Castle Acre Common, the Stanford Training Area, Ringstead Downs, Hunstanton Cliffs, the North Norfolk coast, Weybourne Cliffs, Sheringham and Beeston Regis Common, Beeston Cliffs, East and West Runton Cliffs, Felbrigg Woods, Overstrand Cliffs, Happisburgh Cliffs, Winterton and Horsey Dunes, and Great Yarmouth North Denes.

❏ **Norfolk Coast Partnership**
Norfolk Coast Partnership (NCP; 🖳 norfolkcoastaonb.org.uk) was established in 1991, initially as the Norfolk Coast Project, to promote and co-ordinate policies amongst its member organisations. Established in response to the increased pressure put on the land by burgeoning visitor numbers and the perceived threat to the area's natural beauty that they represented, the partnership's objectives have broadly evolved in line with those of AONB designation, to bring about sustainable use of the Norfolk Coast whilst conserving and enhancing the natural features and ensuring that future generations can enjoy and benefit from the coast.

THE ENVIRONMENT & NATURE

❏ **Other statutory bodies**
● **Historic England** (⌨ historicengland.org.uk) Created in April 2015 as a result of dividing the work done by English Heritage (see opposite). Historic England is the government department responsible for looking after and promoting England's historic environment and is in charge of the listing system, giving grants and dealing with planning matters.
● **Norfolk County Council** (⌨ norfolk.gov.uk).

Special Areas of Conservation (SACs) are designated by the European Union's Habitats Directive and provide an extra tier of protection to the areas they encompass and are a vital part of global efforts to conserve the world's biodiversity. Breckland and the North Norfolk coast both benefit from this increased protection.

For further information about all of these visit Natural England's website (see p58).

The North Norfolk coast is also listed as a **Ramsar site** under the Convention on Wetlands of International Importance, particularly as a waterfowl habitat. It is also recognised internationally as a **UNESCO biosphere reserve**, a label that means that it serves as a 'living laboratory' for testing out and demonstrating integrated management of land, water and biodiversity.

These designations undoubtedly all play an important role in safeguarding the land they cover for future generations. However, the very fact that we require and rely on these labels for conserving small areas begs the question what are we doing to look after the vast majority of land that remains relatively unprotected? Surely we should be looking to conserve the natural environment outside protected areas just as much as within them.

CAMPAIGNING AND CONSERVATION ORGANISATIONS

The survival of so many important natural sites depends on the efforts of a great many. It was in fact on the North Norfolk coast that the Wildlife Trust movement (see opposite) began through the efforts of the Norfolk and Norwich Naturalists Society; the first meeting took place in The George Inn in Cley in 1926 and the purchase of 400 acres of marsh at Cley to be held 'in perpetuity as a bird breeding sanctuary' provided a blueprint for nature conservation that has now been replicated across the UK. The importance of the coast had in fact already been recognised by Professor FW Oliver of London University, who had led the appeal that resulted in the purchase of Blakeney Point by the National Trust in 1912.

The tradition of caring continues today through a variety of diverse organisations, sympathetic landlords and volunteers. The idea of conservation has also gained momentum with an increase in public awareness and interest in environmental issues as a whole. There are now a large number of campaigning and conservation groups in the UK. Independent of the government, they are reliant on public support; they can concentrate their resources on acquiring land that can then be managed for conservation purposes, or on influencing political decision makers by lobbying and campaigning.

The **National Trust** (NT; 🖵 nationaltrust.org.uk) is a charity with some 3.6 million members, which aims to protect through ownership threatened coastline, countryside, historic houses, castles, gardens and archaeological remains for everybody to enjoy. In particular the NT cares for more than 600 miles of British coastline, 248,000 hectares of countryside and 300 historic buildings and monuments. It manages sections of Norfolk including Brancaster (see p144) and Branodunum (p146), Blakeney National Nature Reserve (see box p170) and Sheringham Park (see p182), but also owns properties including Felbrigg Hall, near Cromer.

The **Wildfowl and Wetlands Trust** (WWT; 🖵 wwt.org.uk) is the biggest conservation organisation for wetlands in the UK with over 400 acres of land under their management. Their regional visitor centre at Welney, near Wisbech, in Norfolk is well known and popular with visitors year-round.

The **Wildlife Trust** (🖵 wildlifetrusts.org) undertakes projects to improve conditions for wildlife and promote public awareness of it as well as acquiring land for nature reserves to protect particular species and habitats. The Norfolk Wildlife Trust (🖵 norfolkwildlifetrust.org.uk) manages nearly 10,000 acres of land right across the county, including nature reserves at Thompson Common, Wayland Wood close to Watton, Ringstead Downs, Holme Dunes, Cley Marshes, and Salthouse Marshes set behind a shingle ridge on the way to Sheringham.

The **Royal Society for the Protection of Birds** (RSPB; 🖵 ww2 .rspb.org.uk) was the pioneer of voluntary conservation bodies. It is the largest voluntary organisation body in Europe focusing on providing a healthy environment for birds and wildlife. It is responsible for maintaining 200 reserves across Britain including ones at Titchwell Marsh (see p144), on the Norfolk Coast Path, and Snettisham (see p122) to the south of Hunstanton on The Wash.

Norfolk Ornithologists' Association (NOA; 🖵 noa.org.uk) is dedicated to the scientific study of birds; it has six reserves in Norfolk in addition to its base at Holme Bird Observatory (see p63 and p129).

Butterfly Conservation (🖵 butterfly-conservation.org) was formed in 1968 by some naturalists determined to reverse the decline in the numbers of moths and butterflies in the UK. They now have more than 30 branches including a Norfolk branch and operate a number of nature reserves and sites where butterflies are likely to be found.

English Heritage (🖵 english-heritage.org.uk) looks after, champions and advises the government on historic buildings and places. However, in April 2015 it was divided into a new charitable trust that retains the name English Heritage and a non-departmental public body, Historic England (see box opposite). English Heritage manages the Cluniac priories in both Thetford (see p89) and Castle Acre (p112), as well as Seahenge (see box p140).

THE ENVIRONMENT & NATURE

Flora and fauna

BIRDS

Few birdwatchers, serious or amateur, will not have been to Norfolk or know of its reputation amongst twitchers. This is largely due to the county's strategic location facing Scandinavia, slap bang on a migration pathway, its long coast line and its extremely diverse range of coastal and inland habitats, many of which enjoy protected status as nature reserves (see box opposite). The marshes and inter-tidal mudflats along the coast are important breeding grounds for a vast number of species as they offer feeding and safe roost sites. The county has some of the best year-round birding sites in the country, with locations that consistently attract rare birds. The following lists give just a few of the more than 300 species that have been documented in Norfolk and ought to give you a flavour of what you should see whilst walking the Peddars Way and Norfolk Coast Path.

Scrubland, grassland and heaths

Lapwings (*Vanellus vanellus*) prefer the open country but can be seen on mud-flats, marshes and in meadows; the reserve at Cley and the coast around Holkham are good spots to search them out. These medium-sized waders, which feed on insects and invertebrates close to the surface of ponds or puddles, are also known locally as peewits after their mournful cry. The seemingly black plumage is in fact green and purple, which contrasts with the bird's white under-parts. Once killed for food, their eggs used to be collected and sold as delica-cies, leading to a decline in numbers. Nowadays resident breeding pairs are less common but large flocks of immigrating birds gather briefly in Norfolk during autumn and winter.

    Barn owls (*Tyto alba*) are distinctive, beautifully marked birds that appear totally white but actually have shades of grey, buff and brown on their backs and wings. Seen throughout the year they are most usually spotted hunting along roadsides or ghosting across farmland and coastal fields at dawn and dusk. Holme Dunes is a particularly good spot to look for these birds, which are known in Norfolk as Billywix or hushwing, due to their silent flight. **Short-eared owls** (*Asio flammeus*) are medium-sized owls with mottled brown bodies, paler under-parts and yellow eyes. They commonly hunt during the day but are seen most widely during winter when they can be spotted on coastal marshes and wetlands.

    Stone curlews (*Burhinus oedicnemus*) are easily identifiable by their wail-ing call, which contributes to its local nickname, the wailing heath chicken. They have brown, black and white plumage that provides perfect camouflage against the sandy heaths where they hide during the day before feeding at night. They have long yellow legs and large yellow eyes which are adapted for night-time foraging. Norfolk is a stronghold for the species, which can be particularly spotted in Breckland.

Yellowhammers (*Emberiza citronella*) are types of bunting that can be seen on commons, heaths and farmland, especially around Breckland. They are typically a vibrant golden colour and have an attractive song said to sound like 'a little bit of bread and no cheese'. **Reed bunting** (*Emberizza scheniclus*) are sparrow-sized, slim birds with long, deeply notched tails and a drooping moustache. They are largely seen on farmland or wetlands. **Snow buntings** (*Plectrophenax nivalis*) are large buntings with predominantly white underparts that contrast with a brown and mottled plumage. They breed all around the Arctic then migrate south in winter, arriving in coastal areas from late September, where they remain till February.

Skylarks (*Alauda arvensis*) are small birds with a streaky brown back and white underparts lined with dark brown. Often seen in open country such as grazing marshes, coastal dunes and heaths, they are often spotted and heard at Cley and Holme Dunes, when their melodic, seemingly endless song rings out from late winter to midsummer. In winter they form small flocks and descend on coastal salt-marshes.

Linnets (*Carduelis cannabina*) are reasonably common, slim finches with forked tails and red breasts. Their distinctive twittering call can be heard on heaths and commons, especially in Breckland and on the coast. They are seed-eaters and feed on grains, grass and wildflower seeds, often collecting in flocks to forage in fields or coastal marshes. **Twites** (*Carduelis flavirostris*) look similar to linnet but have brighter, yellowish bills that stand out in contrast to the

---

❏ Reserves

● **Holme Bird Observatory and Reserve** (see p129) Managed by the Norfolk Ornithologists' Association (see p61), this five-hectare patch of pine- and scrub-covered dunes is ideal for migrating thrushes, warblers and finches. Admission is £3 for non-members, under 16s are free.

● **Titchwell Marsh RSPB Reserve** (see p144) Diverse habitats (reedbeds, saltmarsh and freshwater lagoons) attract a wide range of birds. Good café. Free entry for walkers and RSPB members; £6 car park charges.

● **Holkham National Nature Reserve** (see p59 and p153) Managed by Natural England (🖳 holkham.co.uk/naturereserve), this vast 4000-hectare (9580 acres) stretch between Burnham Norton and Blakeney offers fantastic diversity of habitat. Seasonal charges apply.

● **Blakeney National Nature Reserve** (see p61 and p170) Overseen by the National Trust, highlights include **Stiffkey Marshes** and **Blakeney Point**, where you can see vast numbers of birds congregating. There is an information centre at Morston Quay. Free entry.

● **Cley Marshes Reserve** (see p61 and p173) Founded in 1926 this is the Wildlife Trust's oldest bird reserve in England, with boardwalks and hides close to the pools and roost sites. It is run by Norfolk Wildlife Trust and there is an excellent, modern information centre. Entry costs £4.50 for non members (£5 with Gift Aid), children are free.

● **Snettisham RSPB Reserve** (see p61, p122 & p124) Overlooking The Wash, there are bird hides with excellent views out over the islands, ideal for spotting waders and wildfowl. Free entry.

dark feathers of their heads. They breed on moorland and stony areas near to the sea but over-winter on salt-marshes and shorelines, or continue across the North Sea to the Low Countries.

Grey partridges (*Perdix perdix*) often crop up on farmland or grasslands, especially in West Norfolk, when you can most easily spot them during autumn scavenging on ploughed or stubble fields. Plump with short legs and orangey-brown feathers, they spend the majority of their time on the ground.

Red-legged partridges (*Alectoris ruta*) are larger than greys, have large white chin and throat patches bordered with black. They have greyish bodies and bold black flank stripes. Introduced to the UK from Europe they are now seen year-round in England especially in the east, usually in groups and in open fields.

Nightjars (*Caprimulgas europaeus*) are summer visitors from Europe, which inhabit open heathland and moorland in close proximity to small stands of trees that provide roosting sites. They can sometimes be seen in Breckland. Largely nocturnal, they commence their feeding and courtship activities at dusk. This allied to their clever camouflage and tendency to hide in thick cover makes them difficult to see. Their song is very distinctive though and their strange churring song, like a chainsaw, can be heard ringing out over the copse at dusk.

Woodland

Buzzards (*Buteo buteo*) are the commonest bird of prey in the UK and can be seen soaring over farmland, moorland and more arable areas. They are quite large with broad rounded wings and a short neck and tail. Whilst gliding and soaring they hold their wings in a shallow 'V'. **Kestrel** (*Falco tinnunculus*) are another common sight, frequently seen hovering beside roadside verges or above heath and moorland. They have pointed wings and a long tail. Highly adaptable, they have adjusted to life in man-made environments and can be seen in a wide variety of habitats other than dense forests or treeless wetlands.

Hobbies (*falco subbuteo*) are about the same size as a kestrel with long pointed wings similar to a giant swift. The hobby has a similar dashing flight to a swift as well and will chase large insects and small birds, catching prey in its talons in flight. It arrives in the UK from April onwards and is most commonly seen hunting over woodland edges and heathlands until it departs again in September and October.

Sparrowhawks (*Accipiter nisus*) have slate grey backs and white underparts, lined with orange. They are widespread and are identifiable from similar-sized raptors as they never hover like kestrels.

The **rook** (*Corvus frugilegus*) has all-black plumage and a bare, greyish face. They are sociable birds and are usually seen in flocks in open fields. Similar looking is the **crow** (*Corvus corone*), which is identifiable as it has a stockier beak and is more solitary; it is seen usually alone or in pairs. As well as assorted **thrushes**, **tits** and **starlings** look out for **bullfinches** (*Pyrrhula pyrrhula*), which are easily identifiable by their red underparts and black cap. Often spotted in churchyards, tall hedgerows and woodlands including young forestry plantations, they establish territories in March and often pair for life.

Top: Oystercatchers in flight. **Above (left)**: greylag goose; **(right)**: shelduck.

Above, clockwise from top left: Black-backed gull, herring gull, black-headed gull, coot, whooper swans, reed bunting, pochard.

Above, clockwise from top left: Linnet, red kite, grey heron, brent geese, great white egret, chaffinch.

Common seals can often be seen basking off Blakeney Point and by The Wash (© Alex St

Sea Campion
Silene maritima

Sea Holly
Eryngium maritimum

Thrift (Sea Pink)
Armeria maritima

Common Vetch
Vicia sativa

Herb-Robert
Geranium robertianum

Red Campion
Silene dioica

Lousewort
Pedicularis sylvatica

Meadow Cranesbill
Geranium pratense

Common Dog Violet
Viola riviniana

Common Knapweed
Centaurea nigra

Common Centaury
Centaurium erythraea

Old Man's Beard
Clematis vitalba

Common Ragwort
Senecio jacobaea

Yarrow
Achillea millefolium

Hogweed
Heracleum sphondylium

Gorse
Ulex europaeus

Meadow Buttercup
Ranunculis acris

Marsh Marigold (Kingcup)
Caltha palustris

Bird's-foot trefoil
Lotus corniculatus

St John's Wort
Hypericum perforatum

Tormentil
Potentilla erecta

Primrose
Primula vulgaris

Cowslip
Primula veris

Honeysuckle
Lonicera periclymemum

Harebell
Campanula rotundifolia

Foxglove
Digitalis purpurea

Rosebay Willowherb
Epilobium angustifolium

Rowan (tree)
Sorbus aucuparia

Dog Rose
Rosa canina

Forget-me-not
Myosotis arvensis

Scarlet Pimpernel
Anagallis arvensis

Self-heal
Prunella vulgaris

Germander Speedwell
Veronica chamaedrys

Ramsons (Wild Garlic)
Allium ursinum

Bluebell
Hyacinthoides non-scripta

Ox-eye Daisy
Leucanthemum vulgare

Above, clockwise from top left: Redshank, avocet, curlew, sanderling, turnstone, knot.

Wetlands and marshes

The brilliantly camouflaged **bittern** (*Botaurus stellaris*) has warm brown plumage streaked with black markings, which make it difficult to spot in its favoured reed-bed habitat. Sightings of this elusive year-round resident are few and far between; you're more likely to hear the males' distinctive booming call, which carries for up to two kilometres, during the breeding season (March to June). Members of the heron family, they have long legs, a long neck, dagger-like beak and broad, rounded wings. Rarely seen far from reed-beds, they favour wetlands with extensive cover. For the best chance to spot one head to Cley or Titchwell Marshes, particularly in winter when their numbers are boosted by wintering bitterns from abroad. A one-time favourite with taxidermists and egg collectors, the bittern, known locally as a butterbump, was also persecuted and hunted for food.

Bearded tits (*Panurus biarmicus*) are bright, lively characters found in reed-beds. They have warm brown plumage and distinctive long, trailing tail feathers. The males also have blue-grey heads and black moustache-like markings. **Reed warblers** (*Acrocephalus scirpaceus*) are plain, unstreaked warblers with brown feathers and buff-coloured underparts. They are summer visitors to the UK with the largest concentrations descending on Norfolk in mid April, where they concentrate in reed-beds. **Sedge warblers** (*Acrocephalus schoenobaenus*) are small, plump warblers with striking creamy stripes above each eye that arrive all across Norfolk in summer; the best spots to see them though are reed-beds or damp wetlands. They can be differentiated from reed warblers by their long, rambling warble as opposed to the more rhythmic call of the reed warbler.

There are significant breeding colonies of **common terns** (*Stirna hirundo*), which arrive in April and leave in August and September. These silvery-grey and white birds boast long tails that have led to them being nicknamed 'sea swallows'. They breed along the coast on shingle shores, where they collect in noisy groups and can be seen in graceful flight before plunging down into the water to fish.

The breeding colony of **sandwich terns** (*Sterna sandvicensis*) at Scolt Head and Blakeney is also of international importance. They have black caps, short black legs and long, dark bills with a yellow tip. They arrive in late March and stay till September.

Little terns (*Sterna albifrons*) are Britain's smallest tern. They are short-tailed and have a yellow bill with a black tip. They are fast and agile and have an acrobatic courtship display that involves the male carrying a fish and calling to a prospective mate who chases him high before he glides back down with his wings spread into a marked 'V'. The largest breeding colonies are found at Blakeney Point.

Dunlin (*Calidris alpine*) are the commonest small waders seen on the coast, when their flocks can sometimes number thousands. They roost in nearby fields and salt-marshes when the tide is high. They have dark underparts and a slightly down-curved bill. **Redshank** (*Tringa totanus*) are medium-sized waders with

THE ENVIRONMENT & NATURE

long red legs, grey feathers and white underparts, and a long straight bill. They are widespread and can be seen all along the coast, where their numbers are swelled by migrants from Iceland. Unfortunately, the overgrazing of farmland and the draining of coastal marshes has reduced the number of suitable breeding habitats outside of nature reserves.

Oystercatchers (*Haematopus ostralegus*) are large, stocky waders with red-pink legs, black and white feathers and a long orange-red bill used for probing the ground. They are common on coastal stretches and around large estuaries, where they forage for mussels and cockles. In winter their numbers are

---

❏ What to see when

There's plenty to see whatever the time of year; during **spring** there is an excellent diversity of species, and between April and May you'll enjoy the peak months for spring bird migration. Listen out for nightingales as well as the songs of recently arrived warblers, swifts and wheateaters. Watch the acrobatic displays of breeding marsh harriers and nesting avocets and keep an eye out for stone curlews nesting in the heaths. Passage waders in full plumage are particularly striking, especially the large flocks of Icelandic godwits. Rarer birds often spotted at this time include garganey, osprey, spoonbill, common crane, Mediterranean gull, black tern and wood sandpiper. Large colonies of black-headed gulls gather inland at traditional sites whilst common, sandwich and little terns collect on the coast.

In **summer** the heaths of The Breckland and Thetford Forest conceal nightjars, honey buzzards and hobbies. The coast is home to marsh harriers, bearded tits and avocets, who are at their best at this stage of the year. Terns and bitterns, one of the UK's rarest breeding birds, are also present now and the first Arctic skuas begin to appear. Look out too for raptors including kestrels, sparrowhawks and buzzards.

Autumn begins early and even by late July many of the wading birds have begun to return to the marshes, many still in their breeding plumage. By August the south-bound waders will certainly have arrived on the coast, featuring little stints and curlew sandpipers as well as large numbers of geese and ducks. You may also see rare red-backed shrikes or barred warblers, pied flycatchers, robins, goldcrests and impressive arrivals of starlings. Further inland you'll find woodpeckers, grey partridge, kingfishers, barn and tawny owls. With strong onshore winds come fulmars, gannets, Arctic skuas, kittiwakes, sooty shearwaters and occasionally little auks.

Although coldest and with least daylight hours, **winter** offers the best spectacles of the year. The Wash is one of England's most important winter feeding areas for waders and wildfowl. In October, winter thrushes, wild geese and swans arrive; tens of thousands of raucous pink-footed geese, originally from Iceland, quit their night-time roosts to fly inland to feed, the dense flocks of birds forming spectacularly long lines and classic 'V' shapes in the sky. It is calculated that up to 100,000 pink-foots, around 40% of the UK winter population, can be seen on the Norfolk coast at this time. Thousands of wading birds are forced off the mudflats into the air in balletic style as high tide rolls in; this is also when vast wheeling flocks of knot form as they search for somewhere safe to land. Birds of prey also overwinter here; merlin, peregrine, hen harrier and short-eared owls can all be spotted most easily around dusk.

Winter is also a good time to enjoy the area's woodland and farmland species, including Egyptian geese, common buzzards, woodcocks, barn owls, grey wagtails and flocks of thrushes, tits and finches.

THE ENVIRONMENT & NATURE

swelled by migrants from Norway and their shrill calls become quite a cacophony. **Knot** (*Calidris canuta*) are dumpy, short-legged, stocky wading birds with grey feathers and white underparts. They form huge flocks in winter which wheel and turn in flight flashing their pale underwings as they do so. They use UK estuaries as feeding grounds during the winter, with large numbers arriving on The Wash and coastal stretches around Holme from their Arctic breeding grounds in late August.

Woodcock (*Scolopax rusticola*) are large, bulky wading birds with short legs and a very long tapering bill. They are mostly nocturnal and spend daylight hours hidden in dense cover, making them difficult to see. **Bar-tailed godwits** (*Limosa lapponica*) are long-legged wading birds with long, pinkish bills usually seen in their winter plumage of grey-brown feathers when they visit the UK from Scandinavia and Siberia. Huge flocks arrive in the UK between November and February either to over-winter or as they pass through on their way south. **Sanderlings** (*Calidris Alba*) are small, plump waders with pale grey feathers, white underparts and a short straight bill. They don't breed in the UK either but visit during winter from the high Arctic to roost on the long sandy beaches.

Gannets (*Morus bassanus*) are large birds that have long pointed, white wings with black tips, a long neck and a pointed beak. They can be seen wheeling above the water before flying high and circling before plunging into the sea to grab a fish. **Fulmars** (*Fulmarus glacialis*) are grey and white, gull-like birds related to the albatross that are usually seen flying low over the sea. The medium-sized, dark-feathered **Arctic skua** (*Stercorarius parasiticus*) passes through the region in August and September. They are aggressive and will pursue terns to steal the food they have collected.

Wigeon (*Anas penelope*) are medium-sized ducks with round chestnut-coloured heads and small bills. Large numbers winter on the coast, when migrants from Iceland, Scandinavia and Russia add to the flock. **Teal** (*Anas crecca*) are attractive, small dabbling ducks with chestnut-coloured heads, dark green eye patches, spotted chests, grey flanks and black-edged tails. During the breeding months they congregate on northern moors before gathering on low-lying wetlands in winter, where they are joined by large numbers of continental birds from The Baltic and Siberia. **Garganey** (*Anas querquedula*) are similar in size to teal but have more obvious pale eye stripes. They are also scarcer and more secretive. They migrate to Africa during the autumn but return to the reed-beds and shallow wetlands in March, where they flock to areas with plenty of flooded vegetation, making them difficult to see.

Goldeneye (*Bucephala clangula*) are medium-sized diving ducks. They have black and white feathers and either green or brown heads depending on their sex. They can most readily be seen in winter along the coast. **Gadwalls** (*Anas strepera*) are grey-coloured dabbling ducks with a much darker rear. They can be seen in coastal wetlands where there are small numbers of breeding birds making these nationally important populations.

The **common crane** (*Grus grus*) was once quite common in wetlands across East Anglia but it has suffered considerably due to habitat destruction

THE ENVIRONMENT & NATURE

and hunting. One of Europe's largest birds, it has a grey body and black wing plumes making it appear to have a bushy tail. Its deep sonorous call can be heard several miles away.

Little egrets (*Egretta garzetta*) are a type of small heron with white feathers, long black legs and yellow feet. They feed by walking through water in search of small fish and crustaceans, but roost in trees, especially around Holkham and Titchwell, and are reasonably common along the north coast.

Kingfishers (*Alcedo atthis*) can be found on many of Norfolk's rivers. They can appear blue, green or almost black and have a very characteristic shape. Populations are restricted by the lack of suitable breeding sites, with the birds needing areas with plentiful supplies of fish and rivers with vertical sandy banks to nest in. Numbers in Norfolk have increased slightly over recent years as a result of the milder winters.

Marsh harriers (*Circus aeruginosus*), as the name implies, are usually found hunting above reed-beds and grazing marshes. Increasingly though they nest inland in arable land. They are the commonest, largest and broadest-winged harrier in Norfolk, with dark brown or rich rust feathers. They have a sharp yelping call and can be seen or heard at Cley or Titchwell marshes year-round. At one time they were sufficiently widespread and common for ornithologists to dub them the Norfolk hawk, but following persecution and habitat loss their numbers dwindled. Since then successful conservation programmes have seen them re-establish themselves. **Hen harriers** (*Circus cyaneus*), which have pale grey feathers, visit Norfolk in small numbers during late autumn and winter but don't breed here and **Montagu's harriers** (*Circus pygargus*) are summer visitors, arriving in April and departing during early autumn. They are extremely rare breeding birds in the UK, which seem to increasingly frequent arable land rather than coastal marshes.

Pink-footed geese (*Anser brachyrhynchus*) are medium-sized geese that winter on freshwater and salt-marshes, arriving in vast flocks from their breeding grounds in Spitsbergen, Iceland and Greenland in October. They can also be seen feeding on stubble and crop fields, where they are identifiable by their short neck, small head and stubby bill. Don't rely on the pink feet as an identifier as **greylags** (*Anser anser*) also have pink legs and juvenile pink-footed geese have dull orange legs. Greylags are the largest and bulkiest of the wild geese native to the UK. They can be seen easily and often in large flocks in lowland areas. **Egyptian geese** (*Alopochen aegyptiacus*) are a similar size but have brown and pink-buff plumage and a distinctive black eye patch. They breed in open woodlands but winter on lakes and marshes.

Brent geese (*Branta bernicla*) are small, dark geese with black heads, grey-brown backs and dark underparts. They fly in loose flocks and gather on salt-marshes in October, where they over winter until March. **White-fronted geese** (*Anser albifrons*) are actually grey, with a large white patch at the front of their head around the beak. They have orange legs and either pink or orange bills. They do not breed in the UK but migrate here during winter to escape the colder climate in Greenland and Siberia.

Avocets (*Recurvirostra avosetta*) have mostly white plumage, marked with thin black lines, blue legs and an upturned bill which they sweep from side to side through the water when feeding. They breed in shallow lagoons and often near estuaries. They are the symbol of the RSPB and representative of the bird-protection programme in Britain; their return to the UK in the 1940s and successful increase in numbers is indicative of what can be achieved.

BUTTERFLIES AND MOTHS

The best time to spot butterflies is from mid July to mid September. Many of their numbers have declined due to the large loss of inland habitats. Butterflies are also under threat from the large **harlequin ladybird** (*Harmonia axyridis*), an invasive non-native species of ladybird with orange, red or black spots, which feeds on the larvae of the native ladybirds as well as on butterfly and moth eggs. First spotted in Norfolk in 2004 its numbers have grown steadily as has its distribution.

The **cinnabar moth** (*Tyria jacobaeae*) is a night flier but can sometimes be seen during the day, when it is easily spotted due to its bright red spots and stripes on its upper charcoal grey forewings – the name derives from the bright red mineral cinnabar. The caterpillars are distinguished by their jet black and yellow-orange stripes and are often spotted decimating patches of ragwort. Found in open spaces, the moth is resident in heathland, well-drained grassland and sand dunes such as those at Holme. The **garden tiger** (*Arctia caja*) is a striking moth with brown forewings crossed with cream lines and red hind wings spotted with large blue dots, which it flashes when disturbed. The caterpillars are very hairy and known colloquially as 'woolly bears'. The large **ghost moth** (*Hepialus humuli*) is common across much of Norfolk. The name refers to its pale appearance and its tendency to hover over grassy areas at dusk, rising and falling slowly. **Hummingbird hawkmoths** (*Macroglossum stellatarum*) are day moths that can be seen on the wing from June to August, feeding on nectar from flowers in the same fashion as hummingbirds. The **lime hawkmoth** (*Mimas tiliae*) has attractive scalloped forewings that vary in colour from pink to olive green. The caterpillar, which is usually bright green with yellow stripes and a blue horn at the rear, feeds on limes. The **privet hawkmoth** (*Sphinx ligustri*) is the largest hawkmoth in the country and can be found on scrub. It has pink and black barring on the body and hind wings. The caterpillar is more striking, with lilac and white stripes down the length of its luminescent green body and a black horn at the rear.

The **comma** (*Polygonia c-album*) is bright orange with dark brown markings on its wings, on the underside of which is a distinctive white 'comma' shape. The ragged edges of the wings are actually easier to spot. Found in woodland clearings, hedgerows and gardens the comma has recolonised Norfolk over the last 70 years.

The **dingy skipper** (*Erynnis tages*), with its dull grey-brown, mottled appearance, looks like a moth but is in fact a small butterfly. It can be seen flitting quickly across open, sunny habitats such as heathland or stretches of chalk

THE ENVIRONMENT & NATURE

grassland found in Breckland. The **grizzled skipper** (*Pyrgus malvae*) has characteristic black and white patterned wings. Although not very common in Norfolk it can be seen on warm, sheltered spots with sparse vegetation.

The **grayling** (*Hipparchia semele*) is hard to spot as the brown and grey patterns are superb camouflage. It can be found in coastal areas such as dunes, especially around Burnham Overy Staithe, salt-marshes and cliffs as well as heathland and grasslands such as the Brecks. The **orange tip** (*Anthocharis cardamines*) boasts bright orange tips to its white wings. Found on verges, in woodland glades and in damp meadows, unusually its numbers are on the increase and it is spreading. The **swallowtail** (*Papilio machaon britannicus*) is Britain's largest butterfly. It has stunning yellow and black markings and two long tail extensions that resemble a swallow's tail. Increasingly rare and restricted to The Broads you may just spot one if you are lucky.

The **white admiral** (*Limenitis camilla*) is also very striking with a bold white stripe across its wings. Common in woodland clearings and places with plenty of brambles, it is often seen in Norfolk, especially around Sheringham Park.

ON RIVERS AND PONDS

Norfolk is also an important breeding ground for dragonflies, which can be seen in areas of open water. There are some 34 species found here although new migrants swell the numbers. Look out for the **black-tailed skimmer** (*Orthetrum cancellatum*), which has a blue abdomen with a black tip and yellow arcs down each side. The **common darter** (*Sympetrum striolatum*) is widespread and often occurs in large numbers. They are red in colour and have a small patch of yellow at the base of their wings. **Migrant hawkers** (*Aeshna mixta*) are one of four species of hawker dragonfly to be found in Norfolk. They have mainly blue or yellow spots down their abdomen. The **Norfolk hawker** (*Aeshna isosceles*) is a rare dragonfly usually found only on The Broads, where it has its stronghold.

The **common pond skater** (*Gerris lacustris*) is a thin brownish-black bug often seen 'skating' across the surface of still patches of water, as a layer of water-repellent silvery hairs allows them to perch on top of the water. Thompson Water is particularly good for spotting them. You might also see green-black **great diving beetles** (*Dytiscus marginalis*) here. The **white clawed crayfish** (*Austropotamobius pallipes*) is the only native species of freshwater crustacean. Once widespread it is now seen in only a handful of rivers in the UK, amongst which is the River Wissey.

REPTILES

Britain's two snake species are found in Norfolk. **Adders** (*Vipera berus*), Britain's only poisonous snake, can occasionally be seen on open heathland and the edges of woodland although their natural habitat is under threat. Identifiable by the bold dark zig-zag stripe down their back, adders come in a range of colours; the male is grey to white whilst the female is brown or copper coloured.

During colder months they are inactive and hibernate but in spring they emerge to shed their skins and mate. The young are born in late August. More often than not adders move swiftly out of the way when disturbed but should you inadvertently step on one and get bitten, sit still and send someone else for help. The bite is unlikely to be fatal – it is designed to kill small mammals, not humans – but it does still warrant attention.

The **grass snake** (*Natrix natrix*) lives on open heathland, meadows and fens, often close to water. They are longer and slimmer than the adder, and are non-venomous although will emit a foul stench if you try to pick them up. Body colour varies from green to grey or brown although the most common characteristic is a yellow or orange collar immediately behind the head.

Although it looks like a snake, the **slow worm** (*Anguis fragilis*) is actually a legless lizard and differs from snakes in that it has a cylindrical grey-brown body that does not taper at the neck. It can be found on dry grassy meadows, woodland margins and churchyards.

You may also hear or come across the **common frog** (*Rana temporaria*), which frequents woodlands, hedgerows and fields where there is plenty of water. Despite its name, numbers are declining due to the large number of predators including foxes, otters, herons and bitterns that hunt it. The **common toad** (*Bufo bufo*), distinguishable from the frog by its warty skin and tendency to walk rather than jump, is relatively widespread whilst the **natterjack toad** (*Bufo calamita*), which has a bright yellow stripe running down its back, is restricted to a handful of coastal sand dune and salt-marsh sites such as the Norfolk Wildlife Trust reserve at Holme (see p129).

MAMMALS

Badgers (*Meles meles*) are readily identifiable with their black-and-white-striped heads, short legs and broad, thickset bodies. Their distribution across Norfolk is unknown but there is plenty of evidence to indicate they are resident in reasonable numbers. Dawn and dusk are the best times to spot these elusive creatures, which live in family groups in underground 'setts'.

The highly adaptable **red fox** (*Vulpus vulpus*) is the size of a small dog and has a warm reddish-brown coat and white underside as well as a white-tipped bushy tail. Opportunistic feeders, they tend to hunt at night but are not exclusively nocturnal, eat a range of food and will scavenge from rubbish.

The seemingly ubiquitous **rabbit** (*Oryctolagus cuniculus*) can be seen on heaths and commons where well-drained soils are ideal for their warrens. **Harvest mice** (*Micromys minutus*) are widespread in suitable tussocky grassland. Elusive and hard to see, they have orange-brown upperparts and white underparts, a blunt muzzle and a prehensile tail that can be twisted around plant stems to improve balance and help them climb.

Shy and elusive, **otters** (*Lutra lutra*) are mainly nocturnal so difficult to see. Often over a metre in length, they have a broad head and muzzle, small ears and a long tail. They prefer shallow water with plenty of fish and can be spotted in many of Norfolk's rivers including the Nar. **Stoats** (*Mustela erminea*) have long

THE ENVIRONMENT & NATURE

slim bodies, with red-brown fur and creamy undersides, and short legs. Found throughout Norfolk they can be spotted year-round as they do not hibernate. Almost as common are **weasels** (*Mustela nivalis*) which are similarly coloured but slightly smaller; they are tunnel-hunters and mostly prey on rodents. Look out too for various species of **voles**, **mice** and **shrews**.

The **common pipistrelle bat** (*Pipistrellus pipistrellus*) is Britain's smallest bat and its most common. Found feeding over open water, woodland and along hedgerows, they are often spotted on Thompson Common.

Roe deer (*Capreolus capreolus*) are small, native deer that tend to shelter in woodland. They can sometimes be seen alone or in pairs on the edges of fields or clearings in the forest, but you are more likely to hear the sharp dog-like bark they use as an alarm call upon detecting your presence.

The diminutive **Chinese water deer** (*Hydropotes inermis*) stands little taller than a medium-sized dog. They have large rounded ears that stand proud above the head. The males are identifiable by the tusks they grow instead of antlers. These are in fact modified teeth and are used for fighting during territorial disputes. They are common in The Broads and make the most of tall, wet vegetation to remain concealed. Beyond this there are sightings along the coast and in river valleys. **Muntjac** (*Muntiacus reevesi*), which also originated in China, are the smallest deer in Britain, standing only 45cm high at the shoulder and can be seen in coniferous woodland and scrub throughout Norfolk. Generally brown, they are slightly hunched as the hind limbs are longer than the fore. Males have short, straight horns as well as large protruding canine teeth. They are nicknamed the barking deer because of their loud, barking call.

The coast is also home to several marine mammals. **Harbour porpoises** (*Phocoena phocoena*) are the smallest cetaceans found in the UK and rarely reach 2m in length. Preferring shallow coastal waters, the porpoises are hardly ever seen from shore but can be spotted when out on the water, when their small triangular dorsal fin and short rounded head with no beak make them identifiable. **Common seals** (*Phoca vitulina*) can be seen on Blakeney Point (see box p170), where there is a permanent breeding colony which you can visit on foot or on a boat trip from Morston or Blakeney. The seals haul out on the exposed sands at low tide and then move westwards onto the shingle as the tide comes in to ensure they always have access to deep water. There is another population living in The Wash. The seals are brown, tan or grey, with identifiably 'v' shaped nostrils. They also have a proportionally large, rounded head. An adult can grow up to 6ft long and live for 20-30 years. They are gregarious and form good-sized groups, returning to favoured breeding sites. Pups are born during June and July. The largest numbers are seen in August and early September whilst the seals are moulting. **Grey Seals** (*Halichoerus grypus*) share the shingle at Blakeney Point. They are medium-sized seals and are distinguishable from their common counterparts by their straight head profile and wide-spaced nostrils. They also have fewer spots on their bodies. They give birth in November and December, and the adults moult in spring.

TREES

At one stage Norfolk used to be covered with forest. Sadly this is no longer the case. In the course of the trek, what forest there still is, is largely encountered along the Peddars Way, either as you start the trail on the wooded Suffolk–Norfolk border or progress north across a landscape dotted with plantations. The windswept northern coast is more barren but the beaches are also often backed by stands of trees. None of the woodland can be described as completely natural and it has all been managed or altered in some way by man. In the past Neolithic communities stripped the countryside here to dig for flint; this left the countryside denuded. Heavy grazing exacerbated the deterioration of the soil, until the deliberate planting of trees again was the only way to bind the soil and prevent it from worsening further. This policy continues today and many of the clusters of woodland are in fact plantations.

Predominant tree species

Ash (*Fraxinus excelsior*) is widespread in Norfolk. The typical grey bark is smooth at first before developing ridges. The black buds in winter and early spring are also distinctive. The woods around Watton, allegedly the site of the *Babes in the Wood* legend, contain a number of impressive ash trees.

ASH (WITH SEEDS)

Substantial, smooth-silvery-grey **beech** (*Fagus sylvatica*) trees, which often develop strong domed canopies, can also be seen throughout the county. Some experts actually hold that Norfolk is the northern limit for native beech trees. Felbrigg Hall, near Cromer, has a particularly attractive beech woodland adjacent to it. The woodland there also boasts a number of magnificent, ancient **sweet chestnut** (*Castanea sativa*) trees, whose large oval leaves darken with age from pale green to a rich gold in autumn.

The **common oak** (*Quercus robura*) is widespread and easily identifiable by its distinctive leaves and acorns.

Two species of willow, **white willow** (*Salix alba*) and **crack willow** (*Salix fragilis*), also appear throughout Norfolk, and thrive next to waterways.

❏ Oak leaves showing galls

Oak trees support more kinds of insects than any other tree in Britain and some affect the oak in unusual ways. The eggs of gall-flies cause growths known as galls on the leaves. Each of these contains a single insect. Other kinds of gall-flies lay eggs in stalks or flowers, leading to flower galls, growths the size of currants.

THE ENVIRONMENT & NATURE

Catkins in March and April provide an early source of nectar for visiting birds and insects.

Hawthorn (*Crataegus monogyna*) is the most common small tree in Norfolk due in part to its use in roadside and farmland hedging. The trees are most apparent in spring when fragrant white blossom bursts forth during April and May. The red, oblong fruit, or 'haw', produced in autumn is popular with migrating birds, and trees on the coast can often seem alive with migrating thrushes and warblers during October as they feed on the fleshy fruit before moving south. Less widespread is the **common lime** (*Tilia vulgaris*) which can be distinguished by its red twigs and smooth, purplish grey bark. It is commonly found in parks and gardens, including those at Houghton Hall (see box p120).

FLOWERS

Many wildflowers have declined in parts of Norfolk as a result of habitat destruction. With grasslands and heaths ploughed up, flower-filled meadows have given way to arable crops. Elsewhere, the introduction of pesticides and toxins to kill weeds has reduced the successfulness with which plants pollinate.

The coast

Rock samphire (*Crithmum maritimum*) is a succulent plant found on beaches and growing in salt-marshes, which is more commonly known as sea asparagus. The term is thought to be a corruption of the plant's French name *herbe de Saint-Pierre*. Samphire is edible and usually steamed and then coated in butter (see box p23). Shakespeare referred to the dangerous practice of collecting rock samphire from the cliffs in the 17th century, writing in *King Lear*, 'Half-way down, Hangs one that gathers samphire; dreadful trade!' **Marsh samphire** (*Salicornia europaea*) is a different species, but is frequently confused with its namesake. Its jointed green stems, which turn red in autumn, are also edible.

Sea lavender (*Limonium vulgare*) is an attractive plant that thrives in salt-marshes and muddy saline pools. It is particularly prevalent at Titchwell and on Scolt Head Island. It has oval erect leaves and blue-purple flower clusters that give the plant its name; it is not related to true lavender though and does not have its distinctive smell. Nonetheless it is popular with insects, butterflies and bees in particular. **Sea aster** (*Aster tripolium*) is another native of salt-marshes. It has long fleshy leaves and loose flowerheads that resemble daisies in shades of blue, white or yellow.

Sea holly (*Eryngium maritimum*) is an attractive coastal plant found in dune systems and along shingle sections of the coast. It has blue-green spiky leaves and powder-blue flowers that bloom between June and September in cone-like clusters. Up to the end of the 19th century the roots were dug up and candied for use as a sweet treat and aphrodisiac, a practice that had a significant effect on the plant's distribution and from which it is only now recovering.

Sea campion (*Silene maritima*) is a clump-forming plant found on coastal cliffs and shingle, especially on Blakeney Point. In spring the young shoots form a compact cushion of leaves, from which emerge masses of white flowers with distinctive inflated calyces. **Thrift** (*Armeria maritima*) is a compact perennial that grows in low clumps and sends up long stems from which profusions of pink flowers blossom. It is common in marshes and along the coast.

Yellow horned-poppy (*Glaucium flavum*) grows on shingle banks and beaches and can most readily be seen between Blakeney and Weybourne or on Scolt Head Island, where its rosettes of grey-green, waxy leaves and bright yellow flowers, which bloom between June and September, stand out against the stones. Under threat due to declining habitat it is a protected species and must not be picked from the wild. **Bird's-foot-trefoil** (*Lotus corniculatus*) is an attractive trailing plant with yellow pea-like flowers that can be seen in grassy areas. It has easily recognisable seed pods, shaped like a bird's foot, which give it its name. **Alexanders** (*Smyrnium olusatrum*) is a tall plant (up to 1.5m high) with bright green, glossy leaves and yellow-green, umbrella-shaped flower heads, which appear from March to June. Introduced to Britain by the Romans as a food plant, Alexanders was once found only along the coast. With increasingly mild winters the plant has spread inland though and is now common in hedgerows and roadside verges.

Woodland and hedgerows

Bluebell (*Hyacinthoides non-scripta*) flowers are deep purple-blue and very attractive. Growing in light shade they are often found in patches of hundreds or thousands and, when in flower from mid April to late May, form a carpet of colour.

Japanese knotweed (*Fallopia japonica*) is a highly vigorous, invasive plant introduced to the UK from Japan. Growing up to 3m tall, it has fleshy red and green stems that look like bamboo, and small creamy white flowers and can be seen in hedgerows where there is a decent water supply. **Mistletoe** (*Viscum album*) forms rounded clumps often high in a tree canopy, where it can be identified by the white, semi-transparent berries visible between December and February. Although not common in Norfolk it can be seen in lime trees, but also appears in hawthorn and willow.

Other flowering plants to look for include **foxgloves** (*Digitalis purpurea*) with its trumpet-like flowers, **forget-me-not** (*Myosotis arvensis*) with tiny, delicate blue flowers and **cow parsley** (*Anthriscus sylvestris*), a tall plant with a large globe of white flowers.

Heathland and scrub

Bee orchids (*Ophrys apifera*) have a distinctive flower consisting of three pink 'wings' and a central hairy brown 'bee' body patterned with yellow spots and lines – the flowers look as if at the centre of the three petals a small bee is sucking nectar, an illusion designed to attract other bees. The flowers, which appear between May and July, project outwards from a spike that varies in height from just 5cm to more than 30cm. Notoriously unpredictable, bee orchids can be found on areas of grassland and coastal sand dunes or scrub.

The **common poppy** (*Papaver rhoeas*) is found throughout Norfolk on embankments, roadside verges, farmland and gardens. The translucent, papery-petalled scarlet flowers and pepper-pot seed capsules are highly distinctive, particularly when in bloom from June to August. The stretch of coast between Sheringham, Cromer and Overstrand is known as 'Poppyland', a name first given to the area by the writer Clement Scott in the 1880s. Today the common poppy has been voted the county flower for Norfolk. **Cowslip** (*Primula veris*), recognisable by its nodding yellow flowers hanging downwards in loose groups, grows in hedgerows, grassy verges and churchyards. Once picked for May Day celebrations and used to make cowslip wine and herbal infusions, the flower is in decline.

Giant hogweed (*Heracleum mantegazzianum*) can stand up to 5m tall. Introduced from Asia as an ornamental plant, it has run riot and out-competes native species. It has hollow, green stems with reddish blotches and jagged leaves arranged in a rosette around the stem. The stems, edges and undersides of the leaves have small hairs which contain poisonous sap that can cause skin irritation, blistering and sensitivity to the sun.

Another plant introduced as a garden ornamental but which has spread across the county is **Himalayan balsam** (*Impatiens glandulifera*), identifiable by its hollow, jointed pinkish-red stems and fragrant purple-pink slipper-shaped flowers. Growing in dense stands up to 3m in height, it suffocates competing plants.

Harebell (*Campanula rotundifolia*) is easily spotted due to its delicate, bell-shaped, blue flowers suspended from thin, wiry flower stems. Plants usually grow in clumps and are common in parts of Breckland (see p56) where they form blue splashes of colour whilst in bloom from late summer to early autumn. **Meadow saxifrage** (*Saxifraga granulata*) has white, five-petalled flowers that flower between April and June. Declining nationally, it is still prevalent in Eastern England and relatively widespread in Norfolk, where it is found in patches of well-drained soil.

Water mint (*Mentha aquatica*) grows in wet habitats such as wetland nature reserves. The flowers vary from mauve-purple to pink, lilac or blue although it is the distinctive minty aroma when crushed underfoot that often first draws attention to this species.

MINIMUM IMPACT & OUTDOOR SAFETY

Minimum impact walking

In this chaotic world in which people live their lives at an increasingly frenetic pace, many of us living in overcrowded cities and working in jobs that offer little free time, the great outdoors is becoming an essential means of escape. Walking in the countryside is a wonderful means of relaxation and gives people the time to think and rediscover themselves. Of course, as the popularity of the countryside increases so do the problems that this pressure brings. The Peddars Way and Norfolk Coast Path are situated within easy reach of one of the most populated areas of Britain so are particularly vulnerable. Their relative accessibility further adds to their appeal and places more pressure on the land. It is important for visitors to remember that the countryside is the home and workplace of many others. Walkers in particular should be aware of their responsibilities. Indeed, a walker who respects and understands the countryside will get far more enjoyment from their trip.

Minimum impact walking is all about a common-sense approach to exploring the countryside, being mindful and respectful of the wildlife and of those who live and work on the land. By following a few simple guidelines while walking the Peddars Way and Norfolk Coast Path, you can have a positive impact not just on your own well-being but also on local communities and the environment, thereby becoming part of the solution. Simple measures such as not dropping litter, keeping dogs on leads and leaving gates as you find them ought to be second nature to anyone who regularly uses the countryside. However, some things are not as well-known and thus are worth consideration.

ECONOMIC IMPACT

Buy local
Rural businesses and communities in Britain have been hit hard in recent years by a seemingly endless series of crises. Most people are aware of the countryside code (see box p82); not dropping litter and closing the gate behind you are still as pertinent as ever, but in light of the economic pressures that local countryside businesses are under, there is something else you can do: buy local.

Look and **ask for local produce** (see box p23) to buy and eat. Not only does this cut down on the amount of pollution and congestion that the transportation of food creates – so-called 'food miles' – but also ensures that you are supporting local farmers and producers, the very people who have moulded the countryside you have come to see and who are in the best position to protect it. If you can find local food which is also organic so much the better.

Money spent at local level – perhaps in a market, or at the greengrocer, or in an independent pub – has a far greater impact for good in that community than the equivalent spent in a branch of a national chain store or restaurant. It would be going too far to advocate that walkers boycott the larger supermarkets, which after all do provide local employment, but it's worth remembering that smaller businesses in rural communities rely heavily on visitors for their very existence. If we want to keep these local shops and post offices, we need to use them.

ENVIRONMENTAL IMPACT

A walking holiday in itself is an environmentally friendly approach to tourism. The following are some ideas on how you can go a few steps further in helping to minimise your impact on the natural environment while walking the Peddars Way and Norfolk Coast Path.

Use public transport whenever possible

Although there is minimal public transport along the Peddars Way, public transport on the Norfolk coast is good and in the case of the Coastliner 36 and No 4 bus service (see p50 and box p54) specifically geared towards the coast-path walker. By using the local bus you will help to keep the standard of public transport high. Public transport is always preferable to using private cars as it benefits everyone: visitors, locals and the environment.

Never leave litter

Leaving litter shows a total disrespect for the natural world and others coming after you. As well as being unsightly litter kills wildlife, pollutes the environment and can be dangerous to farm animals. Please carry a degradable plastic bag so you can dispose of your rubbish in a bin in the next village. It would be very helpful if you could pick up litter left by other people too.

● **Is it OK if it's biodegradable?** Not really. Apple cores, banana skins, orange peel and the like attract insects and ruin a picnic spot for others. Using the excuse that they are natural and biodegradable just doesn't cut any ice.

● **The lasting impact of litter** A piece of orange peel left on the ground takes six months to decompose; silver foil 18 months; a plastic bag 10 years; clothes 15 years; and an aluminium can 85 years.

Erosion

● **Stay on the main trail** The effect of your footsteps may seem minuscule but when they are multiplied by several thousand walkers each year they become rather more significant. Avoid taking shortcuts, widening the trail or taking more than one path; your boots will be followed by many others.

● **Consider walking out of season** The maximum disturbance by walkers coincides with the time of year when nature wants to do most of its growth and repair. In high-use areas, like that along much of the coast path, the trail never recovers. Walking at less busy times eases this pressure while also generating year-round income for the local economy. Not only that, but it may make the walk a more relaxing experience with fewer people on the path and less competition for accommodation.

Respect all wildlife
Care for all wildlife you come across along the path; it has as much right to be there as you. Tempting as it is to pick wild flowers leave them so the next people who pass can enjoy them too. Don't break branches off or damage trees in any way.

If you come across wildlife keep your distance and don't watch for too long. Your presence can cause considerable stress, particularly if the adults are with young, or in winter when the weather is harsh and food is scarce. Young animals are rarely abandoned. If you come across young birds keep away so that their mother can return. Anyone considering a spot of climbing on the sea cliffs should bear in mind that there are restrictions in certain areas due to the presence of nesting birds. Check with the local tourist information office.

The code of the outdoor loo
'Going' in the outdoors is a lost art worth re-learning, for your sake and everyone else's. As more and more people discover the joys of the outdoors this is becoming an important issue.

In some parts of the world where visitor pressure is higher than in Britain walkers and climbers are required to pack out their excrement. This could soon be necessary here. Human excrement is not only offensive to our senses but, more importantly, can infect water sources.

● **Where to go** Wherever possible **use a toilet**. Public toilets are marked on the trail maps in this guide and you will also find facilities in pubs and cafés along the coast path.

If you do have to go outdoors choose a site at least **30 metres away from running water**. Carry a small trowel and **dig a small hole** about 15cm (6 inches) deep to bury your excrement in. It decomposes quicker when in contact with the top layer of soil or leaf mould. Use a stick to stir loose soil into your deposit as well as this speeds up decomposition even more. Do not squash it under rocks as this slows down the composting process. If you have to use rocks to cover it make sure they are not in contact with your faeces.

Make sure you do not dig any holes on ground that is, or could be, of historic or archaeological interest.

● **Toilet paper and tampons** Toilet paper takes a long time to decompose whether buried or not. It is easily dug up by animals and may then blow into water sources or onto the path. The best method for dealing with it is to **pack it out**. Put the used paper inside a paper bag which you then place inside a plastic bag (or two). Then simply empty the contents of the paper bag at the next toilet you come across and throw the bag away.

You should also pack out **tampons** and **sanitary towels** in a similar way; they take years to decompose and may also be dug up and scattered about by animals.

Wild camping

Unfortunately, wild camping is not encouraged along either the Peddars Way or Norfolk Coast Path. In any case there are few places where it is a viable option. This is a shame since wild camping is an altogether more fulfilling experience than camping on a designated site. Living in the outdoors without any facilities provides a valuable lesson in simple, sustainable living where the results of all your actions, from going to the loo to washing your plates, can be seen.

If you do insist on wild camping **always** ask the landowner for permission. Anyone contemplating camping on a beach should be very aware of the times and heights of the tide. Follow these suggestions for minimising your impact and encourage others to do likewise.

● **Be discreet**   Camp alone or in small groups, spend only one night in each place and pitch your tent late and move off early.

● **Never light a fire**   The deep burn caused by camp fires, no matter how small, damages the turf which can take years to recover. Cook on a camp stove instead.

● **Don't use soap or detergent**   There is no need to use soap; even biodegradable soaps and detergents pollute streams. You won't be away from a shower for more than a day or so. Wash up without detergent; use a plastic or metal scourer or, failing that, a handful of fine pebbles from the beach or some bracken or grass.

● **Leave no trace**   Learn the skill of moving on without leaving any sign of having been there: no moved boulders, ripped up vegetation or drainage ditches. Make a final check of your campsite before departing; pick up litter that you or anyone else has left, thus leaving the place in a better state than you found it.

ACCESS

Britain is a crowded cluster of islands with few places where you can wander as you please; the south-east corner of the country is the most populated area with some of the busiest roads in the country. Most of the land is a patchwork of fields and agricultural land, and the countryside the Peddars Way cuts across is no different. However, there are countless public rights of way, in addition to both this and the coast path, that criss-cross the land. This is fine, but what happens if you feel a little more adventurous and want to explore the beaches, dunes, moorland, woodland and hills that can also be found within the national park boundaries? Most of the land the Peddars Way and Norfolk Coast Path pass through is private land or nature reserve and, unless you are on a right of way, is off limits. However, the 'Right to Roam' legislation (see opposite) has opened up some previously restricted land to walkers.

Rights of way

As a designated National Trail (see box below) the Peddars Way and Norfolk Coast Path is a public right of way – this is either a footpath, a bridleway or a byway; the route is in fact made up of all three.

Rights of way are theoretically established because the landowner has dedicated them to public use. However, very few rights of way are formally dedicated in this way. If people have been using a path without interference for 20 years or more the law assumes the owner has intended to dedicate it as a right of way. If a path has been unused for 20 years it does not cease to exist; the guiding principle is 'once a highway, always a highway'.

Farmers and land managers must ensure that paths are not blocked by crops or other vegetation, or otherwise obstructed, and the route is identifiable and the surface restored soon after cultivation. If crops are growing over the path you have the right to walk through them, following the line of the right of way as closely as possible. If you find a path or right of way is blocked you should report it to the appropriate authority, Norfolk County Council (see box p60) or the National Trail officer (see p46 for the National Trail website).

Right to roam

In October 2005 the Countryside & Rights of Way Act (CRoW) 2000, or 'Right to Roam' as dubbed by walkers, came into effect after a long campaign to allow greater public access to areas of countryside in England and Wales deemed to be uncultivated open country. This essentially means moorland, heathland, downland and upland areas. It does not mean free access to wander over farmland, woodland or private gardens.

Some land is covered by restrictions (ie high-impact activities such as driving a vehicle, cycling, horse-riding are not permitted) and some land is excluded (such as gardens, parks and cultivated land).

❑ **National Trails**

The Peddars Way and Norfolk Coast Path is one of 15 National Trails (🖳 national trail.co.uk) in England and Wales. These are Britain's flagship long-distance paths which grew out of the post-war desire to protect the country's special places, a movement which also gave birth to national parks and AONBs.

National Trails are funded by the government through Natural England with additional contributions from local highway authorities and other partners. The trails are managed on the ground by a National Trail Officer. They co-ordinate the maintenance work undertaken by the local highway authority and landowners to ensure that the trail is kept to nationally agreed standards.

Maintenance of the paths is carried out by the National Trail Officer. Teams of rangers, wardens and volunteers undertake various tasks throughout the year.

Where erosion of the path becomes a problem boardwalks or steps are constructed and particularly boggy areas are drained by digging ditches. Occasionally the authorities will re-route the path where erosion has become so severe as to be a danger to the walker. During the winter some sections of the path can be swamped by storms, requiring the shingle or sand to be cleared.

❏ THE COUNTRYSIDE CODE

The Countryside Code, originally described in the 1950s as the Country Code, was revised and relaunched in 2004, in part because of the changes brought about by the CRoW Act (see p81); it was updated again in 2012, 2014 and also 2016. The Code seems like common sense but sadly some people still appear to have no understanding of how to treat the countryside they walk in. An adapted version of the 2016 Code, launched under the logo 'Respect. Protect. Enjoy.', is given below:

Respect other people

● **Consider the local community and other people enjoying the outdoors** Be sensitive to the needs and wishes of those who live and work there. If, for example, farm animals are being moved or gathered keep out of the way and follow the farmer's directions. Being courteous and friendly to those you meet will ensure a healthy future for all based on partnership and co-operation.

● **Leave gates and property as you find them and follow paths unless wider access is available** A farmer normally closes gates to keep farm animals in, but may sometimes leave them open so the animals can reach food and water. Leave gates as you find them or follow instructions on signs. When in a group, make sure the last person knows how to leave the gate. Follow paths unless wider access is available, such as on open country or registered common land (known as 'open access land'). Leave machinery and farm animals alone – if you think an animal is in distress try to alert the farmer instead. Use gates, stiles or gaps in field boundaries if you can – climbing over walls, hedges and fences can damage them and increase the risk of farm animals escaping. If you have to climb over a gate because you can't open it always do so at the hinged end. Also be careful not to disturb ruins and historic sites.

Stick to the official path across arable/pasture land. Minimise erosion by not cutting corners or widening the path.

Protect the natural environment

● **Leave no trace of your visit and take your litter home** Take special care not to damage, destroy or remove features such as rocks, plants and trees. Take your litter with you (see p78); litter and leftover food doesn't just spoil the beauty of the countryside, it can be dangerous to wildlife and farm animals.

Fires can be as devastating to wildlife and habitats as they are to people and property – so be careful with naked flames and cigarettes at any time of the year.

● **Keep dogs under effective control** This means that you should keep your dog on a lead or keep it in sight at all times, be aware of what it's doing and be confident it will return to you promptly on command.

Across farmland dogs should always be kept on a short lead. During lambing time they should not be taken with you at all. Always clean up after your dog and get rid of the mess responsibly – 'bag it and bin it'. (See also pp231-3).

Enjoy the outdoors

● **Plan ahead and be prepared** You're responsible for your own safety: be prepared for natural hazards, changes in weather and other events. Wild animals, farm animals and horses can behave unpredictably if you get too close, especially if they're with their young – so give them plenty of space.

● **Follow advice and local signs** In some areas there may be temporary diversions in place. Take notice of these and other local trail advice. Walking on both the Peddars Way and Norfolk Coast Path is pretty much hazard-free but you're responsible for your own safety so follow the simple guidelines outlined opposite.

With more freedom in the countryside comes a need for more responsibility from the walker. Remember that wild open country is still the workplace of farmers and home to all sorts of wildlife. Have respect for both and avoid disturbing domestic and wild animals.

Outdoor safety

AVOIDANCE OF HAZARDS

With good planning and preparation most hazards can be avoided. This information is just as important for those out on a day walk as for those walking the entire path.

Ensure you have suitable **clothes** (see pp41-2) to keep you warm and dry whatever the conditions and a spare change of inner clothes. A compass, whistle, torch and first-aid kit should be carried and are discussed on p42. The **emergency signal** is six blasts on the whistle or six flashes with a torch. A **mobile phone** may also be useful.

Take plenty of **food** with you for the day and at least one litre of **water** although more would be better, especially on the long northern stretches of the Peddars Way. It is a good idea to fill up your bottle whenever you pass through a village since stream water cannot be relied upon. You will eat far more walking than you do normally so make sure you have enough food for the day, as well as some high-energy snacks (chocolate, dried fruit, biscuits) in the bottom of your pack for an emergency.

Stay alert and know exactly where you are throughout the day. The easiest way to do this is to **check your position regularly** on the map. If visibility suddenly decreases with mist and cloud, or there is an accident, you will be able to make a sensible decision about what action to take based on your location.

If you choose to walk alone, you must appreciate and be prepared for the increased risk. It's a good idea to leave word with someone about where you are going and remember to contact them when you have arrived safely.

Safety on the Peddars Way and Norfolk Coast Path

Although the Peddars Way and Norfolk Coast Path are both ostensibly fairly easy routes, through gentle terrain, there is always the potential for an accident to happen. Do not become complacent or underestimate the route and the terrain just because it seems straightforward.

Always err on the side of over-caution and think twice about walking if you are tired or feeling ill. This is when most accidents happen. To ensure you have a safe trip it is well worth following this advice:

● Keep to the path – avoid walking on the marshes or muddy inlets at low tide
● Avoid walking in windy weather – the coast can be very exposed

● Wear strong sturdy boots with good ankle support and a good grip rather than trainers or sandals
● Be extra vigilant with children
● Keep dogs under close control
● Wear or carry warm and waterproof clothing
● In an emergency dial ☎ 999 and ask for the police, ambulance or coastguard.

Safety on the beach

Norfolk's beaches are spectacular in any weather but it's when the sun is shining that the sweaty walker gets the urge to take a dip.

The sea can be a dangerous environment and care should be taken if you do go for a swim and even if you're just walking along the beach. Follow this common-sense advice:

● If tempted to take a shortcut across a beach be aware of the tides to avoid being cut off or stranded
● Do not sit directly below cliffs and do not climb them unless you are an experienced climber with the right equipment, or with someone who has experience
● Don't swim immediately after eating, or after drinking alcohol; swimming in itself can be dangerous
● Be aware of local tides and currents – don't assume it is safe just because other people are swimming there; if in doubt consult the tide tables (see below) or check with the nearest tourist information centre
● Be extra vigilant with children
● Keep dogs under close control and be aware of the regulations (see pp231-3)
● In an emergency dial ☎ 999 and ask for the coastguard.

DEALING WITH AN ACCIDENT

● Use basic first aid to treat the injury to the best of your ability.
● Work out exactly where you are. If possible leave someone with the casualty while others go to get help. If there are only two people, you have a dilemma. If you decide to get help leave all spare clothing and food with the casualty.
● Telephone ☎ 999 and ask for the police, ambulance or coastguard. They will assist in both offshore and onshore incidents.

TIDE TABLES

Tide tables are available from 🖥 tidetimes.org.uk. You can also get them from newsagents in the area and tourist information centres along the coast.

WEATHER FORECASTS

The Norfolk coast is exposed to whatever the North Sea can throw at it. Even when it's sunny, sea breezes usually develop during the course of the day so it's worth taking weather forecasts with a pinch of salt.

A warm day can feel bitterly cold when you stop for lunch on a cliff top being battered by the wind. Try to get the local weather forecast from the newspaper, TV or radio, or one of the internet/telephone forecasts before you set off. Alter your plans for the day accordingly.

Internet/telephone forecasts

Weather call (⌨ weathercall.co.uk) provides frequently updated and generally reliable weather forecasts. For detailed online weather forecasts, including local five-day forecasts, also check out ⌨ bbc.co.uk/weather or ⌨ metoffice.gov.uk.

BLISTERS

It is important to break in new boots before embarking on a long walk. Make sure the boots are comfortable and try to avoid getting them wet on the inside. Air your feet at lunchtime, keep them clean and change your socks regularly. If you feel any hot spots stop immediately and apply a few strips of zinc oxide tape and leave them on until it is pain-free or the tape starts to come off.

If you have left it too late and a blister has developed, you should surround it with 'moleskin' or any other blister kit to protect it from abrasion. Popping it can lead to infection. If the skin is broken keep the area clean with antiseptic and cover with a non-adhesive dressing material held in place with tape.

HYPOTHERMIA

Also known as **exposure**, this occurs when the body can't generate enough heat to maintain its normal temperature, usually as a result of being wet, cold, unprotected from the wind, tired and hungry. It is usually more of a problem in upland areas. However, even on the Norfolk coast in bad weather your body can be exposed to strong winds and driving rain making the risk a real one. The northern stretches of the Peddars Way path are particularly exposed and there are fewer villages making it difficult to get help should it be needed.

Hypothermia is easily avoided by wearing suitable clothing, carrying and eating enough food and drink, being aware of the weather conditions and checking the morale of your companions. Early signs to watch for are feeling cold and tired with involuntary shivering. Find some shelter as soon as possible and warm the victim up with a hot drink and some chocolate or other high-energy food. If possible, give them another warm layer of clothing and allow them to rest until feeling better.

If allowed to worsen, strange behaviour, slurring of speech and poor co-ordination will become apparent and the victim can quickly progress into unconsciousness, followed by coma and death. Quickly get the victim out of wind and rain, improvising a shelter if necessary. Rapid restoration of bodily warmth is essential and best achieved by bare-skin contact: someone should get into the same sleeping bag as the patient, both having stripped to their underwear, any spare clothing under or over them to build up heat. Send urgently for help.

MINIMUM IMPACT & OUTDOOR SAFETY

HYPERTHERMIA

Heat exhaustion is often caused by water depletion and is a serious condition that could eventually lead to death. Symptoms include thirst, fatigue, giddiness, a rapid pulse, raised body temperature, low urine output and later on, delirium and coma. The only remedy is to re-establish water balance. If the victim is suffering severe muscle cramps, it may be due to salt depletion.

Heat stroke is caused by failure of the body's temperature-regulating system and is extremely serious. It is associated with a very high body temperature and an absence of sweating. Early symptoms can be similar to those of hypothermia, such as aggressive behaviour, lack of co-ordination and so on. Later the victim goes into a coma or convulsions and death will follow if effective treatment is not given. To treat heat stroke, sponge the victim down or cover with wet towels and fan them vigorously. Get help immediately.

SUNBURN

Even on overcast days the sun still has the power to burn. Sunburn can be avoided by regularly applying sunscreen. Don't forget your lips and those areas affected by reflected light off the ground; under your nose, ears and chin. You may find that you quickly sweat sunscreen off, so consider wearing a sun hat. If you have particularly fair skin, wear a light, long-sleeved top and trousers.

ROUTE GUIDE & MAPS 4

Using this guide

The trail guide has been divided into stages but these should not be seen as rigid daily stages since people walk at different speeds and have different interests. The route summaries below describe the trail between significant places and are written as if walking north towards the coast on the Peddars Way and then east along the Norfolk Coast Path since this is by far the most popular direction for people tackling the trail. To enable you to plan your own itinerary, practical information is shown clearly on the trail maps. This includes walking times for both directions, places to stay and eat, as well as shops where you can stock up on supplies. Further service details are given in the text under the entry for each place.

For an overview of this information see **itineraries** on pp31-3 and the **village and town facilities tables** on pp36-9.

For **overview maps** and **trail profiles** see the colour pages at the end of the book.

TRAIL MAPS   [for map key see p234]
Scale and walking times
The trail maps are drawn at a scale of 1:20,000 (1cm = 200m; $3^{1}/_{8}$ inches = 1 mile). Walking times are given along the side of each map and the arrow indicates the direction to which that time refers. Black triangles show the points between which the times have been taken. See **note on walking times** in box below.

The time-bars are there as a guide and are not to judge your walking ability. Any number of variables will affect the speed at which you actually walk, from the weather conditions to the number of beers you drank the previous evening. After the first few hours' walking you should be able to gauge how your speed relates to the timings on the maps.

❏ **Important note – walking times**
Unless otherwise specified, **all times in this book refer only to the time spent walking**. You will need to add 20-30% to allow for rests, time to stop and stare, photography, checking the map, drinking water etc. When planning the day's hike count on 5-7 hours' actual walking.

Up or down?

The trail on the maps is marked as a broken line. An arrow across the trail indicates an incline: it always points to the higher ground. Two arrows show that the slope is steep. If, for example, you are walking from A (at 80m) to B (at 200m) and the trail between the two is short and steep it would be shown thus: A– – –> > – – –B. If the arrow heads were reversed they would indicate the trail was downhill.

Accommodation

Apart from in the larger towns along the coast where some selection of places to stay has been necessary, almost every accommodation option within easy reach of the trail is marked.

Details of each place are given in the accompanying text. The number and type of rooms is given for each place: **S** = single bed, **D** = double bed, **T** = twin beds ie two separate beds, **Tr/Qd** = triple/quad ie rooms that can sleep up to three/four people, but note that this often means two people sharing a double bed and the other(s) in bunk beds; these rooms can also be used as doubles or twins.

The text also mentions whether the premises have **wi-fi** (WI-FI); if a **bath** is available (◠) in, or for, at least one room; if a packed lunch (Ⓛ) can be pre-ordered and whether **dogs** (🐾) are welcome. Most places will not take more than one dog in a room and also only accept them subject to prior arrangement. Many make an additional charge (usually per night but occasionally per stay) while others may require a deposit which is refundable if the dog doesn't make a mess. See also p20.

Rates given are **per person (pp)** based on two people sharing a room for a one-night stay – rates are almost always discounted for a longer stay. Where a single room (**sgl**) is available the rate for that is quoted if different from the per person rate. The rate for single occupancy (**sgl occ**) of a double/twin is generally higher, and the rate for three or more sharing a room may be lower. Unless specified, rates are for B&B. At some places the only option is a room rate; this will be the same whether one or two people share. See p21 for more details on prices.

Note that many places only accept bookings for a minimum of two nights, particularly in the summer months. However, to help walkers staying for two (or more) nights they may offer a pick-up, drop-off service.

Other features

Other features are marked on the maps when pertinent to navigation. To avoid cluttering the maps and making them unusable not all features have been marked each time they occur.

Peddars Way

Peddars Way follows a Roman road built along the line of an even older trackway. The trail starts in the Brecks and runs north from Knettishall Heath for 46 miles to Holme-next-the-Sea (see p129) where it intersects with Norfolk Coast Path.

If you are arriving by train or bus, Thetford (see below) is the closest stop to the start of the trail at Knettishall Heath some 15 miles away.

THETFORD [see map p90]

Thetford was once the capital of Saxon East Anglia. An important medieval religious centre, its fortunes changed when the Dissolution of the Monasteries meant the religious buildings were destroyed, removing much of Thetford's wealth and prestige.

Nowadays it is pleasant enough and boasts a number of significant historic buildings including a **Cluniac Priory** (see box below) dating from 1107. The extensive remains (free admission), although little more than outlines of structures, are all that's left of one of the most important East Anglian monasteries; see also p112. Other sites include **St Peter's Church** from the 1300s as well as older Iceni-fortified ramparts at **Gallows Hill** dating from AD40, Saxon defences, and a Norman castle built on a massive man-made mound, **Castle Hill**, dating from the 1070s. The earthworks, the tallest in England, stand 81ft high and measure 1000ft around the base. The largest area of lowland pine forest left in Britain, **Thetford Forest**, also stands on the north-western edge of the town.

On King St there is a gilded, bronze **statue of Thomas Paine** who was born in Thetford in 1737. He worked as an exciseman here before going to America, where his pamphlets *Rights of Man* and *Age of Reason* made him famous in the late 1700s. He played an active part in both the American and the French revolutions.

Snetterton Circuit (see p15), 12 miles/20km north-east of Thetford on the A11, is a motor-racing track that hosts British touring cars, Formula Three and superbike events.

Services

Everything of importance, including a **supermarket**, such as Tesco and Sainsbury's, and **banks** with ATMs can be found by turning left out of the station and walking into the centre of town.

There is a **tourist information centre** (TIC; ☎ 01842-751975, 🖳 leapinghare.org; Feb-Nov Mon-Thur 10am-3pm, Fri till 5pm, Sat 9am-3pm; rest of year same but Mon-Thur to 2pm) at 20 King St. They can provide information about accommodation but do not do any bookings.

Transport

● **Getting to Thetford** Thetford is a stop on Greater Anglia's **train** services between Cambridge/Ely and Norwich and East Midlands Trains' between Liverpool and

---

❑ **Cluniac Order**

The Cluniac Order was a medieval organisation of Benedictines centred on the abbey at Cluny in France. Founded in 910, the order became the furthest reaching religious reform movement of the Middle Ages and at its height was second only to the papacy as the chief religious force in Europe. Gradually superseded by the Cistercians and finally suppressed by the French Revolution.

Norwich. Cambridge and Norwich provide services to London and other destinations. See box p48.

National Express **coach** NX490 (see box p49) stops here.

Coach Services' Nos 40, 81, 84, 86, 200/201 and 332 **bus** services connect with surrounding towns and villages; see pp51-4 for details.

● **Getting to the start of Peddars Way**
There are no scheduled bus services from Thetford to Knettishall Heath (for the start of the Peddars Way) so the best way to get there is by booking the Suffolk Links **Brecks Area Bus** (see box p51; £3 for a single journey); it can take you from Thetford (bus or railway station) to the car park nearest to where the Peddars Way begins and the Icknield Way (see p35) ends.

Alternatively, you can take a **taxi** from the railway station. Sometimes cars are waiting but, if not, try: C&S Taxis (☎ 01842-760322), Daley's Taxis (☎ 01842-750777), or A2B Taxis (☎ 01842-755222, 🖳 a2btaxisthetford.co.uk. The journey takes 10-15 minutes and costs £12-15 from Thetford one way.

If planning to drive note that the **car** park opposite the start of the Way has no facilities and it is not secure so you shouldn't leave your vehicle there for any length of time, especially the time it takes to trek the whole trail. At the nearby Knettishall Heath Country Park, however, there is a pay and display car park with public toilets.

There is also a 15-mile **path** from Thetford to Knettishall Heath that forms part of the Iceni Way (see p39) should you want to walk to the trailhead.

Thetford

Where to stay

Should you arrive early enough in the morning, it is possible to walk to Stonebridge (see p96), some 6 miles north east of Thetford for the first night. However, if you choose to overnight in Thetford, try the large *Bell Inn* (☎ 01842-754455, 💻 oldenglishinns.co.uk; 5S/34D/7T, all en suite; ☜; WI-FI; ⓛ; 🐾), on King St, which has B&B for around £43.75pp (sgl around £77.50, sgl occ room rate) but rates vary depending on demand; or the historical *Thomas Paine Hotel* (☎ 01842-750372, 💻 thethomaspainehotel.co.uk; 7D/1T, all en suite; ☜; WI-FI; ⓛ; 🐾), on White Hart St, named after the eponymous local alumnus (see p89); B&B costs from £70pp (sgl occ rates on request).

Wereham House (☎ 01842-761956, 💻 werehamhouse.co.uk; 2S/4D/1T/one room sleeps up to five, all en suite; WI-FI; ⓛ), on White Hart St, has comfortably furnished rooms with B&B for about £43pp (sgl/sgl occ from £59/72) – and a large secluded garden. They also have a boot room, a drying room and laundry facilities.

Elveden Inn (☎ 01842-890876, 💻 elvedeninn.com; 2Qd, both en suite; ☜; WI-FI; 🐾) provides B&B (from £45pp, sgl occ room rate) and has a café (see Where to eat) located within the stylishly converted farm buildings on the Elveden Estate; the buildings also house a series of upmarket shops.

Where to eat and drink

The restaurant in *Thomas Paine Hotel* (see Where to stay; daily noon-2pm & 6-9.30pm) has a range of bar meals (£9.95-17.95) as well as daily specials and a fine dining restaurant alongside locally brewed real ale.

If you're after a sharpener before you start, *The Albion* (☎ 01842-338208; bar Mon-Wed & Sun noon-11pm, Thur till 11.30pm, Fri-Sat 11am-12.30am; WI-FI; 🐾), on Castle St, is a small pub in a row of flint cottages close to the centre of town. The patio overlooks the earthworks of Castle Hill and Castle Park. Food is not served but you are allowed to eat takeaways in the pub.

There are **fast-food restaurants** on Market Place and Guildhall St.

The eclectic menu in the good quality café at *Elveden Inn* (see Where to stay; food Mon-Sat 7.30-9.30am & noon-9pm, Sun 7.30-10am & noon-8pm; WI-FI; 🐾) includes baked hake fillet (£14.95) and beef & venison Guinness stew (£16.95). Sandwiches are available (Mon-Sat 11am-5pm; from £5.95).

ROUTE GUIDE AND MAPS

KNETTISHALL HEATH TO LITTLE CRESSINGHAM MAPS 1-8

Easy-going and well-maintained paths make this first **14½ miles (23km; 5hrs)** from Knettishall Heath, actually in Suffolk, a gentle introduction to the trail and the route ahead. Meandering through tranquil woods the path, formerly a Bronze Age trading route and Roman road, quickly crosses into Norfolk and breaks out across farmland before beginning to cross a series of attractive heaths where you can begin to appreciate the scale of the landscape. Before you begin, bear in mind that accommodation on the early stages of the Peddars Way is scarce so make sure you have something booked. Alternatively, be prepared to detour from the path and try your luck in one of the larger villages close by.

The Peddars Way begins rather quietly from a finger-post adjacent to a road and next to Blackwater Carr – a surprisingly low-key and easy-to-miss way of signalling the start of a National Trail. *(cont'd on p96)*

ROUTE GUIDE AND MAPS

45 MINS TO/FROM STONEBRIDGE (MAP 4)

A11 CROSSING

50 MINS TO/FROM THOMPSON WATER (MAP 5)

STONEBRIDGE

45 MINS FROM/TO A11 CROSSING (MAP 3)

5

BRICKKILN COVERT

THREE LARGE BARNS

TO GREAT HOCKHAM

A1075

STONEHILL PLANTATION

trailblazer

BRIDLEWAY & NATIONAL CYCLE NETWORK 13

Dog & Partridge

JUNCTION SIGNPOSTED 'BATTLE AREA'

WINDMILL TOWER

STONEBRIDGE 006

TO WRETHAM

ALSO KNOWN AS EAST WRETHAM

PASS BETWEEN ABUTMENTS OF OLD RAILWAY BRIDGE AND APPROACH HOUSES

TO CROXTON

0   1/4 mile
0   500m
APPROX SCALE

ILLINGTON ROAD

A1075

TO ATTLEBOROUGH

FARM

TO THETFORD

RESERVOIRS

MAP 4

3

REMAINS OF DISMANTLED RAILWAY

(cont'd from p91) Pass through the gate beyond the finger-post and head roughly straight on into a light wood. After 700m bend right and cross the Little Ouse, leaving Suffolk and entering Norfolk. Your first experience of the new county will be **Breckland** (see p56), a landscape of light, dry, sandy soils bound together by Scots pine and conifer plantations.

Passing through attractive woods, the path climbs gently to a pair of main roads (including the A1066) and then meanders alongside a forest (Boundary Plantation) on a raised Roman causeway (or *agger*) almost 5m wide, until it arrives at the River Thet. To the east of here is Thorpe Woodlands Caravan Park and Campsite; however, campers can stay here only if they have a chemical toilet since there are no facilities on site.

Just before the River Thet there is a section of **duckboards** which continues once you have crossed the river on a small humpback bridge; this is useful as the ground can be wet and marshy here. Then cross a minor road; following the road there are excellent views of **Brettenham Heath** to the north-west, one of the largest areas of heathland in Norfolk and a haven for birdwatchers. Cross the A11 (Map 3), a dual carriageway (London–Norwich), and the Ely–Norwich railway line at a level crossing (Shadwell Crossing), to re-enter the woods.

Beyond a **gas pipeline pump station** the path climbs gently alongside both farmland and piggeries and the disused Thetford–Watton railway line. Having crossed a minor road (Illington Rd) it eventually passes between the abutments of an old railway bridge and arrives at Stonebridge.

STONEBRIDGE [MAP 4, p95]

Named after the stone bridge that used to cross the railway line, the village, which is sometimes referred to as **East Wretham** depending on which side of the road you're standing, is little more than a straggle of houses along a single road. However, it is home to *The Dog and Partridge* (☎ 01953-497014, 🖥 dog-and-partridge.org.uk; food served Mon-Fri 4-8.30pm, Sat noon-8.30pm, Sun noon-3pm; bar Mon-Fri from 4pm; WI-FI; 🐾 bar area). Pause at this homely, traditional pub for a pint and a chance to refuel – evening meals include game pie (£16.95) and mustard rabbit cobbler (£14.95) alongside more typical pub grub, while at the weekend sandwiches go from £4.95 and burgers start at £7.50. Note that if they are not busy the kitchen/pub may close early. Attached to the Grade II listed pub is a more modern building containing three rooms (3Qd, each with two single beds and a double sofa bed; all en suite; 🛏; WI-FI; Ⓛ). Rates for **B&B** are from £40pp (sgl occ from £60).

Turn right when you reach the road and walk past the pub before branching off left at a junction signposted 'Battle Area'. This is also a bridleway and National Cycle Network 13 so expect to see horses and cyclists. The metalled path dwindles to a broad forest track as it strikes off across The Brecks, past **Stanford Military Training Zone** (Map 5), a large, closed military training area that is still used; when you see red flags hanging at the gated entrances to the zone it means the army are on exercise.

On this section you pass the first of a series of modern stone sculptures inscribed with verse; these are part of the **Norfolk Songline** (top box opposite).

To the north and east lies **Thompson Common** (see box opposite).

❏ **A Norfolk Songline**

*...as they hunted and gathered over thousands of years
those first people pressed patterns into the ground with their feet...
track-ways and paths.'*

*'...the eastern-most strand of the final stretch of that tangle of tracks,
between Knettishall Heath and Holme,
between Blackwater Carr and Sea-Gate,
has come to be called the Peddars Way.*

A Norfolk Songline was an arts project inspired by the Peddars Way. A Songline is originally an Australian Aboriginal concept that explores the connection between a track and the landscape it passes though. In the form of a song, the history of the path and the formations around it are told. The Norfolk Songline was created by Hugh Lupton, who wove poetry, imagery and song together to bring the landscape of the Peddars Way to life. A series of temporary sculptures, including arranged stones, reed vanes, earth rings and flint mounds, first accompanied the story, and subsequently five stone sculptures inspired by the project have been created and set along the trail, providing a reminder of the past and history of the countryside whilst acting as way-markers. The sculptures appear on Maps 5, 6, 11, 16 and 23.

Beyond Thompson Water is a path that leads east to **Thompson** village, just over a mile away.

For a side trip consider the **Great Eastern Pingo Trail** (see p33).

THOMPSON [off MAP 6, p99]

This small historic village is thought to have Danish origins and appears in the *Domesday Book* as Tomesteda; it is centred on the 14th-century flint church, **St Martin's**.

There are few facilities but it does have a **post office** (Mon-Tue & Thur-Fri 9am-1pm) containing an **ATM**. *The Chequers Inn Thompson* (☎ 01953-483360, 🖳 thompsonchequers.co.uk; 3D, all en suite; WI-FI; ⓛ; 🐾). This 16th-century inn has a low-slung thatched roof. *(cont'd on p100)*

❏ **Pingo ponds on Thompson Common**

This area is an important patchwork of grasslands, ponds, woods and scrub covering 346 acres. **Thompson Water**, a shallow lake artificially created in 1845 by draining a tributary of the River Wissey, covers 40 acres.

Unusual landscape features include *pingo* ponds. Pingos were low hillocks formed 20,000 years ago during the last Ice Age when spring water below the surface froze to form lenses of ice that pushed the earth upwards. In warmer months, when the ice melted, the surface soil would slough off and gather around the rim of the hillocks. Once all the ice had melted the remnants of the hillocks collapsed to leave shallow craters which have filled with water to become ponds. The name comes from the Inuit word for hill; pingos are currently found only in areas of permafrost, such as the Arctic tundra.

Most pingo ponds in England have been ploughed up or lost, but a number remain in the Brecks, the best examples of which can be seen on Thompson Common. The ponds are home to a unique range of wildlife and are excellent breeding grounds for amphibians, dragonflies and damselflies.

THOMPSON WATER

6

THOMPSON WATER 008

MADHOUSE PLANTATION

FIRST SONGLINE SCULPTURE

FLAG HEATH

GATE

WATERING FARM

STANFORD MILITARY TRAINING ZONE- KEEP OUT

IGNORE TRACKS BRANCHING OFF EAST

DIRT TRACK

007

ARMY ROAD

JUNCTION - TAKE DIRT TRACK BRANCHING RIGHT ALONG EDGE OF STANFORD MILITARY TRAINING ZONE

STANFORD MILITARY TRAINING ZONE- KEEP OUT

HOCKHAM HEATH

TO GREAT HOCKHAM

★ trailblazer

GALLEY HILL

MAP 5

METALLED ROAD

WOODCOCK HILL

HOSPITAL HILL

0   1/4 mile
0   APPROX SCALE   500m

4

90 MINS BETWEEN THOMPSON WATER (MAP 5) AND BRANDON ROAD JUNCTION (MAP 7)

7

NORFOLK SONGLINE SCULPTURE

TO MERTON

SPARROW HILL

MERTON WOOD

TUMULI

TO POCKTHORPE

MILITARY TRAINING ZONE-KEEP OUT

GATE

GATE, RED FLAG & CATTLE GRID

BOSTON PLANTATION

★ trailblazer

TO POCKTHORPE & THOMPSON

GATE & RED FLAG

SHAKERS FURZE

MAP 6

STANFORD MILITARY TRAINING ZONE-KEEP OUT

TUMULUS

GATE & RED FLAG

TO THOMPSON, 1¼ MILES/2KM

GREAT EASTERN PINGO TRAIL

THOMPSON WATER

0   ¼ mile
0   APPROX SCALE   500m

5

(cont'd from p97) The inn has a beer garden and serves up renowned hearty **food** (Mon-Sat noon-2pm & 6.30-9pm, Sun noon-8.30pm) such as breaded scampi (£9.95), homemade mushroom & sweet pepper stroganoff (£10.95) and a substantial mixed grill (£20.95) – booking is recommended. The rooms boast modern amenities and **B&B** costs from £37.50pp (£55 for single occupancy).

B&B at the 600-year-old *College Farm* (☎ 01953-483318, 🖥 collegefarm norfolk.co.uk; 2D both en suite, 1D with private facilities; 🛏; WI-FI; Ⓛ) costs from £60pp (sgl occ from £60) including tea and homemade cake on arrival and a full English breakfast. It is possible to put an additional bed in one of the rooms for three to share and, subject to prior arrangement, they will collect walkers from the Peddars Way and take them back the next morning.

The charming 16th-century *Thatched House* (☎ 01953-483577, 🖥 thatched house.co.uk; 1D en suite/1T private facilities; 🛏; WI-FI; Ⓛ), on Mill Rd, charges from £40pp (sgl occ from £50).

The main Peddars Way path pushes straight on, past **Sparrow Hill**, to arrive at **Merton Estate**, home to the de Grey family since the late 1330s. The current owner, Lord Walsingham, was responsible for allowing a path to be opened along this stretch of the Peddars Way.

Beyond Merton Estate and **Home Farm** the metalled road reaches a (track) crossroads where you can go straight over for Watton. Instead, join a green lane that bears left then right to reach the B1108, Brandon Rd. The Peddars Way continues left from here. About 1½ miles to the right though is the vibrant market town of Watton.

WATTON   [off MAP 7]

An historic market town, these days Watton is still a bustling place. The parish church, **St Mary's**, dates from the 12th century and has a Norman tower and octagonal belfry. In the heart of the village stands an unusual **bell tower** dating from 1679, which was erected after a fire destroyed most of the town in 1674, reputedly so the bells could warn townsfolk of any future disaster.

On the town sign are the two 'babes' from the popular fairy tale *Babes in the Woods*; it is rumoured that nearby **Wayland Wood** is where the two unfortunate children met their fate. A hare ('*wat*' in the local dialect) and barrel ('*tun*') also feature on the sign and account for the town's name.

The town also hosts an annual craft fair (see p14) showcasing locally made products.

Services

For **tourist information** go to **Wayland Visitor Centre** (☎ 01953-880212, 🖥 way land-tourism.org.uk; Easter to mid Dec Mon-Fri 10am-4pm, Sat 10am-1pm; WI-FI), in Wayland House, on the corner of the High St and George Trollope Rd. When open general information is available but there may not be any staff to answer questions.

The town also has a **post office** (Mon-Fri 9am-5.30pm, Sat 9am-12.30pm) and several **banks** with ATMs, all along the High St.

The **market** takes place along the High St on Wednesdays and there is a farmer's market on the first Saturday of every month.

Transport

[See also pp51-4] Konectbus's No 11 **bus** service links Watton to Sporle and Swaffham and their Nos 3 & 6 operate to Norwich. Coach Services' No 81 runs to Thetford.

Where to stay

Half a mile before the village on Brandon Rd is a traditional family pub, *The Hare &*

PATH RUNS ON GRASS VERGE ON NORTH SIDE OF ROAD

FIELD BARN

010

TO LITTLE CRESSINGHAM

BRANDON ROAD JUNCTION

8

BRANDON RD B1108

TO WATTON, 1½ MILES/2.5KM

WATTON PLANTATION

TO WATTON

009

CAPPS' BUSH

TO MERTON

90 MINS FROM/TO THOMPSON WATER (MAP 5)

ORIGINAL ROMAN ROUTE CONTINUED STRAIGHT HERE

THREXTON HOUSE

HOME FARM

METALLED ROAD

MERTON ESTATE

★ trailblazer

GATE

0   ¼ mile
0   APPROX SCALE   500m

MAP 7

STANFORD MILITARY TRAINING ZONE— KEEP OUT

6

ROUTE GUIDE AND MAPS

Barrel (☎ 01953-882752, 🖳 hare-and-bar
rel-hotel-norfolk.co.uk; 4S/2D/4T/3Tr/
1Qd, all en suite; WI-FI; (L); 🐾 in some
rooms but not in the actual bar), which
serves standard pub grub (**food** Mon-Sat
noon-2pm & 6.30-9pm, Sun noon-2pm) and
which charges from £37.50pp (sgl/sgl occ
from £55) for **B&B**. The pub closes at 5pm
on Sundays and is closed on bank holidays.

Close by, on Richmond Rd, is **Broom
Hall Country Hotel** (☎ 01953-882125, 🖳
broomhallhotel.co.uk; 11D/4T, all en suite;
🍴; WI-FI; (L); 🐾), a rather grand Victorian
country house set in two acres of gardens,
which offers **B&B** for £43.50-85pp (sgl occ
£78-100); the highest rates are for their four
poster room. Note that they generally do
not accept a single-night stay for Saturdays
between early April and mid October. There
is an indoor pool and massage treatments
are available (if booked in advance; separate charge for the latter) for aching limbs.

Watton itself has very limited accommodation options. Most reliable is probably
The Willow House (☎ 01953-881181, 🖳
thewillowhouse.co.uk; 3S/2D or T/2Qd, all
en suite; WI-FI; 🐾), on the High St, which
is a Grade II listed thatched building dating
from the 16th century. Converted into a
period hostelry full of low beams, it has
chalet-style rooms from £40pp (sgl/sgl occ

from £65); rates include a full breakfast.
This would be handy if the only place to
stay in Little Cressingham (see below) is
fully booked.

Where to eat and drink

Food is available in the **Ivy Room** (Tue-Sun
noon-2pm & daily 6.30-8.30pm) and
Swallowtails Restaurant (Mon-Sat 6.30-
8.30pm, Sun noon-2pm & 6.30-7.15pm), at
Broom Hall Country Hotel (see Where to
stay); where the former serves sandwiches,
light lunches and selections from a daily
specials board, the latter offers more formal
dining – a three-course meal will set you
back around £24. Light lunches and cream
teas are also served (daily 10am-4.15pm) in
the Conservatory or on the Terrace.

The Willow House (see Where to stay;
food Mon-Thur noon-2pm & 6-8.30pm,
Fri-Sat noon-2pm & 6-8.45pm, Sun noon-
2.30pm) has bar meals as well as more
elaborate à la carte dishes including a best
end rack of lamb (£19.50), or brace of sea
bass fillets (£17).

If you're after a snack, **Express Fish
Bar** (Mon-Sat 11.30am-11pm, Sun from
11am) sells fish & chips, and fried chicken
and salad boxes – walkers get a free bottle
of water with every meal.

Once on the B1108 pick up a grassy path running alternately along the
verge or following the edges of adjoining fields. At a crossroads look right and
you'll see **All Saints' Church**, seemingly stranded amidst fields to the north,
and at a fork bear left to stroll downhill into Little Cressingham.

LITTLE CRESSINGHAM   [MAP 8]

Another small hamlet, centred on a crossroads just off the main road, Little
Cressingham is a sleepy place with no services and just the one accommodation
option. Over the crossroads and just down
the hill stands a partially collapsed church,
St Andrews, whose ruined tower makes for
a striking silhouette whilst the nave is still
in use for services.

A little further on is a striking **water
and wind mill** built around 1821; this mill
boasts an unusual double action where two
pairs of stones at the base of the tower were

driven by power from the waterwheel and
two in the upper half of the tower were
powered by the sails. The mill ceased using
wind power in 1916 and water power in
1952 but has been well maintained and
restored since.

Where to stay and eat

There is a distinct lack of accommodation
actually on the early stage of the Peddars
Way, and the only place to stay here is
Sycamore House (☎ 01953-881887, 🖳
j.wittridge@btinternet.com; 1D en suite,

ROUTE GUIDE AND MAPS

MAP 8

TO ASHILL

⑨

📱012

TO GREAT CRESSINGHAM,
1¾ MILES/2.75KM

TO SAHAM
TONEY

ROAD CROSSING

10–15 MINS

LIMEKILN
FARM

★ trailblazer

0   ¼ mile
0   APPROX SCALE   500m

THE
NUNNERIES

PILGRIMS
WAY

LITTLE
CRESSINGHAM 📱011

WATER &
WINDMILL

ST ANDREWS

DISUSED PHONE BOX

TO SAHAM
TONEY

ALL SAINTS

CHURCH
FARM

LITTLE CRESSINGHAM

TO GREAT
CRESSINGHAM

CROSSWAYS ⑦

Sycamore
House

THREXTON
HILL

B1108

B1108

TO
BODNEY

PATH RUNS ON GRASS
VERGE AND EDGE OF FIELDS
ON NORTH SIDE OF ROAD

LITTLE CRESSINGHAM ◀ 30 MINS FROM/TO BRANDON ROAD JUNCTION (MAP 7) ▶

1S/1D/1T share facilities; 🛏; WI-FI; (🔒), which offers **B&B** in a very welcoming, chintzy house. The rate is from £32.50pp (sgl £45, sgl occ rates on request). The shared bathroom has a Jacuzzi. Evening meals are not available but the owner will kindly run you to and from The Olde Windmill Inn in Great Cressingham (see

below) for supper. In the morning he will serve a substantial breakfast to set you up for the day and prepare a packed lunch (if requested in advance; additional charge), which is very handy as there are no food stops on the first part of the following day's walk.

LITTLE CRESSINGHAM TO CASTLE ACRE   MAPS 8-13

These **11½ miles (18.5km; 4hrs 10 mins to 4½hrs)** again form an almost arrow-straight track, much of it metalled, which continues to push across the broad farmland and lightly wooded countryside. The landscape of rolling hills, cultivated, chequered fields and the occasional stand of trees is subtle rather than dramatic, but nonetheless charming.

Leave Little Cressingham from the crossroads in the middle of the hamlet, on a road called Pilgrims Way, and follow the Peddars Way as it undulates gently north. Cross the road to **Great Cressingham** and continue northwards towards South Pickenham.

GREAT CRESSINGHAM
[off MAP 8, p103]

Almost two miles from the Peddars Way, Great Cressingham is a picturesque village with a fine church, **St Michaels**. There is also a **priory**, set inside the moat of an earlier manor house that dates from the 16th century. In addition the village boasts a good pub with accommodation and a B&B.

The Olde Windmill Inn (☎ 01760-756232, 🖥 oldewindmillinn.co.uk; 9D/5D or T, all en suite; 🛏; WI-FI; (🔒); 🐾), at Water End, has been operating since the mid 17th century. It is a rambling, rustic building supported by oak beams, with three bars, separate dining areas, a modern extension and a beer garden. The extensive

menu (**food** daily 11.30am-2.30pm & 5.30-10pm, Sun till 9.30pm) includes lamb shank in red wine (£15.95), steaks from £13.95, and vegetarian dishes such as Indian-style vegetable masala (£10.95). Their signature sandwich, a bacon & cheese hoagie prepared 'Windmill style', costs £7.50. Wash the meal down with a pint of the house beer, Windy Miller, or one of the 30 malt whiskies stocked behind the bar. The smart rooms are traditional in style but have modern amenities. **B&B** costs £40-43.75pp (sgl occ from £69.50). Breakfast is served 7.30-9.30am and a full English costs £9.50 for non-residents.

As you ease gently northwards past **Caudle Common** and approach Hall Farm, keep an eye out for the chimneys of **Pickenham Hall** to the north-west, looming over the trees. It is owned by the Packiri family, who are still landlords for many of the properties in the village of South Pickenham. There has been a hall at Pickenham since Tudor times, but the present red-brick building was enlarged and rebuilt in the style of the Arts and Crafts movement in the first few years of the 20th century. Surrounded by parkland, the hall is relatively modest, built for comfort rather than to impress, a factor which has ensured its survival as it is easy to maintain.

MAP 9

10

TO BRICK
KILN FARM
¼ MILE/400M
& ASHILL,
¾ MILE/1.2KM

DISUSED
PHONE
BOX

PICKENHAM
HALL

013

B1077

ALL
SAINTS

HALL
FARM

VIEWS OF
PICKENHAM HALL
THROUGH WOOD

SOUTH
PICKENHAM

BRIDLEWAY &
ACCESS TO
BRICK KILN
FARM CARAVAN
& CAMPING PARK,
1 MILE/1½ KM

COUSIN'S
WOOD

GATE

TO GREAT
CRESSINGHAM

PICKENHAM
CARR

RESERVOIR

CAUDLE
HILL

trailblazer

CAUDLE
COMMON

0   ¼ mile

ELEVEN ACRE
PLANTATION

0   APPROX SCALE   500m

PRIORY ROAD

TO GREAT
CRESSINGHAM

8

30-45 MINS FROM/TO ROAD CROSSING (MAP 8)

ROUTE GUIDE AND MAPS

There is a crossroads immediately after Hall Farm; to the left is **South Pickenham**. There are no facilities in the village but just beyond Pickenham Hall is an historic church, **All Saints**; it has a distinctive Norman round tower and medieval crown and flint walls dating from 1075. Inside are some well-preserved historic memorials, a 15th-century wall painting of St Christopher, an elegant piscine and 14th-century font as well as an impressive organ with winged doors, considered to be one of the great East Anglian art treasures of the 19th century. The wings open out to show images of the Nativity and the Adoration of the Magi, and the keys still produce a fine sound.

One mile to the east of Hall Farm crossroads is ***Brick Kiln Farm Caravan & Camping Park*** (☎ 01760-441300, 🖳 norfolk-camping.co.uk; WI-FI; 🐾), which has **tent pitches** (£10pp for walkers and cyclists) and decent shower & washroom facilities. They also have three '**camping pods**', a timber-built beach hut, barrel and pod with mattresses and basic equipment consisting of a kettle, mini fridge, crockery and cutlery. You must bring your own bedding and towels. Each sleeps two adults; rates are £38 per pod per night. Advance booking for the pods is recommended.

A short distance beyond the crossroads the path leaves the road and runs parallel to it behind a hedge before dropping into the River Wissey valley to cross the river. Before descending though there is a side track that climbs to **St Mary's Church** (🖳 houghtonstmarys.co.uk; summer daily 2-4pm, winter Sat-Sun 2-4pm), set on the summit of a small hill to the east. The rather pretty 11th-century church, all that remains of the hamlet of **Houghton**, has been restored; during the restoration Romanesque wall paintings were uncovered which are held to be the largest surviving collection of medieval paintings in England. The round-trip diversion takes 15-20 minutes.

Having skirted around a series of fields to descend to the river, the path crosses it and climbs away alongside a further series of fields before edging around a school and joining a road opposite a **war memorial** commemorating the American airmen stationed here during WWII. More than 500 members of 42nd Bomb Group lost their lives in 64 missions flown over three months in 1944. The airfield has been converted and is now home to eight wind turbines, visible on the skyline. Turn right and walk to a T-junction. The Peddars Way continues left, whilst right takes you into North Pickenham.

There's little in **North Pickenham** to keep you here, although there is a **church**, St Andrews, that's part medieval and part 19th century, and a one-time friendly local pub ***The Blue Lion***, though it was closed at the time of writing.

❑ **Peddars Way cycle route**
People who are cycling the Peddars Way should note that, at the point the trekking path drops into the River Wissey valley, the cycle route continues on the road before taking a left onto Houghton Lane and entering North Pickenham. At the T-junction in the village centre, turn left to round a bend and re-join the Peddars Way trekking path.

West Norfolk Community Transport's No 12 **bus** service operates from here to Swaffham; see box p51.

From the T-junction turn left onto Manor Farm Hill Rd and continue along the tarmac road. Cross over the next road to Swaffham and join **Procession Lane**, a wide dirt track that begins by the remains of two supports for an old railway line bridge that used to cross the path here. Undulate north passing another **Norfolk Songline Sculpture** (see box p97) until you reach the A47, connecting King's Lynn to Norwich. Just to the left, before a roundabout, is a petrol station where you can pick up snacks and cold drinks, and a McDonald's fast food restaurant. There are also public **toilets** and a **phone box** here. Beyond the roundabout the road left continues to **Swaffham** which is 1½ miles from the Peddars Way.

SWAFFHAM   [off MAP 11]

Swaffham is a small market town that developed during Norfolk's wealthy medieval agricultural past and was once a bustling social centre with a theatre, race-course and dance hall. Although the Market Place still has Georgian buildings and a domed rotunda the other features and entertainments are now gone.

Set on a slight rise, the town's two wind turbines are easily identifiable against the skyline while the Georgian and Victorian façades hide mostly medieval houses. The tall, slender church of **St Peter and St Paul** is particularly impressive, with 88 flying angels set in its roof and medieval carving still evident in the Victorian benches and choir stalls. Once home to Howard Carter who famously discovered Tutankhamen's tomb, the town has various useful services for the walker.

The Carter connection is explored at **Swaffham Museum** (☎ 01760-721230, 🖳 swaffhammuseum.co.uk; mid Feb-Dec Mon-Fri 10am-4pm, Sat 10am-1pm; £3), housed in a Grade II listed town house at 4 London St; the museum has local historical information as well as material on ancient Egypt.

The **Green Britain Centre** (☎ 01760-726100, 🖳 greenbritaincentre.co.uk; Mon-Fri 9am-4pm, Sat 10am-4pm; Aug Sun 10am-4pm; free) is an award-winning sustainable environmental education centre that offers guided turbine tours (11am, 1pm & 3pm; adults £6, children £4; booking is recommended) during which you are shown to the top of the E66 wind turbine up

a flight of 305 steps, at the top of which is a glass-encased viewing platform designed by Sir Norman Foster. There's a small organic and vegan *café* here as well.

Services and transport

There is a **tourist information centre** (☎ 01760-722255, 🖳 swaffhamtic@gmail .com; opening hours as for the museum plus Dec-mid Feb Fri 10am-3pm, Sat 10am-1pm) in Swaffham Museum (see column opposite). They have information on accommodation but don't do bookings.

National Express **coach** service NX375 (see box p49) calls here. Konectbus No 11 runs to Dereham via Sporle and Watton and the Swaffham Area Flexibus can be booked to travel to Sporle; see pp51-4 for details.

Where to stay

If you're **camping** head to *Breckland Meadows Touring Park* (☎ 01760-721246, 🖳 brecklandmeadows.co.uk; WI-FI; 🐾) to the west of Swaffham on Lynn Rd. It's a caravan touring park that has a few tent pitches (from £8/12 for a one-/two-man tent), washrooms, laundry facilities and a small shop which is open daily. Booking is recommended in the summer months and note that they do not accept children.

Lydney House Hotel (☎ 01760-723355, 🖳 lydney-house.co.uk; 1S/5D/1T/1Tr, all en suite; �; WI-FI; Ⓛ), located next to the town's medieval church, has good-quality rooms and charges from £45pp (sgl/sgl occ from £80) for **B&B**.

MAP 11

Strattons Hotel (☎ 01760-723845, 🖳 strattonshotel.com; 14D, all en suite; 🛏; WI-FI; 🐾), at 4 Ash Close, is a more upmarket boutique hotel with excellent green credentials and it charges accordingly. The rooms are individual and funky; B&B costs £59-87.50pp (sgl occ £120-130). Note that the hotel has its own two cats.

Where to eat and drink
For fish & chips pop into *Mother Hubbard's* (☎ 01760-721933, 🖳 motherhubbards.com; Mon-Thur 11.30am-2pm & 4.30-9pm, Fri 11.30am-10pm, Sat 10.30am-10pm, Sun 2-9pm), at 91 Market Place, where good-sized portions of award-winning grub cost from £6.20.

Market Cross Café (☎ 01760-336671; Mon-Thur 9am-5.30pm, Fri-Sat 9am-6pm, Sun summer 9.30am-6pm winter 10am-4pm; WI-FI), in Market Place, serves good coffee as well as light lunches and evening meals, and is licensed.

The bar in *Lydney House Hotel* (see Where to stay; daily 11am-10.30pm) is a relaxing place to unwind with a pint of real ale; you can also try playing one of their traditional pub games.

The award-winning restaurant at *Strattons Hotel* (see Where to stay; daily 6.30-8.30pm) serves locally sourced produce such as monkfish cheek pie with smoked dapple mash & Swiss chard (£15), or grilled mackerel with German potato & runner bean salad and creamed horseradish (£12); afternoon teas are available (noon-4.30pm). They also have a **coffee shop and deli** (Mon-Fri 7.30am-5pm, Sat & Sun 8.30am-5pm) which serves morning coffee and light lunches; you can also get the ingredients for a packed lunch here.

For something less local there's good Chinese food at *East Garden Chinese Restaurant* (☎ 01760-725722, 🖳 eastgarden.net; Tue-Sun noon-2pm & 5-11pm), on London St.

Beyond the A47 a metalled road continues, passing over a disused railway line (Map 12; the old King's Lynn to Dereham line) before zigzagging abruptly and branching off the road that leads to the pretty village of **Sporle**, just over a mile to the east, to join Palgrave Rd to Palgrave Hall.

SPORLE   [off MAP 12]
There is a small shop, **Threeways General Store** (☎ 01760-724300; Mon-Sat daily 6.30am-7.30pm, Sun 8am-7pm), where you can buy basic supplies.

Konectbus No 11 stops outside the store and the Swaffham Area **Flexibus** can be booked to come here; see pp51-4 for details.

The Peddars Inn (☎ 01760-788101, 🖳 thepeddarsinn.com; bar Tue 6-10.30pm in the summer only, Wed-Fri noon-3pm & 6-11pm, Sat 3-11pm, Sun noon-6pm; WI-FI; 🐾) serves **food** (Wed-Fri noon-2pm & 6-9pm, Sat 4-9pm, Sun noon-3pm); the menu includes burgers, pies, seafood and meat from the grill (most mains cost £9.95-11.95). However, note that The Peddars Inn is not open on Mondays and has limited opening hours on Tuesdays.

Pass **Palgrave Hall** before turning left at a T-junction and following the minor road that skirts Hungry Hill and descends to cross the A1065 Swaffham to Fakenham road at **Bartholomew's Hills**. A metalled track then descends towards South Acre and another crossroads. Cross straight over and take the road signed 'Ford, unsuitable for motors' and descend to the **River Nar** on a

---

❏ **Important note – walking times**
All times in this book refer only to the time spent walking. You will need to add 20-30% to allow for rests, photography, checking the map, drinking water etc.

narrow road, with glimpses through the trees and hedgerow of Castle Acre and its ruined priory in the distance. There is a footbridge over the river or you can splash through the shallow ford to emerge opposite the ruins of Cluniac Priory (see p112). There is a short path beyond a stile that curves round to the ruins and provides access to the site. Turn right along the river briefly and ascend into **Castle Acre**, entering the centre of the village by passing beneath a bailey gate.

CASTLE ACRE

The medieval village occupies a strategic location overlooking the River Nar and controlling traffic on the Peddars Way. Roughly halfway along the Peddars Way it makes for a good base. The village itself lies within the outer bailey of an 11th-century castle and the road into the village still passes under the **Bailey Gate**, the former north gateway to the planned walled town. The village takes its name from the Norman **castle**, built soon after the Conquest by William de Warrene, first Earl of Surrey. Initially a stone country house it was converted into a keep defended by stone walls and a system of ditched earthworks. Although now only its walls and ramparts remain, it still provides an impressive indication as to what the castle must once have looked like, and some consider these the finest village earthworks in England. Access is from Bailey St, adjacent to the Old Red Lion (see Where to stay) and is free. Interpretative panels dotted about the site provide information and reveal just how extensive the planned village and fortifications were in their prime.

The remains of the **Cluniac Priory** (Map 13; 🖳 english-heritage.org.uk; Apr-Oct daily 10am-5 or 6pm, Nov-Mar Sat-Sun 10am-4pm; adult/child £7/4.20, English Heritage members free) here are worth exploring. The priory is thought to have been founded in 1089 and was inspired by the monastery at Cluny in France. Originally built within the walls of the castle it was too small for the monks, so was moved to its current location by the River Nar.

Although tumbledown, the ruins, which are in the care of English Heritage, are still in good condition. It's possible to see the great west front of the building, complete with tiered ranks of intersecting round arches, and much of its core structure including a 15th-century gate house and porch.

The substantial prior's lodgings are also well preserved and boast traces of wall paintings and two fine oriel windows. At its height 25 monks resided here in fine style, but all of this was wiped away with the Dissolution in 1536. Next to the priory is a recreated herb garden. There is also a visitor centre with a display of artefacts, a site model and exhibition as well as a small shop selling snacks and public toilets. There is another ruined priory in Thetford (see p89).

Centred on Stocks Green, Castle Acre itself is an attractive place with plenty of pretty houses. The church of **St James the Great** stands at one end of the Green and enjoys sweeping views out over the countryside. The interior of the substantial church is bright and lofty. An unusual font and pulpit make popping in worthwhile.

Services & transport

The good-sized Spar **supermarket** (☎ 01760-755274; Mon-Sat 6am-8pm, Sun 8am-6pm) in the village sells groceries and

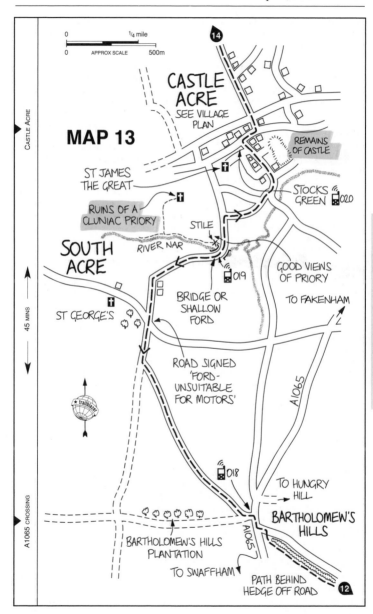

0   ¼ mile
0   APPROX SCALE   500m

14

CASTLE ACRE

SEE VILLAGE PLAN

MAP 13

REMAINS OF CASTLE

ST JAMES THE GREAT

STOCKS GREEN 📟020

RUINS OF A CLUNIAC PRIORY

STILE

SOUTH ACRE

RIVER NAR

📟019

GOOD VIEWS OF PRIORY

ST GEORGE'S

TO FAKENHAM

BRIDGE OR SHALLOW FORD

ROAD SIGNED 'FORD - UNSUITABLE FOR MOTORS'

★ trailblazer

A1065

📟018

TO HUNGRY HILL

BARTHOLOMEW'S HILLS

BARTHOLOMEW'S HILLS PLANTATION

A1065

TO SWAFFHAM

PATH BEHIND HEDGE OFF ROAD

12

CASTLE ACRE

45 MINS

A1065 CROSSING

ROUTE GUIDE AND MAPS

newspapers and also offers **cashback** when you spend £5 or more. In addition they have a coffee machine, bake bread and pasties in the shop, sell sandwiches and they provide fish & chips (daily 11am-2pm & 4-8pm). There is also a **post office** (Mon-Fri 9am-5pm, Sat 9am-noon) in the shop.

The Swaffham Area **Flexibus** can be booked to call here; see box p51.

Where to stay, eat and drink

Good-value accommodation can be had at the *Old Red Lion* (☎ 01760-755557, ☐ old redlion.org.uk; 1 x 3 bunk-bed dorm, 1 x 2-bunk bed dorm with four single beds/1D/2T all share facilities, 2D both en suite; ♥; WI-FI; 🐾), on Bailey St (main entrance round the back), just before Bailey Gate. This former 17th-century pub has been lovingly converted into a cosy **hostel-cum-B&B -cum-retreat** with dorm beds from £22.50pp and private rooms for £25-35pp (sgl occ rates on request). There is a small but fully equipped kitchen as well as a very cosy snug where you can meet fellow guests. All rates include bedding, a towel and a vegetarian wholefood self-service breakfast with homemade breads. The kindly owner will lead you in a couple of yoga stretches before you head on if you're feeling the aches and pains of the previous day – she gives classes for locals on Monday (morning and evening), and Friday (morning). They know their email is unreliable so please call if you don't get a response.

On Stocks Green, *The Ostrich Inn* (☎ 01760-755398, ☐ ostrichcastleacre.com; 3D/1T/1Qd, all en suite; ♥; WI-FI; (Ⓛ) is an impressive 16th-century coaching inn with striking décor and a good atmosphere. It wears its 400 years well although the walls aren't all straight and the ceiling is slightly skew-whiff. Accommodation is available in bright, generous-sized rooms, most of which look out over the Green; **B&B** costs £45-55pp (sgl occ from £70). The menu (**food** Mon-Sat noon-3pm & 6-9pm, Sun noon-3pm) changes regularly (see the website for the latest) but the lunch menu may include fish & chips (£13.50), or a substantial Swaffham sausage ciabatta (£8). In the evening, look out for spiced chicken Shawarma (£12.95), grilled sea bass, steamed octopus & shrimp mash (£17.95), or an 8oz Norfolk sirloin steak (£19). They serve a range of pizzas (£8.95-12.95) as well. If you've got space, puddings are old school and substantial, or there is a great cheeseboard that includes Binham Blue and Norfolk Dapple; see box p23. The beer garden is well-maintained and tranquil.

Barnfields Café (☎ 01760-755577; Wed-Sat 10am-4pm, winter to 3pm; WI-FI), also on Stocks Green, serves breakfast till 11.15am and lunch till 2pm. A good breakfast here will set you up well for what's ahead, as will the Welsh rarebit and their sandwiches. However, note that the café is closed when the owner is away. The small **shop** next door sells local produce and local ice-cream.

CASTLE ACRE TO RINGSTEAD   MAPS 13-22

The path from Castle Acre to Ringstead doesn't look all that appealing on a map. Much of the **17-mile (27km; 6-6¼hrs) route** appears to be along minor roads. However, the route usually follows a grassy path parallel to the metalled surface alongside rolling, cultivated fields, meaning you can take in the wide, expansive views that lend the section a particularly remote feel. There are no food options actually on this section of the path, so bring a packed lunch or be prepared to deviate from the route to find a pub.

After leaving Castle Acre the path shadows the road north from the village on a grassy verge behind a hedge. Beyond a **stile** immediately before a cross-roads and Old Wicken Cottages it rejoins the road to descend into a hollow.

(cont'd on p118)

ROUTE GUIDE AND MAPS

CROSSROADS

15 MINS

TRIG POINT

15 MINS

CROSSROADS

16
METALLED ROAD
TO GREAT MASSINGHAM
Hartswood
COTTAGE
B1145
TO GAYTON
BETTS' FIELD BARN
TO ROUGHAM
MASSINGHAM HEATH
BROAD GRASSY TRACK BRANCHES OFF ROAD
SHEPHERD'S BUSH
022
OLD TRIG POINT - 92M/302FT PEDDARS WAY HIGHEST POINT
PATH SWITCHES TO GRASS VERGE ON RIGHT SIDE OF ROAD
TO GAYTON

MAP 15

0   1/4 mile
0   APPROX SCALE   500m

PATH IS ON GRASSY VERGE ALONGSIDE ROAD
TO WEST ACRE
14

(cont'd from p114) At the bottom of the slight depression following the cross-roads the path once again takes to the grass verge and climbs to another cross-roads (Map 15), where it switches from left to right.

At a pronounced bend in the road, **Shepherd's Bush**, a broad grass track continues straight on north-west past an old **triangulation pillar**. At 92m (302ft), this signifies the highest point on the Peddars Way. The grass track descends alongside **Massingham Heath**, an expanse of land littered with evidence of Stone Age man, where axes, arrowheads and other implements are frequently unearthed.

The path continues towards the B1145, following which a metalled road continues straight ahead, past Betts Field Barn. There's a small, tent-only **campsite** here, *Hartswood* (Map 15; ☎ 07501-726089; 🐾; (Ⓛ)), with basic facilities including a toilet block and washing up area. The friendly, helpful owner charges £5pp and if requested in advance is happy to offer breakfast and/or a packed lunch; booking is recommended.

Continuing over two roads that lead to Great Massingham it climbs to yet another (track) crossroads, to the right of which two **radio masts** can be seen. To the left on the second road, Lynn Lane, is *West Heath Barn* (☎ 01485-521748, 🖳 westheathbarn.com; 1D/1D or T/1T, all en suite; 🖤; WI-FI; (Ⓛ)), a stylish, well-equipped **B&B** in three converted barns dating from the 1850s. B&B costs from £47.50pp (sgl occ from £80). The owners offer a luggage-transfer service and will also take guests to and from the local pub for an evening meal (it is about a 25-minute walk).

The broad grass track which heads east past the radio masts here also goes to **Great Massingham**, three-quarters of a mile away.

GREAT MASSINGHAM
[off MAP 16, p117]

There is a village **shop and post office** (☎ 01485-520272; shop daily 8am-5.30pm, post office Mon-Tue & Thur-Fri 9am-1pm & 2-5.30pm, Wed 9am-noon, Sat 9am-1pm) here in addition to the well-known traditional country pub, *The Dabbling Duck* (☎ 01485-520827, 🖳 thedabbling duck.co.uk; 1S/7D/1Tr, all en suite; 🖤; WI-FI; (Ⓛ); 🐾), at 11 Abbey Rd. The pub is set between two ponds that have their origins as fish ponds and is connected to an 11th-century Augustinian Abbey. Its tastefully decorated rooms cost £55-65pp (sgl from £75, sgl occ £85-90) for **B&B**. The changing menu in the bar (**food** served daily noon-9pm) showcases seasonal local produce, in particular game such as pheasant, pigeon, woodcock, rabbit and venison. In the garden, there's a pizza oven that they fire up on Friday and Saturday (6-10pm); note though that pizza is only served in the garden or for takeaway. There's always a good selection of local ales on handpump at the bar, which is shaped from a giant slab of tree trunk. Breakfast is available 8-10am (non residents welcome) and afternoon tea is served (3-5.30pm).

The Peddars Way passes a striking **Norfolk Songline sculpture** (see box p97) and then descends gently past Clarke's Farm (Map 17) followed by a fuel pipe installation to arrive at a **disused railway line** running parallel to the busy A148 Hillington to Fakenham road.

Cross the A148 carefully and push on over the minor road beyond that which is the most pleasant way of walking to **Harpley**, 1½ miles away.

18

TO ANMER

TO NEW HOUGHTON, 3 MILES & HOUGHTON HALL, 4 MILES

TO HARPLEY

MARWICKS WOOD

★ trailblazer

60 MINS TO/FROM ANMER MINQUE (MAP 18)

TO HARPLEY, 1½ MILES/2.5KM & FAKENHAM

BUSY ROAD- CROSS CAREFULLY

HARPLEY DAMS COTTAGES

A148

024

A148

TO HILLINGTON

HARPLEY DAMS

FUEL PIPE INSTALLATION

HARPLEY DAMS

TO LITTLE MASSINGHAM

DISUSED RAILWAY LINE (KING'S LYNN TO FAKENHAM LINE)

MAP 17

45 MINS FROM/TO LYNN LANE (MAP 16)

CLARKE'S FARM

0   ¼ mile
0   APPROX SCALE   500m

16

HARPLEY   [off MAP 17, p119]
B&B is available at *Meadow House* (☎ 01485-520240, 🖳 meadowhousebandb.co.uk; 2D or T, both en suite; 🛏; WI-FI; Ⓛ) for £40-47.50pp (sgl occ £45-55). The *Rose and Crown* (☎ 01485-521807, 🖳 roseand crownharpley.co.uk; food daily noon-9pm; WI-FI; 🐾) is a rustic themed pub offering up classic fare from a menu that changes daily and is cooked to order from fresh and local ingredients.

To reach **Houghton Hall** (see box below) follow the path north-east as shown on Map 17 and head to New Houghton around three miles away; from there you head north a further mile to the Hall.

Ascend slowly past Harpley Dams Cottages and then **Marwicks Wood** on your left and Harpley Common on your right. A broad grass path makes its way imperiously across the unspoilt countryside of crop fields, with a number of **tumuli** visible to both east and west. There is access to one of these Bronze Age burial mounds, dating from 1500BC to 1300BC via a stile just before a tarmac road.

Beyond the tarmac road a grassy track ambles past a triangular field, **Anmer Minque**, crosses the B1153 to Great Bircham and continues to head straight across the countryside. Eventually, to the east amidst undulating fields are views of the white-capped **Bircham Windmill** and a number of giant cranes at a construction-industry training site. The best way to Great Bircham from Peddars Way is via Fieldbarn Farm (see Map 19).

❏ **Houghton Hall**

The 18th-century politician Robert Walpole, generally considered to be Great Britain's first Prime Minister, was educated in Great Massingham. He also built near-by Houghton Hall (🖳 houghtonhall.com; late Mar/Apr to end Sep Wed, Thur, Sun & Bank Holiday Mondays 11am-5pm, with access to the house itself available noon-3.30pm; adult £10, child 16 and under free, 10% discount if tickets booked online).

The Hall, set in 350 acres of parkland that are home to a herd of white fallow deer, is one of the finest surviving Palladian mansions in England. Designed for entertaining on a grand scale, the hall was meant to symbolise the great power of its owner. In fact, plans for the Hall were so grand that it was feared the village of Houghton wouldn't be in keeping with the house so it had to be destroyed and rebuilt a mile further away. During Walpole's heyday the Hall was filled with magnificent treasures including china, tapestries, sculptures and a collection of Old Masters. Sadly in 1779 the paintings were sold by Walpole's grandson to Catherine the Great of Russia and now form part of the collection in The Hermitage in St Petersburg. The Hall does still boast an impressive collection of more than 20,000 model soldiers gathered together by the 6th Marquess, who was fascinated by the campaigns of the Napoleonic period. Complex battle scenes are depicted from the Battle of Waterloo to the Second World War.

The walled garden was renovated at the start of the 1990s and now features a series of ornamental gardens in various styles. The rose garden is planted with around 150 varieties, whilst the box-edged parterre is based on the ceiling design in the Hall's White Drawing Room.

Stables Restaurant (days/hours as for the Hall) on the premises serves light lunches and homemade cakes and pastries as well as hot drinks.

The **Houghton International Horse Trials** (see p14) are held here in May.

ANMER MINQUE

60 MINS FROM/to HARPLEY DAMS (MAP 17)

ROUTE GUIDE AND MAPS

19

TO GREAT
BIRCHAM

025

B1153

0 .... 1/4 mile
0 .... 500m
APPROX SCALE

TO
ANMER

ANMER
MINQUE

GRASSY
TRACK

TO
FLITCHAM

TUMULUS

★ trailblazer

STILE &
ACCESS TO
TUMULUS

TUMULUS

BUNKER'S
HILL

TO NEW
HOUGHTON

TUMULI

TO
HARPLEY

MAP 18

BROAD GRASSY
PATH LINED BY
HEDGES EITHER
SIDE

HARPLEY
COMMON

17

GREAT BIRCHAM   [off MAP 19]

Easily identifiable courtesy of the restored Bircham Windmill, one of the few remaining working mills in the region, Great Bircham is a sleepy place 1½ miles from the Peddars Way.

Visitors to the village can explore **Bircham Windmill** (☎ 01485-578393, 🖳 birchamwindmill.co.uk; Easter-end Sep daily 10am-5pm; adult/child £5.50/3.75; see also Where to stay and eat) built in 1846, and climb five floors to the fan stage; on windy days it's still possible to see the sails turn and the machinery in action.

Services

Bircham Stores and Café (☎ 01485-576006, 🖳 birchamstoresandcafe.co.uk; shop Mon-Sat 8am-6pm, Sun 9am-noon) sells groceries and other provisions and also has a café (see Where to eat).

Where to stay, eat and drink

Bircham Windmill (see above) allows **camping** (WI-FI; 🐾 on lead; £9pp per night) when the windmill is open. Shower facilities are available and there is 24hr access to toilets, wash basins and an outdoor tap. The price also entitles you to a discount on visiting the mill. Breakfast is available for campers from 9am and in the school holidays. They also have two quirky, handbuilt **shepherd's huts** (sleeping two adults, and two adults and a child respectively). The wooden huts are warm and cosy with seating inside or out, an outdoor cooking area and a shower unit. Each hut costs £55-65 per night. Bring your own sleeping bag or hire linen (£8) from the mill. There's a small *tearoom* and bakery that still uses its original coal-fired oven. Cream teas are a speciality but you can also buy bread and the flour milled on the premises.

The King's Head Hotel (☎ 01485-578265, 🖳 thekingsheadcountryhotel.co .uk; 11D or T/1D, all en suite; ➧; WI-FI; Ⓛ; 🐾) is a Grade II listed coachhouse that has been tastefully made over into a stylish modern hotel with contemporary rooms. **B&B** costs £57.50-92.50pp (sgl occ from £95). There's a restaurant (see Where to eat) on site and also a drawing room to relax in. The restaurant (food Mon-Sat noon-2.30pm, Sun noon-3pm & daily 6-9pm) overlooks a sheltered courtyard. **Food** is carefully prepared and sourced locally. The menu changes regularly and, depending on the season, may include pan-fried wood pigeon (£7.95), saffron gnocchi with wild mushroom (£6.50), while mains might include sesame pan-seared tuna with wasabi mash (£16.50), or salt & pepper pork fillet with dauphinoise potato (£17.95). You can choose from a lighter bites menu in the bar, where you'll also find a decent range of ales and wines.

Bircham Stores and Café (see Services; Easter to end Oct 8am-3.30pm, Sun 9am-2.30pm; WI-FI; 🐾 in enclosed courtyard) sells hot snacks, homemade soup and sandwiches to eat in or take away and the food is made, if not baked, on the premises.

At a couple of points the path crosses minor roads (Map 20) heading east to the hamlet of **Fring** hidden amidst the trees and west to the larger village of **Snettisham** 2½ miles away. Fring has no facilities for the walker, but Snettisham boasts a pretty, warm and welcoming pub and a bus service.

SNETTISHAM   [off MAP 20, p125]

St Mary's church in Snettisham has what is reputed to be one of the finest windows in England, containing a complex tracery pattern all the more remarkable given that it dates from the late Middle Ages. Many of the other windows were destroyed by a bomb dropped from a Zeppelin in 1915, making this the first church in England to be attacked from the air.

Snettisham RSPB Reserve (see p61) faces The Wash and provides sanctuary for large numbers of wading birds which, on high tides when water covers the vast mud-flats, are pushed off their feeding grounds

20

WILDLIFE
PROTECTION
AREA

TO GREAT BIRCHAM
& BIRCHAM WINDMILL

VIEW EAST OF
BIRCHAM WINDMILL
& NUMBER OF
GIANT CRANES

FIELDBARN
FARM

MAP 19

ARROW STRAIGHT ROMAN
ROAD HERE, APPEARING AS
A STANDARD-WIDTH GRASSY
TRACK MAKING ITS WAY
ACROSS COUNTRYSIDE

GRASSY PATH
BETWEEN HEDGES
& BRACKEN VERGES

0   ¼ mile
0   APPROX SCALE   500m

18

60 MINS BETWEEN ANMER MINQUE (MAP 18) AND ROAD CROSSING (MAP 20)

ROUTE GUIDE AND MAPS

★ trailblazer

and on to the banks and islands adjacent to the RSPB hides.

Snettisham is a stop on Lynx's Nos 34, 35 and Coastliner 36 **bus** services; see p50 and box p54.

The *Rose and Crown* (☎ 01485-541382, 🖳 roseandcrownsnettisham.co.uk; 11D/5D or T, all en suite; 🛏; WI-FI; Ⓛ; 🛏), near the church and opposite the cricket pitch. Complete with winding passages, low ceilings and an uneven floor, the relaxed pub-cum-restaurant-cum-boutique-hotel is quintessentially English. **B&B** in rooms varying in style from traditional oak panelling to contemporary pastel paints, is available from £60pp (sgl occ from £100). Breakfast (7.30/8-10am) is also available to non-residents, while the pub (**food** daily noon-9pm, Fri & Sat till 9.30pm, Sun till 8.30pm) serves staples such as shoulder of lamb shepherd's pie (£15), or beer-battered haddock & chips for £13.

A metalled road climbs past a house towards **Hill Plantation**, where it dwindles to a dirt track and descends past **Sedgeford Plantation** before crossing a small, frequently dry, stream via a ford or short bridge just before Fring Rd. Climbing towards **Dovehill Wood**, the path switches from the east side of a hedge to the west and turns left then right to reach Littleport, a small string of terraced houses on a dirt track connected to the B1454. About a mile to the left from here is **Sedgeford**.

SEDGEFORD [off MAP 21, p126]

Listed in the *Domesday Book*, Sedgeford, lying in the fertile Heacham River valley, is an old village centred on a flint and stone church thought to be at least partly Saxon in origin. The remains of Roman villas, pottery shards and a gold torc from the Iron Age have been uncovered in the area, underlining its historical importance.

There is an inn with rooms and a B&B. *The King William IV Country Inn* (☎ 01485-571765, 🖳 thekingwilliamsedgeford.co.uk; 8D or T/1D, all en suite; 🛏; WI-FI; Ⓛ; 🛏), on Heacham Rd, has luxurious, characterful rooms; **B&B** costs £62.50-70pp (sgl occ £80-100). This popular and often packed pub (bar Mon 6-11pm, Tue-Sat 11.30am-11pm, Sun noon-10.30pm)

has both indoor and alfresco dining areas (**food** served Apr-Oct Mon 6-9pm, Tue-Sat noon-2pm & 6-9pm, Sun noon-2.30pm & 6-8.30pm, rest of year from 6.30pm) in which it serves sandwiches and pasta dishes at lunchtime, and classic mains such as venison suet pudding (£14.95), or pork & black pudding wellington (£14.95), in the evenings.

Park View Bed and Breakfast (☎ 01485-572248, 🖳 www.parkviewbandbsedgeford.co.uk; 1S/1T/2D, all en suite; WI-FI; Ⓛ) on Heacham Road has pleasant rooms and hearty breakfasts. Rates start at £37.50pp (sgl/sgl occ from £55) and include tea/coffee and homemade cakes on arrival.

Join the B1454 road briefly heading right then branch left past **Magazine Cottage**, a Victorian folly that is occasionally claimed to have been a Civil War ammunition store. *(cont'd on p128)*

❏ **Peddars Way cycle route**
Cyclists on Peddars Way should turn left on Fring Rd (Map 20) and pedal towards Sedgeford. In the heart of the town pick up Ringstead Rd and continue north to the village, where you'll rejoin the trekking route.

CYCLISTS ON THE PEDDARS WAY DIVERT FROM THE MAIN TRAIL HERE

027

OLD PLANTATION

SEDGEFORD PLANTATION

HALL PLANTATION

TO DOCKING

FRING HALL

TO SEDGEFORD

FORD SMALL STREAM OR USE BRIDGE ADJACENT TO PATH

FRING ROAD

CHURCH FARM

HILL PLANTATION

METALLED ROAD TO HOUSE GIVES WAY TO GRASSY TRACK AFTERWARDS

ALL SAINTS

FRING

TO SNETTISHAM, 2½ MILES/4KM

30 MINS

TOP PLANTATION

★ trailblazer

TO SNETTISHAM

RED BARN FARM

MAP 20

0   ¼ mile
0   APPROX SCALE   500m

TO GREAT BIRCHAM & BIRCHAM WINDMILL

026

19

FRING ROAD CROSSING

ROAD CROSSING

ROUTE GUIDE AND MAPS

MAP 21

TO OLD
HUNSTANTON
& HUNSTANTON,
3 MILES/5KM

23

TO
THORNHAM

GEDDING'S
FARM

ST
ANDREW'S

WAR
MEMORIAL

RINGSTEAD

GENERAL
STORE

030

BURNHAM RD

TO COURTYARD FARM
& BUNKHOUSE BARN,
1½ MILES/2.5KM &
DOCKING

DOCKING ROAD

Gin
Trap Inn

PEDDARS
WAY
SOUTH

TO RINGSTEAD
DOWNS
NATURE
RESERVE

BROAD
GRASSY PATH
SIMILAR TO A
GREEN LANE

PEDDARS
WAY CYCLE
ROUTE

TO
HEACHAM

MAP 22

PATH ON EAST
SIDE OF HEDGE

SEDGEFORD
BELT

PATH ON WEST
SIDE OF HEDGE

21

0   ¼ mile
0   500m
APPROX SCALE

30-45 MINS TO/FROM HOLME CROSSROADS (MAP 23)

RINGSTEAD

60 MINS FROM/TO B1454 ROAD CROSSING (MAP 21)

★ trailblazer

ROUTE GUIDE AND MAPS

(cont'd from p124) Also here is ***Magazine Wood Luxury B&B*** (Map 21; ☎ 01485-570422, 🖳 magazinewood.co.uk; 3D, all en suite; 🛏; WI-FI; 🐾) boasts rooms with king-sized beds that are fitted out to the highest standard, available for around £49.50-70pp (sgl occ room rate). However, there is generally a two-night minimum stay at weekends.

After Magazine Farm the path descends to cross another **disused railway line**, the old Heacham to Wells line, evident as a dark cinder streak across the countryside. After a turn to the left and then to the right continue north; a long gentle straight – which offers you a last chance to savour the country you have been crossing – leads past **Sedgeford Belt**, towards Ringstead where you join a road called Peddars Way South. At a roundabout turn left, then veer right shortly after a T-junction to reach the main street.

RINGSTEAD   [MAP 22, p127]

This unspoilt village, the last before Holme-next-the-Sea and the coast, used to be famous for the iron-rich spring just to the west on Ringstead Downs. Today the village is full of charm and has a number of shops selling period furniture and art.

Services

The **General Store** (☎ 01485-525270; Mon-Wed 8am-1pm, Thur-Sun 8am-5.30pm), at 41 High St, has a wide selection of groceries and meats, sourced from local suppliers, as well as rolls, pastries and snacks, wines and a number of real ales. **Cashback** is available when you spend more than £5. There is also free **internet access** here.

Where to stay, eat & drink

As you approach Ringstead there are signs for *Courtyard Farm* (☎ 01485-525251, 🖳 courtyardfarm.co.uk; 🐾 in kennels only and must be on a lead) just over 1½ miles to the east. A working organic farm, it has a **bunkhouse barn** (1 x 4- /1 x 8-bed dorm) offering basic shelter as well as toilet/shower and cooking facilities for £15pp), although you need to supply your own bedding and towels. Check availability in advance as the barn is sometimes booked by groups. They also have **tent pitches** (£10pp) with access to basic toilets but there are no showers for campers.

In Ringstead village itself ***Gin Trap Inn*** (☎ 01485-525264, 🖳 thegintrapinn.co .uk; 8D/1T, cottage with 2D or T, all en suite; 🛏; WI-FI; 🐾) is an award-winning,

white-painted, coaching inn that has been a public house since 1668. The inn's name derives from the old gin traps, used to catch game, which used to adorn the interior of the pub, though it is now perhaps better known for its collection of gins (see below). It offers **B&B** in rooms with wonky walls, low ceilings and masses of character. Three of them include a freestanding cast-iron roll-top bath. They charge from £60pp (sgl occ £100-110).

Within the grounds there's also an attractive 2-bedroomed cottage: the Brewhouse is luxuriously appointed and has a small kitchen and cosy snug. A minimum two-night stay is required for advance bookings at weekends in the peak season.

Food (Mon-Thur noon-2.30pm & 6-8.30pm, Fri & Sat noon-2.30pm & 6-9pm, Sun noon-4pm & 6-8pm) is served in either the rustic bar, which has an open fireplace with a wood-burning stove, or in the light, airy dining conservatory, which overlooks the beer garden. The menu changes regularly but often includes a scotch egg of the day (look out for the onion bhaji version, £6.50), lamb meatballs (£6.75), a harissa-spiced beef burger (£14.50), beer-battered coley & chips (£12.50), kedgeree fish pie (£13.50) and a GT lamb balti pie (£13.50). If you've room there are date sticky toffee puddings, pavlova and a drunken cherry parfait (all £6.50).

There is a short but decent wine list. However, their **gin collection**, drawn from all corners of the globe, numbers more than 120 types, including their own Thai-inspired

Gin Trap Gin, brewed in Norwich; you can buy it by the bottle to take away. Ask staff for a recommendation or try a gin-tasting board (£16-22). There's a folk night held in the bar on the first Tuesday of every month (other than July and August) and a gin festival in mid August.

RINGSTEAD TO HOLME-NEXT-THE-SEA (AND HUNSTANTON)
MAPS 22-23 (MAPS 23-25)

This **2½-mile (4km; ¾-1hr) walk** sees you begin to leave the farmed remoteness of the earlier days before you finish the Peddars Way when you arrive at the beach below Holme-next-the-Sea. This is also the point at which you join the Norfolk Coast Path and enter another world, where sand, sea and salt-marshes merge beneath vast skies, and small harbours, flint villages and fishing communities replace the farming hamlets you have previously passed through.

The route from Ringstead to the coast is comfortable and straightforward. Pass **St Andrew's church** and **war memorial** on the way north out of Ringstead, then turn right at the first T-junction and then first left to track past an old **windmill** at Mill Farm. Leave the road and pick up a path to the left that follows the field boundaries, giving you your **first view of the sea**.

The path turns right and descends gently, passing the final **Songline sculpture** (see box p97), before developing into a heavily overgrown green lane seasonally lined with blackberries, elderberries and rose hips. This crosses the A149 between Hunstanton and Thornham, and continues to the beach on the appropriately named Beach Rd. Just before you reach the coast there is a turning right to the main part of Holme-next-the-Sea.

HOLME-NEXT-THE-SEA
[MAP 23, p130]

An attractive, quiet hamlet, Holme-next-the-Sea (the 'l' in Holme is pronounced) is the gateway to the coast, where the North Sea meets The Wash. Historically this would have been the point merchant and naval vessels would have sailed to Lincolnshire and further afield.

From here to Holkham (see p153) is an interconnected series of nature reserves making the area a mecca for wildlife enthusiasts and birdwatchers in particular; **Holme Dunes Nature Reserve** (Map 26) managed by Norfolk Wildlife Trust (NWT; see p61), which includes **Holme Bird Observatory** (see p63) is one such reserve rich in birdlife, insects and plants such as marsh orchid and sea lavender. The rather harshly beautiful dunes and salt-marshes below the village are often whipped by winds, but are no less appealing or bracing because of this. Note that there are no toilet

ROUTE GUIDE AND MAPS

❏ **Peddars Way cycle route**
Cyclists on the Peddars Way Cycle Route should continue on the road at the point where the path turns left (Map 23). Descend gently on the road, crossing the A149 to join a road confusingly called Peddars Way, but which isn't actually part of the official trail. Follow this into the village of Holme-Next-the-Sea and turn left at a T-junction close to the White Horse pub (see p131). At the end of this road, you will turn right on to Beach Rd and re-join the Peddars Way proper as it pushes towards the coast.

ROUTE GUIDE AND MAPS

BEACH / END OF PEDDARS WAY ← 15 MINS → ← HOLME CROSSROADS → ← 30–45 MINS FROM/TO RINGSTEAD (MAP 22) →

~ HUNSTANTON ~
~ ~ THORNHAM ~

26

TO HOLME DUNES
NATURE RESERVE

FINGER POST MARKING THE
END OF PEDDARS WAY.
JOIN NORFOLK COAST PATH

033

24

CAR PARK &
SEASONAL KIOSK

TOILETS
& WATER
TAP

HOLME-NEXT-THE-SEA

RIVERSIDE
CARAVAN PARK

Home Farm
Stables

The
White Horse

KIRKGATE

RIVER HUN

SEA
GATE

PHONE

BEACH
ROAD

WESTGATE

HOLME
CROSSROADS

032

PEDDARS
WAY

BUS
STOP

BUS
STOP

BUS
STOP

TO
THORNHAM

BUS
STOP

A149

BUS
STOP

NAME OF
ROAD ONLY!

TO OLD
HUNSTANTON

TO OLD
HUNSTANTON
& HUNSTANTON

trailblazer

LAST
NORFOLK
SONGLINE
SCULPTURE

PEDDARS
WAY CYCLE
ROUTE

DIRT
TRACK

FIRST VIEW
OF THE SEA

031

MAP 23

0   ¼ mile
0   500m
APPROX SCALE

MILL
FARM

WINDMILL

TO
RINGSTEAD

22

facilities at the NWT centre as the building is not connected to the mains.

There are no services of note, though Lynx's Coastliner 36 **bus** service stops at the Holme Crossroads; see p50 and box p54 for details.

Note that the road marked Peddars Way on the map is not part of the official route.

Although mainly geared up for equestrians, *Home Farm Stables* (☎ 01485-525350, 🖥 homefarmstables.com; 3D or T/1Qd, all en suite; ☞; WI-FI; 🐾; mid Mar-end Nov), on Westgate, has accommodation in a converted barn. There's a communal, galleried sitting room, and two garden courtyards, a terrace and a deck overlooking

a pond. **B&B** costs from £49pp (sgl occ rates on request). They also have full stable facilities for people riding sections of the route.

The White Horse (☎ 01485-525512; **food** served daily noon-9pm in school summer holidays; rest of year Mon-Fri noon-3pm & 5-9pm, Sat-Sun noon-9pm; 🐾) is a good place to pause and toast your achievement in getting this far. The menu includes fisherman's pie (£8.50), tiger garlic prawns (£10.95), and a generous baked ham dish (£8.75); depending on the weather conditions, you can either take advantage of one of their two beer gardens or a cosy fire.

OLD HUNSTANTON ← 30–45 MINS FROM/TO BEACH / END OF PEDDARS WAY (MAP 23) →

MAP 24

23

PATH RUNS ALONG BROW OF DUNES

DUNES

GOLF COURSE CLUBHOUSE

GOLF COURSE

BEACH HUTS

★ trailblazer

Old Boathouse Café

TO HOLME-NEXT-THE-SEA

TOILETS

A149

CP

OLD LIGHTHOUSE

CP

REMAINS OF EDMUND'S CHAPEL

TO RINGSTEAD

BUS STOP

STRIPED CLIFFS

BUS STOP

B1161

OLD HUNSTANTON

SEE TOWN PLAN

CLIFF PARADE

A149

25

0   ¼ mile

0   500m
APPROX SCALE

ROUTE GUIDE AND MAPS

Beach Rd continues, crossing the River Hun and passing Riverside Caravan Park before arriving at a car park. There are public toilets and a fresh-water tap here as well as a seasonal **snack shack** (daily; hours vary) that sells drinks and ice-cream. Push on to the beach, keeping a wary eye out for golf balls being hit across the path from the large course running parallel to the sea, and arrive at a finger-post just before the dunes indicating the direction of the Norfolk Coast Path. This is the **finish point for the Peddars Way**.

You can now either turn right and continue on to **Thornham** (see p140) and the other villages strung along the coast, or turn left and take the detour to the traditional seaside town of **Hunstanton** (see pp134-8), where you may choose to overnight. It is also where you need to go if you want to walk the whole of the Norfolk Coast Path. If you don't want to walk so far consider stopping in Old Hunstanton (see below) where there are also places to stay and some fine restaurants.

Holme-next-the-Sea to Hunstanton

The 2½-mile (4km) route to Hunstanton begins by meandering along the top of the dunes, on the seaward side of Hunstanton Golf Course. Follow the path and allow yourself to look out over the broad expanse of beach. Although wide and generally clean, this section of sand can be windswept and is consequently often empty. Ostensibly flat it is deceptive on a calm day in that the returning tide can race in, potentially catching people who are straying far out onto the sands unaware.

The path passes behind a string of pastel-coloured **beach huts** and then dips inland past the golf-course clubhouse to arrive at the **RNLI lifeboat shed** just below Old Hunstanton.

OLD HUNSTANTON

Unlike its brasher, slightly contrived newer neighbour, Old Hunstanton is quieter, more traditional and retains some of its original charm. Climbing away from the beach, there are some good-quality accommodation options (and a very good restaurant) that provide viable alternatives to those on offer in Hunstanton itself.

Le Strange Old Barns (☎ 01485-533402, ⌨ lestrangeoldbarns.com; daily summer 10am-6pm, rest of year 10am-4/5pm), opposite the Ancient Mariner Inn (see Where to eat), is considered to have the largest collection of arts, crafts and antiques in Norfolk. Browse paintings, pottery, ceramics, jewellery, glassware and other collectables or watch craft demonstrations.

Services and transport

There are public **toilets** next to the RNLI lifeboat shed. Set back from the sea, up the hill is **Post Office & Stores** (☎ 01485-533197; Mon-Fri 7.30am-5.30pm, Sat 7.45am-5.30pm, Sun summer to 4pm, winter till 1pm; post office Mon-Fri 9am-1pm & 2-5.30pm, Sat to 12.30pm) where you can pick up local produce at reasonable rates.

Lynx's Coastliner 36 **bus** service (see p50 and box p54) stops on Old Hunstanton Rd, the A149.

Where to stay

Dominating the seafront is the modern ***Best Western Le Strange Arms Hotel*** (☎ 01485-534411, ⌨ lestrangearms.co.uk; 3S/39D or T/1Qd, all en suite; ☛; WI-FI; Ⓛ), where the rooms are graded – standard, superior and suite – and come in various styles complete with mod-cons. Rates are flexible depending on demand and are best if booked in advance and direct; standard/

superior rooms cost from £49.50/72pp (sgl occ rates on request) and suites go for upwards of £180pp (sgl occ rates on request).

The Lodge (☎ 01485-532896, 🖥 thelodgehunstanton .co.uk; 1D or T/1D/2T, all en suite; ➖; WI-FI; ①; 🐾), on Old Hunstanton Rd, is an imposing place at the top of Sea Lane. It has put people up since 1912 although the farmhouse the lodge was converted from has stood since 1542. A grade II listed building, it still has a number of original features and lets rooms on a B&B basis for £60-85pp (sgl occ £75-95);

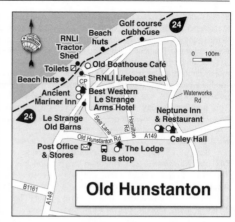

Old Hunstanton

dinner, bed and breakfast rates are also available.

On the same road to the east is *The Neptune Inn and Restaurant* (☎ 01485-532122, 🖥 theneptune.co.uk; 4D/1T, all en suite; ➖; WI-FI; closed three weeks in Jan and one week in Nov), which was a store for seized contraband until the 1880s when it became a coaching inn. Subsequently renovated in tasteful and fine style, it is now an exceptional restaurant with pristine rooms. Prices start at £135pp (sgl occ rates on request) for dinner, bed and breakfast with a three-course meal from their à la carte menu (see Where to eat). They only take advance bookings for a two night stay at weekends but nearer the time may be able to accept a single-night stay.

Adjacent is *Caley Hall Hotel* (☎ 01485-533486, 🖥 caleyhallhotel.co.uk; 38D or T, all en suite; ➖; WI-FI; ①; 🐾; Feb-Dec), which was originally a manor house dating from 1648. The house and outbuildings have been converted into a motel-style stopover and there are now masses of fairly plain rooms. B&B costs £44.50-70pp (sgl occ from £69).

Where to eat and drink

Immediately opposite the RNLI lifeboat shed is *Old Boathouse Café* (Mar-end Oct Mon-Fri 10am-3pm, Sat-Sun 9am-3pm but longer during the summer high season,

Nov-early Mar Fri-Sun only but depends on the weather; WI-FI; 🐾), which is good for homemade cakes, hot snacks and sarnies.

For more substantial fodder, *Best Western Le Strange Arms Hotel* (see Where to stay) has a lounge looking out over attractive gardens, where you can have tea and coffee from 10am, take lunch (daily noon-2pm; booking essential for Sundays) or enjoy afternoon tea (Mon-Sat 2.30-5pm), evening meals are also served here (Mon-Sat 6-8.45pm). Next door and part of the Best Western is the *Ancient Mariner Inn* (food daily noon-9pm), a great sprawling place overlooking the sea, created from the barns and stables of the original Victorian hotel. It has an eclectic menu of staples – try their beer-battered fish (£12.95), or any of the substantial sandwiches (from £6.25; served noon-6pm) – and a good selection of cask ales.

The bar in *The Lodge* (see Where to stay; food Apr-Sep daily noon-9pm, Oct-Mar daily noon-2pm & 6-9pm, afternoon tea 2.30-5.30pm) has some original features. Food is served in the restaurant; the menu changes but may include fish & chips (£12.95), stone-baked pizzas (from £7.95) and slow-braised local estate venison (£17.50).

Down the hill, *Caley Hall Hotel* (see Where to stay; daily breakfast 8-9.30am, bar meals noon-9pm, evening meals 6-9pm) has

ROUTE GUIDE AND MAPS

a restaurant in a converted stable block that's open to both guests and non-residents. Sandwiches cost upwards of £5.25, more substantial lunchtime meals start at £11.95, and evening mains such as salt-marsh lamb rump with ratatouille, or pan-fried sea bass with samphire & parmentier potatoes, will set you back from £16.95. The popular Sunday lunch (from £14; noon-2.30pm) includes generous roasts. The bar boasts free wired high-speed internet access as well as wi-fi.

Best of all though is *The Neptune Inn and Restaurant* (see Where to stay; Tue-Sun 7-9pm, Sun noon-1.30pm), where the fine dining restaurant decorated in subtle coffee-coloured tones serves award-winning modern British food; they have retained a Michelin star since 2009. Start with Brancaster lobster & star anise mousse, or Norfolk quail, and then follow that with red mullet, Brancaster crab & aubergine compôte, suckling pig, or sirloin of dry-aged Dexter beef with baked beetroot. Puddings such as Columbian white chocolate mousse are sumptuous. Appetisers, tasty breads, pre-desserts and petits fours mean you won't go away wanting. Two courses cost £45 or three for £60. Alternatively, there's an adventurous 9-course tasting menu for £75pp. Sunday lunch is good value, with two/three courses costing £30/38; be sure to book in advance though. There's also a cosy lounge and small bar adjacent to the understated dining room.

Passing in front of the RNLI lifeboat shed and then behind another row of attractive beach huts, the path climbs on a grassy path to a car park set atop Hunstanton's famous **striped cliffs**. If the tide's out you can in fact walk along the beach all the way to Hunstanton and thereby get a great view of these 18m (60ft) high white and red walls, made of chalk and a mixture of red limestone and carrstone. Due to the lack of sea defences the cliffs are subject to a high rate of erosion, meaning that fossils, including large mussel shells, sea urchins and ammonites buried in the rocks, frequently come to light.

Follow the tarmac path along Lighthouse Close, past the out-of-service **lighthouse** and the **ruins of St Edmund's Chapel**, dating from 1272. The road turns into Cliff Parade which becomes Esplanade Gardens before finishing at the sloping Green in the middle of **Hunstanton**.

HUNSTANTON   [MAP 25, p137]

Colloquially known as 'Sunny Hunny', the town is a traditional British family seaside resort that still has traces of Victorian sedateness about it. Lauded for being a safe, family resort it can be brash and tacky too. Originally known as Hunstanton St Edmunds in recognition of the fact that Edmund landed here in AD855, became King of East Anglia and was later martyred by the Danes. It has since developed into a popular destination for day-trippers and holidaymakers although visitor numbers have declined since their peak in the 1980s. It is the only east-coast town to face west and from which you can watch the sun set over the sea, a fact the locals are particularly proud of. Weather permitting you can also see Lincolnshire and the outline of Boston's famous church, The Stump, on the far side of The Wash.

The town owes its success to Henry Styleman Le Strange who decided to develop the area as a bathing resort. In 1861 Le Strange became a director of the regional railway and arranged for the line to be extended to Hunstanton, opening up the area to tourists. Sadly he died in 1862 having never seen his dream fully realised, although his son reaped the benefits of his ambition. The remains of an ancient cross stand atop a set of tiered steps on The Green. This was placed there by Le Strange to mark his intention and as a focal point for the town.

Along the seafront there are various **entertainment complexes** and **amusement arcades** with slot machines and computer games. The most substantial, comprising a bowling alley and arcade, stands on the site of the town's Victorian pleasure pier, which was damaged by fires in 1939 and the 1950s before being wrecked by storms in 1978. The remaining stub was finally destroyed by another fire in 2002 and it was then demolished.

Further south, on the long promenade, is a seasonal **fairground** with typical rides and **Hunstanton Sea Life Sanctuary** (☎ 01485-533576, 🖳 visitsealife.com/hunstanton; daily 10am-4pm, till 3pm in winter; general admission £16.60, but book online to save up to 40% or buy tickets from the tourist information centre for £9.90); this is one of three national seal sanctuaries responsible for the rescue, rehabilitation and release of wild animals.

The centre combines a seal hospital, otter and penguin sanctuary, aquarium and an underwater tunnel that allows you to come face to face with Bonnethead sharks. There's also a small gift shop and *café*.

If you want to get on to the water, **Searles Sea Tours** (☎ 01485-534444, 🖳 seatours.co.uk) runs a quirky fleet of craft from Hunstanton including two amphibious landing craft used in Vietnam that still sport their distinctive shark's head livery. The Wash Monsters (tours £10/5 adult/children under 14; approx 30 mins), as they are affectionately known, are the most popular means of enjoying this stretch of coast, during the course of which you get good views of the striped cliffs, the lighthouse and even a couple of wrecks. Call in the morning between 9.30 and 10am to find out which tours are available as they depend on the weather and the tides.

Better though is their seal safari (£17/8.50 adult/child; approx 1hr), where you are ferried out to a boat in The Wash which takes you to see some of the 3000 common seals that live on the sandbanks here. Book in advance for this.

For a more relaxing form of entertainment **Princess Theatre** (☎ 01485-532252, 🖳 princesstheatrehunstanton.co.uk), by

The Green, stages plays, pantomimes, live music and comedy, and screens films.

The town also hosts a number of **annual events** including the Lifestyles Festival, the District Festival of Arts, Hunstanton Carnival and a kite festival. For more information see pp14-15.

Services and transport

Overlooking The Green is the Town Hall dating from 1896 and designed by the eminent architect George Skipper. The town council still convenes there and it is also now home to a **tourist information centre** (TIC; ☎ 01485-532610, 🖳 visithunstanton.info; daily Apr to May 9.30am-4pm, late May to late Sep 9.30am-5pm, late Sep to Oct 9.30am-4.30pm, Nov to Mar Mon-Sat 10am-2pm, Sun 11am-2pm), which has a good supply of leaflets and flyers regarding attractions in the area as well as comprehensive accommodation listings and notes on where there are vacancies each evening. They will make bookings for you; they charge 10% of the first night's accommodation but this will be deducted from the bill you pay.

The local **library** (Mon-Tue & Fri 10am-5pm, Wed 10am-7pm, Thur 10am-1pm, Sat 10am-1pm), on Westgate, has free **internet access**.

There are **banks** and **ATMs** at the crossroads of High St and Greevegate, as well as an ATM on High St itself. There is also a **pharmacy**, a branch of Boots (Mon-Sat 8.30am-5.30pm, Sun 10am-3pm), on High St, as well as a Londis **supermarket** (Mon-Sat 7am-7pm, Sun 7.30am-6pm), inside which is a **post office** (Mon-Fri 9am-5.30pm, Sat 9am-1pm). There is a Sainsbury's (Mon-Sat 8am-10pm, Sun 10am-4pm), on Westgate, which is much larger than the Londis and will have everything you need to resupply. **Norfolk Deli** (☎ 01485-535540, 🖳 norfolk-deli.co.uk; generally Mon-Sat 8.30am-5pm, Sun 10am-4pm but check especially in winter), 16 Greevegate, offers more than 60 cheeses, antipasti, meats and other local produce, along with East Anglian wines, Norfolk gins and regional ales. They serve snacks to eat in or takeaway too.

On Wednesdays and Sundays (9am-5pm) throughout the year there is a **market** in Southend car park on the seafront, selling fresh fish and general goods.

Lynx's Nos 34, 35 & Coastliner 36 **bus** services (see p50 and box p54) call at the bus station.

Where to stay

Hunstanton Backpackers & YHA (☎ 01485-532061, 🖳 norfolkbeachholidays.co.uk; 2 x 2- /1 x 3- /3 x 4- /3 x 6-bed rooms; some en suite, rest shared facilities; WI-FI; ⓛ; late Mar-Nov) is an independently run hostel but it can also be booked through the YHA. Meals are available but they also have a self-catering kitchen as well as a drying room. A dorm bed costs from £24pp and private rooms are from £65.

There are masses of B&Bs and guesthouses in Hunstanton, most of them in the quiet residential streets set back from the seafront.

Deepdene (☎ 01485-532460, 🖳 deepdenehouse.co.uk; 2D/1T, all en suite; ☛; WI-FI; ⓛ), at 29 Avenue Rd, has generously sized rooms meaning that spending time in them is peaceful and relaxing; the double rooms in particular are well turned out. B&B costs from £45pp (sgl occ from £55).

The Bays (☎ 01485-532079, 🖳 the bays.co.uk; 1S/1T/4D, all en suite; ☛; WI-FI; ⓛ), next door at No 31, is a lovingly refurbished Victorian house that retains many of its original features. Two of the double rooms have king-sized beds. Rooms come with numerous extras including a fridge (stocked with soft drinks, crisps and chocolate though there is a charge for these) and dressing gowns; rates for B&B are £50-55pp (sgl £50, sgl occ rates on request). Breakfast includes homemade breads and jams; they'll also provide an evening meal (three-courses £25) if asked

in advance. Also worth a look on this street is *Ellinbrook* (☎ 01485-532022, 🖳 ellin brookhouse.com; 4D/2D or T, all en suite; ☛; WI-FI; mid Mar-mid Nov), at No 37; they charge £37.50-42.50pp (sgl occ from £50).

The Richmond (☎ 01485-532601, 🖳 richmondhousehunstanton.co.uk; 1S private facilities, 7D/1T all en suite; ☛; WI-FI; ⓛ; Easter-Oct), a large Victorian property centrally located at 6-8 Westgate, offers B&B from £40pp (sgl from £55, sgl occ from £65). They also have a licensed bar and restaurant (daily 6-8pm) that caters for both guests and non-residents.

Gate Lodge (☎ 01485-533549, 🖳 gate lodge-guesthouse.co.uk; 6D/1T, all en suite; ☛; WI-FI; Mar-Nov), No 2 Westgate, offers superb-value accommodation with lots of little extras. The upper rooms have sea views. Rates, which include a hearty breakfast, start from £45pp (sgl occ room rate); the highest rate is of course for their luxury double, complete with king-size four-poster bed. They require a minimum stay of two nights for advance bookings, but at short notice it may be possible to stay for one night.

On Cliff Terrace are two well-equipped B&Bs that have communal lounges and their own bars; the welcoming *Shellbrooke* (☎ 01485-532289, 🖳 theshell brooke.co.uk; 1S with private facilities, 8D/1T/1Tr/2Qd, all en suite; ☛; WI-FI; ⓛ) has well-presented, tastefully furnished rooms (£36-55pp, sgl/sgl occ from £55/75). Evening meals (daily 6-8pm) are available if booked at least the day before.

Close by is the marginally more upmarket but better-value *Burleigh* (☎ 01485-533080, 🖳 theburleigh.com; 2D with private facilities, 1S/2D/2T/4Tr, all en suite; WI-FI; ⓛ), which charges £35-44.50pp (sgl from £45, sgl occ room rate).

❏ Where to stay: the details

In the descriptions of accommodation in this book: ☛ means at least one room has a bath; ⓛ means a packed lunch can be prepared if arranged in advance; 🐾 signifies that dogs are welcome in at least one room but also subject to prior arrangement, an additional charge may also be payable; WI-FI means wi-fi is available. See also p88.

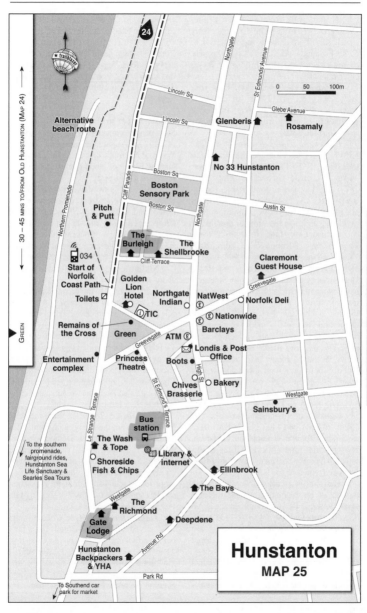

Hunstanton
MAP 25

A short walk from the town centre, *Glenberis* (☎ 01485-533663, 🖳 glenberis .co.uk; 4D/1T, all en suite; ☞; WI-FI; Ⓛ), at 6 St Edmunds Ave, has large, homely rooms and charges £36-47pp for B&B (sgl occ from £60).

Rosamaly (☎ 01485-534187, 🖳 rosa maly.webs.com; 1D/1T/2Tr, all en suite; WI-FI; Ⓛ; 🐾), 14 Glebe Ave, is a cosy guesthouse charging from £40pp (sgl occ from £60) for B&B.

Claremont Guest House (☎ 01485-533171, 🖳 claremontguesthousehunstan ton.co.uk; 1S/4D/1T/1Qd, all en suite; ☞; WI-FI; 🐾), at 35 Greevegate, dates from 1873 and has large, comfortable rooms. B&B costs £37.50-42.50pp (sgl £55, sgl occ room rate). They have a minimum two-night stay policy in the summer months.

Golden Lion Hotel (☎ 01485-532688, 🖳 www.coastandcountryhotels.com; 20D/ 7T/1Tr, all en suite; ☞; WI-FI; 🐾), built in 1846 and originally known as the Royal Hotel, was the first building in Le Strange's new town and it dominates the original centre poised as it is above The Green and looking out to sea. For a while it stood alone and was nicknamed Le Strange's folly; today it's a pleasant-enough place to stay. The majority of the rooms have sea views. Standard rooms start at £54.50pp (sgl occ room rate), rooms with a view start from £61.50pp (sgl occ room rate). Breakfast costs an additional £8.95pp.

The Wash & Tope (☎ 01485-532250, 🖳 washandtopepubhunstanton.co.uk; 5D/ 1T, all en suite; ☞; WI-FI; Ⓛ; 🐾), at 10-12 Le Strange Terrace, just opposite the beach, is a pub with rooms above. All the rooms look out over the coast and cost from £40pp (sgl occ from £55) for B&B.

Hunstanton's most stylish place to stay though is on Northgate, where there is smart boutique B&B accommodation at *No 33 Hunstanton* (☎ 01485-524352, 🖳 33hunstanton.co.uk; 5D, all en suite; ☞; WI-FI; 🐾), in a handsome, restored Victorian building. The generously-sized, stylish rooms are decked out in muted shades of fashionable grey and are full of attractive furniture. Rates, which include a cream tea on the day of arrival and a full English or Continental breakfast, are from £65pp (sgl occ from £120), except for Room 3, which has a large balcony terrace and goes for £75pp (sgl occ from £140) but this may vary according to the season. There is a minimum two-night stay at weekends.

Where to eat and drink

Surprisingly, considering the high standard of pubs and restaurants along the Peddars Way and Norfolk Coast Path, Hunstanton is largely bereft of good-quality eateries or places to grab a pint.

Fast food is available from numerous **stalls** along the seafront, otherwise a portion of cod & chips from *Shoreside Fish & Chips* (open daily) will set you back £5.60.

A wide range of decent Indian dishes starting at £6.50 are on offer at *Northgate Indian* (☎ 01485-535005; daily 5-11pm), at 8-9 Northgate Precinct. They have a takeaway service as well.

For largely Mediterranean-themed dishes try *Chives Brasserie* (☎ 01485-534771; daily from 9am, lunch Mon-Sat noon-3pm, Sun to 4pm, evening meals daily 6-9.30pm, winter Sun noon-8pm), at 11 High St; the menu changes weekly but always has pizza (from £10.25), pasta (from £10.95) and steaks (from £18.95). Light lunches and afternoon tea (cream tea £5.15) are also available, or you can simply perch at their bar to have a drink.

The Wash & Tope (see Where to stay; food served summer daily noon-9pm, winter Mon noon-3pm, Tue-Sat noon-3pm & 5-9pm, Sun noon-5pm), on Le Strange Terrace, is a large town pub popular with locals and tourists alike. The main bar has a large-screen television and there's a second smaller sports bar behind this. Generic pub grub is available from £8.95.

Golden Lion Hotel (see Where to stay; food served daily noon-8.30pm) has a long bar overlooking The Green and the sea. There's a selection of cask ales and a lunchtime bar-snack menu during the low season and a more substantial lunch and evening menu during the high season.

Norfolk Coast Path

HUNSTANTON TO BURNHAM OVERY STAITHE
(MAPS 25-23 & 26-31)

This **13½-mile (21.5km; 5¼-6¼hrs) route** is your first real experience of the North Norfolk coast. From The Green the path drops down onto the promenade. There's a route along the cliff tops and another that runs below the famous striped cliffs along the beach, all the way to **Holme** (see p129).

From Holme you can join the Peddars Way and trek inland along this route to Ringstead. For the Norfolk Coast Path, once you arrive at Holme continue to follow the finger-posts arrowing along the top of the dunes. Follow the path east towards Gore Point and Holme Dunes Nature Reserve; the latter is managed by Norfolk Wildlife Trust (see p61) but it includes a Bird Observatory which is maintained by Norfolk Ornithologists Association (see p61). To the seaward side are lavender marshes and shingle bars that provide refuge for roosting and migrating birds. During the autumn and spring keep an eye out for oystercatchers and knot roosting in vast numbers. A section of boardwalk ends just before **Gore Point** (Map 26), the headland beyond which was the original location of Seahenge (see box p140).

An undulating, rolling **boardwalk** weaves across the dunes before entering a stand of Corsican pines, just before **Norfolk Wildlife Trust Visitor Centre** (see p61 for website details; Apr-Oct daily 10am-5pm, Nov-Mar Sat & Sun 10am-4pm), which has lots of interesting information on the reserve and its inhabitants. Drinks, snacks and ice-cream are available and there is a deck overlooking Broad Water and the marshes on which to enjoy them. They have an emergency telephone and toilets.

The path then bends inland, rounding **Broad Water** and heading south past **Ragged Marsh** on a sea defence bank. Ahead you'll see an old coal barn, the subject of lots of paintings and photographs over the years, stood alone overlooking the marshes. Drop off the sea defence and join a dirt track. Turning left at the stump of an old windmill, the path veers east and then enters **Thornham**.

ROUTE GUIDE AND MAPS

❏ **Important note – walking times**
Unless otherwise specified, **all times in this book refer only to the time spent walking**. You will need to add 20-30% to allow for rests, photography, checking the map, drinking water etc. When planning the day's hike count on 5-7 hours' actual walking.

❏ **Seahenge**

The mysterious Bronze Age monument Seahenge was discovered in 1998 close to the low-tide mark on Holme beach. Despite the similarity in names, there's no direct connection with Stonehenge and no-one really knows to what purpose it was built. Some archaeologists consider it to have ceremonial or astronomical importance; others think it was a site for excarnation, where bodies were laid out after death so that their spirits could escape as the flesh decomposed.

The site consists of a rough timber circle comprising 55 small split oak trunks centred on an enormous upturned oak-tree stump; it was the first intact timber circle discovered in Britain – usually all that remain of the circles are soil markings where the timber has crumbled away – and is the best-preserved example in Europe. One of the trunks had a narrow 'Y' in it allowing access to the circle, whilst another stood in front of this entrance, blocking the view of the interior. The trunks were set a metre below the current surface but it isn't known how high they originally stood. The trees have subsequently been dated to 2049BC using *dendrochronology* (tree-ring dating). Between 16 and 26 trees were used to make the monument and evidence suggests these came from nearby woodland. The central stump was hauled into place using ropes made from honeysuckle stems, which were found under the stump. It is thought to have been turned upside down as Bronze Age people are supposed to consider death an inversion of life.

Forty centuries ago the circle would have been much further inland and constructed on swampy ground rather than a beach. Having been covered by the sea and slowly hidden from sight beneath layers of soil though, the monument was only discovered as a result of the sea eroding the peat layers to reveal the ancient landscape. Since the logs had been preserved in a waterlogged state with no oxygen, they hadn't rotted. Exposure to the air immediately put them at risk though, and as the sea water that had soaked into the timbers drained away so they began to dry and crumble. The successive tides that swept Holme Beach also threatened to damage the site.

Shortly after its discovery English Heritage controversially arranged to move the site to an archaeological centre at Flag Fen, near Peterborough, in order to work on preserving the wood. Despite sit-in protests by druids and modern-day pagans who argued much of the significance of the site was its location, this went ahead. Since then a recreated Seahenge has been set-up at Lynn Museum in King's Lynn.

Subsequently, a second, older ring has been discovered a hundred metres east of the Seahenge site. Consisting of two concentric rings Holme II, as it has become known, dates from around 2400BC. Despite facing the same dangers, this set of posts has been left in situ, largely as a result of the controversy associated with preserving the original site.

THORNHAM   [MAP 27, p143]

Once a busy harbour (there used to be sea access via the creeks for shallow draught boats until it silted up) and a centre for trade in timber, coal and farm stuffs, Thornham went into decline with the arrival of the railways as business moved elsewhere. Nowadays it's a quiet, traditional village. Depending on how far you're hoping to walk, Thornham can make a wonderful lunch break, with three very good pubs to entice you to stop awhile. Alternatively, each also offers accommodation in case you want to stay for a night.

Services and transport

There is a small village **shop** (Mon-Wed & Fri-Sat 8am-5pm, half-day Thur & Sun) selling a variety of food and drink.

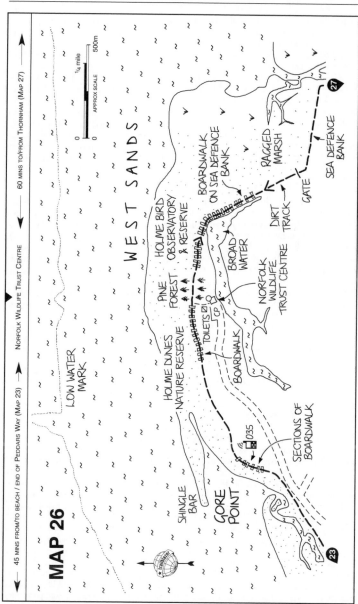

MAP 26

← 45 MINS FROM/TO BEACH / END OF PEDDARS WAY (MAP 23) →   NORFOLK WILDLIFE TRUST CENTRE   ← 60 MINS TO/FROM THORNHAM (MAP 27) →

LOW WATER MARK

WEST SANDS

APPROX SCALE
0   500m
0   ¼ mile

SHINGLE BAR

GORE POINT

035

SECTIONS OF BOARDWALK

HOLME DUNES NATURE RESERVE

PINE FOREST

HOLME BIRD OBSERVATORY & RESERVE

TOILETS
CP

BOARDWALK

NORFOLK WILDLIFE TRUST CENTRE

BROAD WATER

DIRT TRACK

BOARDWALK ON SEA DEFENCE BANK

GATE

RAGGED MARSH

SEA DEFENCE BANK

23

27

(Thornham *cont'd*) On the outskirts of the village there's **Thornham Deli** (☎ 01485-512194, 🖥 thornhamdeli.co.uk); this fine food shop sells local, seasonal produce but also includes a *café* (daily summer 7.30am-4.30pm, winter 8.30am-3pm; WI-FI) serving a wide range of tasty homemade treats, and a lifestyle shop selling homeware and crafts. You can sit indoors or on their outside, south-facing terrace.

Lynx's Coastliner 36 **bus** service stops in front of **All Saints church**; see p50 and box p54 for details.

Where to stay

There is B&B at *The Lifeboat Inn* (☎ 01485-512236, 🖥 lifeboatinnthornham .com; 13D or T, all en suite; ☞; WI-FI; ⓛ; 🐾), set back from the main road on Ship Lane. This charming country pub has been operating since the 16th century when it was reputed to be a smuggler's alehouse. It's been through some changes since then but the history and character of the place have been preserved. In keeping with the Inn's history, each room is named after the crew of the *Licensed Victualler's III*, the last pulling lifeboat at Hunstanton lifeboat station, which started service in 1900. The stylish, good-sized rooms (many of which have sea views) are spacious and bright with neutral colours that reflect the landscape outside. B&B costs £72.50-107.50pp (sgl occ £130-200); note an extra bed can be put in some rooms and there is a two-night minimum stay at weekends.

At the other end of town, on the High St, is The Lifeboat Inn's sister establishment, *The Chequers Inn* (☎ 01485-512229, 🖥 chequersinnthornham.com; 11D, all en suite; ☞; WI-FI; ⓛ; 🐾). Warm and welcoming, combining rustic charm and contemporary style, the rooms here are airy and include king-size beds and freestanding baths. B&B costs £60-90pp (sgl occ rates on request); note there is also a two-night minimum stay at weekends here.

Between these two, on the High St close to the church, is *The Orange Tree* (☎ 01485-512213, 🖥 theorangetreethorn ham.co.uk; 14D/1T/2D or T, all en suite; ☞; WI-FI; ⓛ; 🐾), a stylish gastro pub that has contemporary rooms decorated in shades of cream and chocolate, set around a courtyard. B&B costs £44.50-54.50pp (sgl occ room rate). You can also stay in the neighbouring **Old Bakery Annexe**, which has four themed bedrooms, or **Manor Lodge**, snuggled between the two properties and offering seven luxurious en suite double rooms, three of which have their own enclosed, terrace gardens. Rates for these start at £55pp (sgl occ room rate) but suites can set you back up to £132.50pp (sgl occ room rate) per night. In each instance, call the hotel for their best rates.

Above Thornham Deli (see above) there is smart B&B accommodation at *No 33 Thornham* (☎ 01485-524352, 🖥 33hunstanton.co.uk/thornham.html; 2D, both en suite; ☞; WI-FI; 🐾). The sister property of the similarly named boutique B&B in Hunstanton, this branch of the No 33 brand has just two elegant suites (with a sitting area and bathroom with both bath and shower) painted in a soothing palette and full of stylish flourishes. Rates are from £80pp (sgl occ room rate) and include a sumptuous breakfast. Guests are also given a discount voucher towards lunch at the Deli below.

Where to eat and drink

The Lifeboat Inn (see Where to stay; food daily noon-9pm) is firmly established as a local favourite. The bar area is full of guns, swords, mattocks, traditional tools and other antique equipment; you can sense the history of the place as you ease into one of the pews around the carved oak tables with a pint of one of their real ales. There are several nooks and five open fires, ideal if the weather hasn't been co-operating. The kitchen offers an extensive menu of local staples, with blackboard specials which change daily; people have been known to travel a long way for a chance to enjoy a bowl of mussels (gathered from the beds nearby), or a smoked fish & shellfish platter (£9.95), which along with perhaps merguez sausage linguine (£13.95), fillet of bream (£15.95), or slow-cooked pork belly

MAP 27

60 MINS FROM/TO NWT CENTRE (MAP 26)

75-90 MINS TO/FROM BRANCASTER (MAP 29)

ROUTE GUIDE AND MAPS

chilli (£15.95) will set you up for the onward journey. They also serve snacks and cream teas (£6.95) all day if you're feeling peckish. There's a good value Sunday lunch menu as well with 2/3 courses costing £20.45/24.95.

Stiff competition is available from *The Orange Tree* (see Where to stay; food daily noon-3.30pm & 5.30-9pm, Sunday lunch noon-5pm), which has won high praise and a string of awards for its exceptional cuisine. From the menu choose linguine fruits de mer using Brancaster cockles & mussels (£11), or one of the chef's signature dishes which include rolled fillet steak (£28.50) and pan-fried halibut (£22.95). Their free-range chicken & wild mushroom pie (£16.75) has won awards. If arranged in advance non-residents can have breakfast here (8.30-10am).

During the summer months, and if the weather is good, they have BBQs, with local seafood and meats, in their substantial, shady beer garden.

The Chequers Inn (see Where to stay; food daily noon-9.30pm), completes the local dining scene and provides a contrasting option with a seasonal à la carte menu (think pan-seared breast of duck with pickled blackberries for £20, or butter-roasted wild hake for £22) alongside homemade stone-baked crispy based pizzas (from £11.95) and Norfolk tapas, where plates of crispy chilli squid, local quails' eggs and fishcakes among others will set you back £4 each. Breakfast is available for non-residents as well if booked in advance (daily 8-10am; £14.95).

About a mile west of Thornham on the A149 is **Thornham Drove Orchard**, a working farm with a great little farm shop selling fresh produce. On-site is also *Eric's Fish & Chips* (☎ 01485-472025, 🖳 erics fishandchips.com; daily noon-9pm, take-away menu available as well; closed early to late Jan), where the eponymous Eric, head chef at Titchwell Manor, moonlights, rustling up great traditional beer-battered fish cooked in beef dripping, served with chips (from £9/7.50 for a medium-size eat in/takeaway). Look out too for their gruyère & spinach arancini, battered squid, and Kansas City chicken wings (all from £6.50/5 eat in/takeaway) and don't miss the black garlic mayo. Dip into the concise wine list or sample their range of Prosecco,

champagne, craft beers and lagers.

Look out too for *Shucks* (☎ 01485-525889, 🖳 shucksattheyurt.co.uk; Mon-Fri 10am-9pm, Sat 9.30am-9pm, Sun 9.30am-6pm; WI-FI; 🐾; closed early to late Jan), a venture by award-winning local chef Philip Milner that serves up rustic food within an atmospheric yurt setting. With the emphasis on farm to table, there's a menu of classics such as Red Poll beef burgers (£14.50), that use ingredients sourced from the gardens at Drove, complemented by a range of ever-changing specials that might include lin-guine vongole using Brancaster cockles & Palourde clams (£14.75), or Nepalese Ghurka curry with tandoori buttermilk chicken (£14.50). Desserts cost from £6.75.

Assuming you can drag yourself away from Thornham's fine pubs, walk east along the High St. There is no coast path to Brancaster so you must head inland briefly. Turn right and head away from the sea along a metalled road (Choseley Rd) that climbs a small hill, from the top of which, if you look back over your shoulder, you can see the large windfarm at work in The Wash. The path cuts east through farmland. At one point, it crosses a road heading north; it is two miles along this road to Titchwell and half a mile more to **Titchwell Marsh Nature Reserve** where you can walk past reedbeds and shallow lagoons to the beach, all the while looking for a wide variety of birds. Norfolk Coast Path continues on, before once more turning to the sea and descending to **Brancaster** along a country lane.

BRANCASTER [MAP 29, p147]

Although sleepy and fairly quiet at first glance there's actually more to this small village, set above an attractive stretch of sand, than first meets the eye, with a huge area of bird-rich salt-marsh and sandflats nearby.

To the right at the crossroads, on the A149, is *The Ship* (☎ 01485-210333, 🖳 shiphotelnorfolk.co.uk; 5D/4T, all en suite; ➤; WI-FI; 🐾) run by the same Flying Kiwi chain behind The Crown in Wells (see p160). Centred on an inviting bar area it also boasts a decent restaurant (Mon-Sat noon-2.30pm & 6-9pm, Sun noon-8pm) whose

wholesome menu uses local ingredients; look out for chargrilled sirloin steak (from £24.95), the rump-steak Ship burger (£16.95), or seared sea bass fillets with crab mash (£19.95). The elegant rooms decked out in interesting and varied designs are well equipped and spotless. **B&B** rates are £45-90pp (sgl occ £70-160); note, there is a minimum two-night stay at the weekend.

Lynx's Coastliner 36 **bus** service stops further along this road; see p50 and box p54 for details.

To stay on the path, carry straight on over the A149, past **St Mary's church**, and before the salt-marsh turn right onto a path running east alongside

MAP 28

75-90 MINS BETWEEN THORNHAM (MAP 27) AND BRANCASTER (MAP 29)

29

SCHOOL FARM

038

FARMLAND

FARMLAND

CHALKPIT ROAD

FARMLAND

FARMLAND

HEDGE ON LEFT/NORTH OF PATH

BARNS

HEDGE ON LEFT/NORTH OF PATH

TO TITCHWELL, 2 MILES/3.2KM & TITCHWELL BIRD RESERVE, 2½ MILES/4KM

FARMLAND

BROAD GRASSY TRACK WITH GOOD VIEWS NORTH TO THE COAST

DIRT TRACK

FARMLAND

¼ mile

500m

0

0

APPROX SCALE

VIEW NORTH OF COAST & WINDFARM OUT AT SEA

METALLED ROAD

037

TO DOCKING

27

❏ **Branodunum**

Built during the 3rd century AD, Branodunum was once part of a defensive network of 11 Roman shore forts that lined the south and east coast of Britain. Initially designed to protect and control shipping and trade, the forts were later used to repel the incursions of Angles, Saxons and German tribes, who began to harry the coast. One of the regiments to defend the position is thought to have been the Equites Dalmatae, a cavalry unit from modern-day Croatia. The site remained a garrison for 150 years until being abandoned when the Romans withdrew from Britain.

Since then the site has been plundered and much of the building material spirited away to be used elsewhere; some of the materials have been traced to St Mary's church, Brancaster. Consequently, the site, which is managed by the National Trust, isn't all that impressive and it requires a little imagination to transform the grassy ramparts remaining in a field into the fort as it once would have been.

extensive reed beds and continue past the site of the Roman ruin of **Branodunum** (see box above) on Rack Hill. Branodunum is best reached from the path and is open all the time.

On the outskirts of **Brancaster Staithe** the path winds left then right past the yacht club and through some fishermen's sheds.

BRANCASTER STAITHE   [MAP 29]

Staithe is the Norfolk term for quay or landing place. In the 1700s this quay would have been used by fishing boats and larger cargo ships packed with coal and grain.

Behind the quay once stood an enormous malt house, described by John Chambers in his 1829 *History of Norfolk* as, 'one of the most remarkable curiosities in the county.' This giant building, which could process up to 120 tons of barley grain into malt each week, would have stretched 100m from the quay to the main road, through the village. Sadly by 1840 malting was no longer taking place here and the building was destroyed by 1870, leaving almost no trace.

The seasonal **snack kiosk** in the quay car park, called *The Crab Hut* (Apr-Oct daily 10am-5pm), sells fresh pots of prawns, whelks and cockles (from £2.50/5 small/large), dressed crab and lobster caught from their own boat as well as mugs of tea. During the right season, you can also pick up bags of freshly collected mussels from outside fishermen's houses at very reasonable rates.

If you're after something more substantial, on the main road is the 18th-century *Jolly Sailors* (☎ 01485-210314, 🖳 jolly sailorsbrancaster.co.uk; food summer daily noon-9pm, Oct-Apr Mon-Thur noon-2.30pm & 6-9pm, Fri-Sun noon-9pm; WI-FI; 🐾), which has local seafood, specials from their Smokehouse including brisket and bean chilli (£10.95), rack of ribs (£13.50) and pulled pork burger (£10.50) and stone-baked pizzas (from £8.50). Takeaway is available during food service times and until 10pm on Friday. The bar serves Brancaster Brewery ales that are brewed nearby and boasts a rum menu with more than 30 variations from around the world that will leave you a very jolly sailor. The main bar has country charm while the cosy snugs are more rustic. There is also a good-sized enclosed garden, where you can buy ice-cream from a beach hut (school summer holidays only), and an outdoor play area for any little pirates with you.

Lynx's Coastliner 36 **bus** service calls at the **bus** stops near the Jolly Sailors; for details see p50 and box p54.

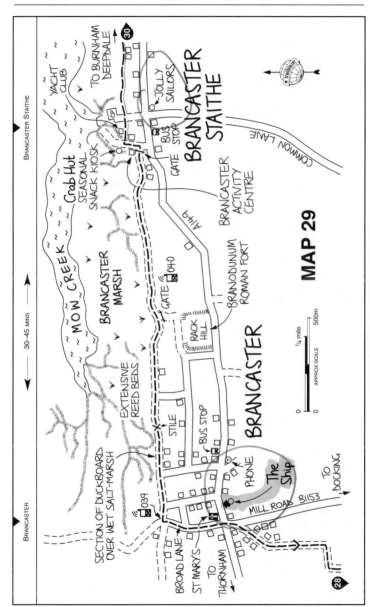

The Coast Path continues along the edge of the marshes and intertidal mud-flats that are so popular with sea birds. After passing an entrance to the garden of The White Horse (see below) the coast path curves left and crosses a dirt track, The Drove, which leads to Burnham Deepdale.

BURNHAM DEEPDALE

This small village straggles along either side of the A149. Next to a petrol station is a Nisa Local **supermarket** (daily 7am-9pm) with a reasonable range of groceries and food; it also offers **cashback**. Opposite is **St Mary's church**, a mostly Victorian structure with a round tower that still retains traces of its Saxon heritage. Inside is an unusual square stone font of Norman origin and a smattering of medieval glass, the best bits of which can be found in the north aisle west window.

Adjacent to the church is a stop for Lynx's Coastliner 36 **bus** service (see p50 and box p54 for details) to Wells/Cromer. On the corner of the A149 and Dalegate Lane is the stop for the equivalent service going to Hunstanton.

Deepdale Backpackers and Campsite (☎ 01485-210256, 🖳 deepdalebackpackers .co.uk; 1D/1T/5Tr/1Qd/3 x 6-, 1 x 8-bed dorm, all en suite; WI-FI; 🐾) is a fantastic hostel-style stop centred around a covered stable courtyard. **Dorm beds**, in the carefully converted stables, cost £12-18pp (all bedding provided, just bring towels) while **private rooms** cost £20-30pp (sgl occ room rate). There's a minimum of two nights booking at weekends (Fri & Sat or Sat & Sun) and three nights over bank holidays or during school holidays for the private rooms.

If you're **camping**, there are 85 pitches suitable for tents, campervans and motor homes (no caravans though). Standard tent pitches cost £7-16/8-26 for one/two people. A strict noise policy means the site remains tranquil after 10pm. As well as a modern kitchen and lounge, eco-friendly hot showers, laundry and drying room, there is a very well-stocked **information centre** and shop (Easter-end Oct Mon-Sat 9am-6pm, Sun 10am-4pm, rest of year Mon-Sat to 5pm) where you

can pick up all sorts of leaflets, get advice, buy postcards and maps. They have a range of **bikes** for hire for all ages and can also provide free route maps and lots of suggestions for where to ride. Rates start from £12/day for adult bikes and children's bikes half that.

There is also a hostel for groups, *The Deepdale Granary*, which sleeps up to 18 (2 x 6- / 1 x 4- / 1 x 2-bed room) with a fully fitted kitchen and dining room, and costs £252-288 per night.

Look out for the Deepdale Hygge, their celebration of the North Norfolk Coast in March and a small music festival hosted on site during September (see pp14-15).

Deepdale Café (☎ 01485-210200, 🖳 deepdalecafe.co.uk; daily 8am-4pm, breakfast 8-11.45am, lunch noon-3pm; WI-FI; 🐾), an eatery that makes substantial breakfasts (Classic full English £9.50) as well as lunch snacks such as loaded jacket potatoes (from £6.50), burgers (from £10.95), good-sized sandwiches (from £6) and tasty salads (from £8.95). Food is also available for takeaway and they have various lunch-pack options from £5.

About five minutes back up the road to Brancaster is *The White Horse* (☎ 01485-210262, 🖳 whitehorsebrancaster.co.uk; 11D/4T, all en suite; 🍺; WI-FI; Ⓛ; 🐾),

Burnham Deepdale

15 MINS FROM/TO BRANCASTER STAITHE (MAP 29) →

BURNHAM DEEPDALE

← 90-120 MINS TO/FROM BURNHAM OVERY STAITHE (MAP 31) →

MAP 30

SCOLT HEAD ISLAND & NATURE RESERVE

DEEPDALE MARSH

TAKE CARE NOT TO STRAY OFF THE PATH AND INTO THE MARSHES. DON'T TRY TO WALK OUT TO SCOLT HEAD EITHER AS IT CAN BE DANGEROUS

ST MARY'S

THE DROVE

MARSH BARN CARR

A149

TO BURNHAM NORTON, 1¼ MILES/2KM & BURNHAM MARKET, 2½ MILES/4KM

BURNHAM DEEPDALE
SEE VILLAGE PLAN

ACCESS TO PUB

The White Horse

¼ mile
APPROX SCALE
500m

which can also be accessed directly from the coast path. The rooms at this splendid pub-cum-hotel are split between the main building and the surrounding grounds. Relaxed and stylish they are contemporary but classic and many boast superb views across the marshes to Scolt Head. **B&B** ranges from £75pp to £120pp (sgl occ rates on request), the highest rate being for the Room at The Top, which has split-level accommodation with a viewing balcony looking out over the marshes to Scolt Head Island. Stays for one night on a Saturday are subject to availability. The bar stocks real ales from Brancaster Brewery, including The Wreck, as well as East Anglian favourites such as Woodforde's Wherry. The locals' bar has scrubbed pine furniture and old photographs from the area displayed on the walls. Food

is served in the **bar** (daily 9am-9pm) and includes Norfolk tapas at £3.95 each, salads from £10.95 and flatbreads (chilli tempura soft shell crab with avocado) from £13.50 at lunchtime, along with classics such as the White Horse burger (£14) and cod cheek & tiger prawn laksa (£16). There is also a smart conservatory **restaurant** (daily noon-2pm & 6.15-9pm) that has an adjoining sundeck, from where you can see the wild salt-marshes. The extensive menu changes daily and boasts shellfish from the beds at the bottom of the garden as well as delicious local fish. Confit trout with saffron potato costs £16.95, smoked pork tenderloin caponata costs £17.95, while roast Norfolk quail with a marmite jus will set you back £18.50. Desserts are all £7.50.

The path follows a wide sweep of shore out towards **Scolt Head**, a mass of dunes, marsh and shingle, where there is an **island nature reserve** (£3.50/2.50 adult/child) and nature trail. The reserve, just offshore, is usually cut off by an intricate pattern of salt-marsh and rivulets of sea water that is treacherous to try and cross on foot but is accessible by boat. Weather and tide permitting, a private **ferry** (Apr-Oct) operates between the quay at Burnham Overy Staithe and the reserve. Alternatively you can explore with **Branta Cruises** (☎ 01485-211132, 🖳 brantacruises.co.uk), which sails from Brancaster Staithe along the creek to Scolt Head offering a rarely seen view of the coastline. The guided cruise lands on the island as well, allowing you to explore the shoreline.

Curving round **Deepdale Marsh** the path meanders past a series of silted creeks, where the break between land and sea is poorly defined and changes all the time, before bending right and aiming inland along a bank towards a prominent 6-storey **windmill**, Burnham Overy Tower Mill, now a self-catering holiday let, on the horizon. Crossing the River Burn, the trail traverses a field then meets a road. Turn right here for **Burnham Market** (see below), 1½ miles inland, and some (luxurious) accommodation options. The path turns left to run parallel to the main road and enters **Burnham Overy Staithe** (see p153).

BURNHAM MARKET   [off MAP 31]

In addition to the accommodation options there's a host of art galleries, trendy boutiques and tempting delis huddled around a small green.

Lynx's Coastliner 36 **bus** service stops at The Green; for details see box p54.

The Hoste Hotel (☎ 01328-738777, 🖳 thehoste.com; 37D or T, all en suite; ☛; WI-FI; 🐾), is a 17th-century coaching inn on

The Green. Nowadays the very smart, sophisticated inn has country-house-style rooms including standard doubles, four posters, suites and a penthouse. Rates (inc a continental breakfast) start at £87.50pp (sgl occ rates on request) but are likely to be double that for the 'Divine' rooms particularly over the weekend and may also be subject to a minimum two-night stay. The

MAP 31

32

GUN HILL

OVERY CREEK

OVERY MARSH

¼ mile

500m

APPROX SCALE

0

0

GATE

BURNHAM OVERY STAITHE

EAST HARBOUR WAY

A149

TO BURNHAM THORPE

CONC LANE

The Hero

BUS STOPS

A149

BURNHAM OVERY WINDMILL

TO BURNHAM MARKET

PATH RUNS PARALLEL TO ROAD

BRIDGE

RIVER BURN

NORTON MARSHES

FOLLOW THE BANK RIGHT – DO NOT CONTINUE INTO THE MARSHES AS IT'S UNSAFE

BURNHAM NORTON

A149

TO BURNHAM MARKET

30

ROUTE GUIDE AND MAPS

Hoste Arms (bar open all day) has a good atmosphere, log fire and friendly staff. There's also an attractive walled garden. The Hoste has several food options: bar and lounge menu (daily noon-9.15pm; Burnham Market Brasserie menu (summer daily noon-9.30pm, winter Fri-Sat noon-2.30pm & 6-9.30pm) and the fine dining menu (Fri-Sat 6-9.30pm), which is served in the wood-panelled dining room. Dishes are interesting, inventive and where possible, ingredients are locally sourced. The Brasserie menu changes but may include sweetcorn pannacotta & Cromer crab (£14), Hoste beef burger (£16), while seared fillet of wild sea bass with hand-dived scallops, baby gem lettuce & peas

costs £29; pan-roasted Angus beef fillet & slow-cooked cheek costs £32. An excellent and extensive wine list completes the restaurant's appeal.

The team behind The Hoste also operate *Railway House* (8D, all en suite; WI-FI; 🐾), a second hotel 10 minutes' walk from The Hoste where rates (inc a continental breakfast) start from £75pp (sgl occ rates on request), and *Vine House* (8D, all en suite; ☞; WI-FI), an opulent adult-only Georgian townhouse just a short stroll across the village green from the original property, where rates (inc full breakfast) start from £100pp (sgl occ rates on request) and include many other benefits.

ROUTE GUIDE AND MAPS

❑ Lord Nelson

I am a Norfolk man and glory in being so (Horatio Nelson)

Horatio Nelson was born at **Burnham Thorpe**, a village some 2½ miles from Burnham Market, on September 29, 1758. Sent to school in Norwich by his father, he went on to sign up with the navy aged just 12. However, in 1787, he retired to Burnham Thorpe with his wife. Drawn back to the sea in 1793 he proved to be a brave and courageous sailor, although the reputation came at the cost of first an eye then his right arm. The crucial victory over the French and Spanish fleets at the Battle of Trafalgar in 1805 cemented his reputation and paved the way for Britain's dominance of the high seas. Nelson himself was fatally wounded in the battle and died of gunshot wounds to the chest. Pickled in a cask of brandy in order to preserve his body on the return journey, he was eventually laid to rest in St Paul's Cathedral in London, despite his express wish to be buried in Burnham Thorpe.

Although there are any number of pubs named after or in honour of Nelson, *The Lord Nelson* in Burnham Thorpe was the first. It used to be known as The Plough but changed its name around 1800 to commemorate the victory over the French at the Nile. Nelson frequented the pub and they've held onto his high-backed settle. Upon being given his command he is reputed to have celebrated by treating the entire village to a meal in the restaurant upstairs. Sadly, at the time of writing, the pub was closed, looking for a new landlord and it is likely it will also be refurbished so therefore it may be a while before it reopens.

A previous landlord was the originator of **Nelson's Blood**, a blend of rum and spices made to commemorate the drinking of the rum from around the body of Nelson on the journey home from Trafalgar; you can still treat yourself to a tot and toast the eponymous hero by buying a bottle online from 🖥 nelsonsbloodnorfolk.co.uk.

To get there take Lynx's Coastliner 36 **bus** service (see p50 and box p54) from Burnham Overy Staithe towards Burnham Market, getting off opposite Friars Lane, then walk to Burnham Thorpe along Joan Short's Lane and then Walsingham Rd. The bus journey is just over five minutes and the walk would be around 25 minutes, meaning the whole journey would take you about half an hour. Check in advance though whether the pub has reopened.

BURNHAM OVERY STAITHE
[MAP 31, p151]

This is yet another small hamlet strung along the A149.

Lynx's Coastliner 36 **bus** service stops by The Hero; see p50 and box p54.

The Hero (☎ 01328-738334, 🖥 the heroburnhamovery.co.uk; 3D; all en suite; 🛥; WI-FI; 🐾), named after local man Horatio Nelson (see box opposite), is a spacious, comfortable pub run by the team behind The Anchor Inn in Morston. B&B costs £47.50-85pp (sgl occ rates on request). Open every day, the pub is decorated in smart contemporary pastel colours and serves a wide range of **food** (daily noon-3pm & 6-9pm) including Brancaster mussels (£16.50) alongside pub classics and sandwiches (from £7.50; available noon-3pm), as well as cask ales, a plethora of gins and wine by the glass.

BURNHAM OVERY STAITHE TO STIFFKEY   MAPS 31-36

This is a very attractive stretch of the coast path, including as it does Holkham Beach, the gem set in the centre of the chain of beaches strung along the shore. The **10-mile (16km; 3½-4hrs) section** also sees you leave the relative calm and tranquillity of the empty Norfolk beaches for Wells-next-the-Sea, one of its bustling holiday towns and the only working port along the route.

Leaving the village, the path follows **Overy Creek** as it heads northwards alongside Overy Marshes (Map 32), towards Gun Hill. Cresting a row of dunes, the path reaches **Holkham Beach**, a lovely, wide area of white sand comprising more than 10,000 acres. When the sea has retreated it's almost invisible from the pine-backed, wind-rippled dunes and a walk to its edge past isolated sea pools, streams and rivulets can take an age. Even on a dull day, when the colours are muted and moody, the views encompassing enormous swathes of sky, sand and sea are spectacular. On clear sunny days it is simply one of the best beaches in England. Plus there's plenty of room even at the height of summer thanks to its size and the lack of public transport to access it.

Holkham National Nature Reserve (see box p63) stretches east towards the horizon. The path technically wanders amidst the dunes but it may be easier to head onto the compacted sands once the tide has gone out. The beach becomes busier as you continue towards **Holkham Gap** (Map 33) and **Lady Ann's Drive**, the main access point to the beach and one of the most impressive approaches to a beach anywhere in the UK. There is a car park but no other facilities, although you can buy ice-creams and drinks from a **seasonal snack van**. Turn right here for **Holkham** and **Holkham Hall** (see box p156).

Beyond the car park at the end of Lady Ann's Drive a stand of pines (**Holkham Meals**) shield the beach from the onshore breezes. Having trailed the beach east behind this screen, the path emerges next to **Abraham's Bosom Lake**, now a boating lake, and enters a car park. *Beach Café* (☎ 01328-713055; daily Apr-June & early Sep-Oct 10am-5pm, July-early Sep 9am-6pm, Nov-Mar 10am-4pm; WI-FI; 🐾) in the corner of the car park is backed by mature pinewoods and just a stone's throw from the beach. *(cont'd on p156)*

MAP 32

← 45–60 MINS TO/FROM HOLKHAM GAP (MAP 33) →

LOW WATER MARK

ON ACCESSING THE BEACH EITHER FOLLOW THE PATH THROUGH THE DUNES OR VENTURE ONTO THE FIRMER SAND AND HEAD EAST

HOLKHAM BEACH

HOLKHAM BEACH

MEALE HOUSE

BURROW GAP

REMARS OF IRON AGE FORT EARTHWORKS

¼ mile
500m
APPROX SCALE
0
0

HOLKHAM NATIONAL NATURE RESERVE

DUNES

CROSS DUNES TO REACH THE BEACH HERE

OVERY MARSHES

GUN HILL

MAP 33

45–60 MINS FROM/TO
HOLKHAM BEACH (MAP 32)

HOLKHAM GAP

60 MINS TO/FROM WELLS BEACH (MAP 34)

WEST SANDS

HIGH CAPE

HOLKHAM MEALS

DUNES

HOLKHAM NATIONAL
NATURE RESERVE.

HOLKHAM GAP

34

32

ABRAHAM'S
BOSOM LAKE
(BOATING LAKE)

trailblazer

¼ mile

APPROX SCALE

500m

0

0

OLD SEA
WALL

PATH
DOG LEGS ☎ 🏠 043

CAR PARK &
SEASONAL
SNACK VAN

LADY ANN'S DRIVE

SECTION OF
BOARDWALK

TO HOLKHAM, HOLKHAM HALL,
THE VICTORIA & BUS STOP

(cont'd from p153) Eat indoors, al fresco on the terrace, or picnic on the beach, enjoying tasty snacks, sausage rolls and pasties, and good homemade cakes. There are traditional board games and free wi-fi if you need it. In winter, warm up by their wood-burning stove. There are public **toilets** opposite.

Some steps give access to the vast, clean **beach** that you have just walked behind. The beach is backed by pine-topped dunes and a cluster of colourful

---

❏ Holkham Hall

The imposing stately pile Holkham Hall (☎ 01328-710227, 🖥 holkham.co.uk) is three miles south of Holkham Gap and can be reached on Lynx's Coastliner 36 **bus** service (see box p54) which stops at The Victoria (see below) from where you have to walk.

Built under the instruction of Thomas Coke, 1st Earl of Leicester, in homage to the buildings he saw whilst on a grand tour of Italy in the mid 18th century, and designed by the 18th-century architect William Kent, this vast sandy-coloured house has a severe Palladian exterior, concealing a much more intimate interior. There is a grand marble hall and richly decorated state rooms complete with paintings by Gainsborough, Rubens and Van Dyck as well as a selection of classical landscape pictures.

You get access to the **Hall** (late Mar/earlyApr-late Oct Sun, Mon & Thur noon-4pm) and **Field to Fork Experience**, an interactive opportunity to learn about food and farming at Holkham and the six-acre **walled gardens** (late Mar/earlyApr-Oct daily 10am-5pm), which are undergoing extensive restoration to preserve the glasshouses and other buildings within the walls, for £16/8 (adult/child). Each attraction is also available to visit individually: Field to Fork Experience/Walled Gardens £5/3; children half price).

The sweeping 3000-acre grounds of **Holkham Park** (daily 9am-5pm) are centred on an obelisk set atop a small knoll. The lake inside the grounds is a good place to spot water fowl; there is also a resident population of about 800 fallow deer. Follow the designated trails to explore, or hire a bike to cover more ground.

Courtyard Café (late Mar/early Apr-Oct daily 10am-5pm, Nov-mid Dec to 4pm), outside the hall and next to the Field to Fork Experience, has a decent range of hot food and snacks. Ideal for sitting in the courtyard with a cream tea or ice-cream made from local milk and cream, flavoured in the relevant season with lavender or plums grown on the estate.

The Victoria at Holkham (☎ 01328-711008, 🖥 holkham.co.uk/victoria) is an inn that was built close to the gates of Holkham Hall to accommodate the aristocrats that used to drop in on its residents. Nowadays the shabby chic hideaway has an interesting colonial feel to it with a collection of handsome Rajasthani furniture and intricate carved doors. The kitchen's stock in trade is modern British **food** (daily breakfast 8-10am, bar snacks noon-6pm, restaurant noon-2.30pm & 6.30-9pm), with the estate providing game and other meats while crab is sourced from Cromer. The Victoria is open to non-residents; booking is recommended for the evening. If you just fancy a drink there's a good range of real ale in their two bars. You can also stay in individually decorated, opulent rooms, named after shooting drives on the estate, which feature a mix of contemporary and antique pieces of furniture gleaned from the attics and basement of Holkham Hall; some of the rooms have their own attractive sitting rooms. Half of the 20 rooms are located at '**The Victoria'** (7D/2D or T/1Qd, all en suite; 🛏; WI-FI; 🐾) and half in **Ancient House** (6D/2D or T/4Qd, all en suite; 🛏; WI-FI), a building located opposite. If you're thinking of pushing the boat out, B&B costs £85-125pp (sgl occ from £150).

The Country Fair (see p15) is held here on odd-numbered years: 2019, 2021 etc.

BEACH HUTS

STEPS TO BEACH 🖥044

LODGE MARSH

LIFEBOAT STATION

33

JETTY

PINEWOODS CARAVAN & CAMPING PARK

CAR PARK, BEACH CAFÉ, TOILETS & PHONE

HOLKHAM NATIONAL NATURE RESERVE

BEACH ROAD, ON RAISED SEA DEFENCE

0   ¼ mile

0   500m

APPROX SCALE

MAP 34

MINIATURE RAILWAY

PATH JOINS THE QUAY 🖥045

WELLS SALT MARSHES

TOILETS

WELLS-NEXT-THE-SEA
SEE TOWN PLAN

35

TO THE WELLS & WALSINGHAM LIGHT RAILWAY, BLUE SKIES CAMPSITE AND BLAKENEY

WELLS BEACH

15 MINS

WELLS-NEXT-THE-SEA

45–60 MINS TO/FROM STIFFKEY TURNING (MAP 36)

beach huts, many perched on stilts, looking out to sea from the edge of West Sands. The sea here can retreat up to a mile at low tide, but returns quickly.

The vast **Pinewoods Caravan and Camping Park** (☎ 01328-710439, 🖳 pinewoods.co.uk; mid Mar to late Oct) does not accept tent campers but has a well-stocked supermarket and coffee shop. You can also rent one of the attractive **beach huts** by the day (£14-31), complete with deckchairs and windbreak; it's a good way of sampling this quirky British tradition.

The path climbs onto **Beach Rd,** a causeway and sea defence, from the top of which there are good views of the beach and the lifeboat station. Following a creek, the path heads inland towards Wells-next-the-Sea, the only usable harbour on the North Norfolk coast. Parallel to the path runs a **miniature, narrow-gauge railway** (Easter-Sep daily from 11am; £3/2 adult/child, return fare), which shuttles between the beach and the town roughly every 20 minutes.

WELLS-NEXT-THE-SEA
[see map p161]

Wells, the name derives from the clear springs found in the area, is a traditional seaside town with a split personality. It has been a harbour for more than 700 years and benefited from easy access to the sea; in its heyday it was one of eastern England's great ports and even as recently as 1986 it handled up to 200 large vessels and tons of cargo annually. Nowadays though, and despite its name, the town is actually a mile from the open water and its only connection to the sea is an inlet harbour. The town itself sits on an estuary of mudflats and salt-marsh, while the pristine sandy beach is at the end of a long sea defence, from the top of which you get great views of the estuary. Nonetheless Wells remains the only func-tioning port on this stretch of coast. Many of the granaries and maltings reminiscent of the town's heyday remain, but have been converted into luxury flats.

The waterfront unfortunately is tar-nished by the familiar arcades, gift shops and chip shops that tend to blight British seaside towns. It's worth being on the quay at high tide though as this is prime time for crabbing (see box p168). Step inland from the quay, however, and the town becomes a delightful maze of narrow streets, old alleys and yards, with some impressive Georgian and Victorian housing.

The parish **church of St Nicholas** dates from 1460, although much of it was careful-ly rebuilt after it was struck by lightning.

Set back from the quayside lies **The Buttlands**, a quiet rectangular green lined with lime trees whose name derives from the days it was used for archery practice.

Wells & Walsingham Light Railway is a narrow-gauge steam railway (see box p49; ☎ 01328-711630, 🖳 wwlr.co.uk; mid Mar-late July & early Sep-end Oct daily departures from Wells 10.30am-3.30pm 4/day, late July to early Sep 10am-4.15pm, 5/day) that connects Wells to Little Walsingham five miles east, where there is a celebrated ruined Augustinian abbey that has drawn visitors and pilgrims since medieval times; for centuries **Little Walsingham** rivalled Canterbury and Bury St Edmunds as a place of pilgrimage. The journey takes half an hour one way, stop-ping at Warham St Mary and Wighton; a return fare costs £9/7 (adult/child). Wells station is three-quarters of a mile along the A149 from the edge of the town plan. Lynx's 36 Coastliner and X29 **bus** services (see box p54) stop at or near the station.

With several upmarket delis and shops, a couple of good restaurants serving excel-lent local fare and some high-quality accommodation, Wells is justifiably popu-lar during the summer months when visi-tors descend in their droves to explore the haberdashery and tool shops that rub along-side more modern galleries, gift stores and eateries.

Wells also hosts an annual poetry festi-val and carnival (see pp14-15).

Services

The **tourist information centre** (TIC; ☎ 01328-710885, 🖳 wellsmaltings.org.uk; daily 10am-2pm, longer in the summer months, winter Fri-Tue 10.30am-2.30pm) is in Wells Maltings, on Staithe St. Wells Maltings is a new arts and culture centre that opened in spring 2018. The centre also includes a cinema, theatre, café and more besides. The TIC staff are friendly and provide an accommodation-booking service (£3 booking fee; see also box p20); the centre has masses of leaflets and information on both the town and the surrounding attractions.

Also on Staithe St is a Londis **supermarket** (Mon-Sat 7.30am-8pm, Sun 7.30am-7pm) with a good selection of groceries; it offers **cashback** on any purchase for a 50p charge. There is a Nisa Local (Mon-Sat 8am-8pm, Sun 8.30am-6pm) on Station Rd.

The renowned **Wells Deli** (☎ 01328-711171, 🖳 wellsdeli.co.uk; daily 9am-5pm) is on the waterfront and has a great range of well-sourced treats including cheeses, jams, chutneys, honey and ice-cream. You can also pick up pies, pastries, tarts and fresh bread as well as 'Builder's Tea', decent coffee and a special house hot chocolate. Sandwiches start at £3.65 whilst a panini will cost £4.50.

You can also drop into the **bakery** (daily 8.30am-4.30pm), on Staithe St, for fresh bread, pastries and cakes.

Well-known local **butcher**, Arthur Howell's, also has a shop on Staithe St where you can pick up excellent cuts of meat and specialist sausages (try the lamb & mint) if you're self-catering or camping. Close by is a well-stocked **greengrocer**.

The shop (Easter to end June, Sep & Oct Sat & Sun 10.30am-5.30pm; July & Aug daily 10.30am-5.30pm) for **Whin Hill Cider** (see box p24) is in the main car park; you can pick up freshly pressed cider and perry here.

The **library** (☎ 01328-710467; Mon 2-7pm, Tue & Sat 9am-1pm, Wed & Fri 9am-5.30pm), on Station Rd, has free **internet access**. The **post office** (Mon-Sat 9am-5.30pm) is also on Station Rd and there is a

Barclays **bank** and ATM on the corner of Station Rd and High St.

Transport

[See also pp50-40] Lynx's Coastliner 36 **bus** service stops on the seafront where Freeman St turns into The Quay and also on Station Rd by The Buttlands; Sanders No 4 service also calls here.

Where to stay

YHA Wells-next-the-Sea (☎ 0345-371 9544, 🖳 yha.org.uk/hostel/wells-next-sea; 1 x 2-, 3 x 3- and 5 x 4-bed room; shared facilities but 1 x 3-bed room is en suite; WI-FI communal area only; late Mar to end Oct), on quiet, residential Church Plain, is a converted church hall with basic dorm beds from £13pp and private rooms from £29; note that some of the rooms have a double bed. The hostel is self catering only but there's a good kitchen and large communal areas.

A little way out of town there are two **camping** options as well. To the west of Wells is *Mill Farm Stables* (☎ 01328-710226, 🖳 millfarmwells.co.uk; 🐾 on leads), a working arable farm. It is a quiet site with showers, toilets and a washing up shed. The pitches (from £8pp) are on raised ground overlooking the marshes.

To the east, close to Wells & Walsingham Railway and just off the coast road, is *Blue Skies Campsite* (☎ 07557-021660, 🖳 blueskiescampsite.co.uk; 🐾 on leads), about a 10-minute walk from the quay. On site they have 25 pitches in a 1½-acre dell for either tents or caravans, with toilets and shower facilities; there is also a communal barbecue area. A pitch costs £9-14 per night plus £4 for each adult over 16. There are smaller pitches for up to two walkers (without a car) that cost £7 per night plus £4 per adult (as above).

In town *Manor Farm Guesthouse* (☎ 01328-711392, 🖳 manorfarmguesthouse .co.uk; 2D/1T/1Tr, all en suite; WI-FI; Ⓛ; 🐾), on Market Lane, offers **B&B** for £40-47.50pp (sgl occ £75-85). They have a minimum three-night booking during the peak season. Breakfast is locally sourced and includes free-range eggs.

The Old Custom House (☎ 01328-711463, ☐ eastquay.co.uk; 1D/1T both en suite, 1D private facilities; ☛; WI-FI; ❄), on East Quay, was built in 1560 and served as its original incarnation until the early 1900s. Homely rooms, look out across the creeks and marshes and B&B starts at £50pp (sgl occ from £80).

Arch House (☎ 01328-710112, ☐ archhouse.co.uk; 10D/1T, all en suite; WI-FI), on Mill Rd, is a more substantial, listed house overlooking the town. They charge £35-60pp (sgl occ £65-85) for B&B.

On Freeman St, close to the harbour, is *The Quay B&B* (☎ 01328-710898, ☐ the quaybandb.co.uk; 2 rooms with bunks/6D, all en suite; WI-FI; ❄). This smart B&B stands in a Grade II listed building that has been carefully renovated. B&B in a double costs £57.50-67.50pp (sgl occ room rate); the two cosy rooms containing adult-size bunks cost £37.50-47.50pp (sgl occ room rate). There's a communal lounge on the ground floor as well and, within reason, the host can arrange extras such as restaurant reservations or a beach hut. Breakfasts are served in its sister venue, Golden Fleece (see Where to eat), on The Quay.

The Merchant's House (☎ 01328-711877, ☐ the-merchants-house.co.uk; 1D en suite/1D private bathroom; ☛; WI-FI), at 47 Freeman St, occupies one of the oldest buildings in Wells, with parts dating from the 15th century. The interior is rather more contemporary and de luxe though, and has just two intimate bedrooms; B&B costs from £50pp (sgl occ from £80). They generally require a minimum two-night stay in July and August but it is worth calling them.

The Edinburgh Inn (☎ 01328-710120, ☐ edinburghinnwells.co.uk; 1S/2D, all en suite; WI-FI; Ⓛ; ❄), on Station Rd, has simple rooms and charges from £37.50pp (sgl from £45, sgl occ rates on request).

Nearby, in an historic Grade II-listed Georgian building at the top of Staithe St, is *Bang in Wells* (☎ 01328-712149, ☐ bang inwells.co.uk; 3D/1D or T, all en suite; ☛; WI-FI; Ⓛ; ❄), a hip addition to the accommodation scene with Scandi-inspired guest

bedrooms that are spacious, high-ceilinged and kitted out with antique furniture and smart bathrooms good enough for an upmarket boutique. B&B costs £52.50-62.50pp (sgl occ rates on request).

The Globe Inn (☎ 01328-710206, ☐ theglobeatwells.co.uk; 12D/3T, all en suite; ☛; WI-FI; ❄), overlooking the tree-lined green known as The Buttlands, is a handsome Georgian inn with bright, spacious rooms with oak flooring and decorated in a fresh contemporary style. Rates, which include a hearty breakfast, are generally £55-95pp (sgl occ £100-180); however, it is always worth calling them to get the best rate. They also have three self-catering apartments sleeping up to three people.

Smarter though is *The Crown Hotel* (☎ 01328-710209, ☐ crownhotelnorfolk.co .uk; 13D/4T/3Qd, all en suite; ☛; WI-FI; Ⓛ; ❄), a former coaching inn also overlooking The Buttlands. It has attractive contemporary rooms; B&B (with a generous, locally sourced breakfast) costs £70-130pp (sgl occ £120-240), however, there is a mandatory policy that bookings for the weekend must be for at least two nights.

If you fancy trying life at sea without getting sick, you can also hire one of the former crew cabins on *Albatros* (☎ 0797-908 7228, ☐ albatroswells.co.uk; six cabins: 1D/1T/3 x 2-bunk-bed cabins for up to two adults, one for one adult and one child; shared facilities; ❄), the 33-metre, twin-masted Dutch clipper dating from 1899 and now moored permanently in the quayside – it's not posh but the experience is authentic and includes anything off the menu for breakfast. You'll need to be able to clamber up the steep steps leading from the deck to the cabins. Berths cost from £32.50pp (sgl occ from £45) per night.

Where to eat and drink
For exceptional local produce try *Wells Deli* (see Services), on the quayside.

Grey Seal Coffee (daily 9am-4pm) have a branch on the quayside as well close to the famous granary building and its over-hanging gantry. The coffee is good and they sell a range of cakes and pastries all baked back at their base in Glandford.

There are also several cafés and coffee bars on Staithe St; try *Picnic Hut* (daily summer 9am-6pm, winter 11am-3pm) for Fairtrade coffee, smoothies and sandwiches priced from £3, or head to the top of the street to try the coffee at *Bang in Wells* (see Where to stay; daily 8.30am-5pm), where you can enjoy a full English (£9.50), or buttermilk pancakes (£8), in their funky dining room. Lunch might include a DIY crab sandwich (£8.50), corned beef hash (£8.50), or lobster wrap (£9). They are fully

licensed and there's a pretty courtyard out the back of this historic building.

For fast-food drop into the cafés, burger bars and fish & chip joints along the quayside; *French's* (☎ 01328-710396, 🖳 frenchs .co.uk; summer daily 11.45am-10.30pm, winter Tue-Thur 11.45am-7.30pm, Friday till 9pm, Sat 11.45am-9pm, Sun 11.45am-7pm) is your best bet for superior fish & chips. For seafood in slightly smarter environs, try *Wells Crab House* (☎ 01328-710456, 🖳 wellscrabhouse.co.uk; Tue-Sat

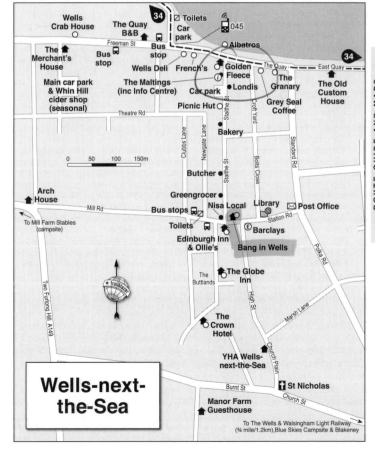

Wells-next-the-Sea

noon-2.30pm & 6-9pm, Sun noon-3pm), on Freeman St. The menu changes monthly but you may be able to bait your appetite with Brancaster oysters (£2 each); then enjoy a main catch of Wells dressed crab (£14), or steamed half lobster (£18). Fish & chips costs £14. Book ahead for a table on Friday and Saturday nights as they can be very busy.

Golden Fleece (☎ 01328-710650, 💻 goldenfleecewells.co.uk; WI-FI; 🐎 downstairs only) on The Quay is a well-located, comfortable pub with views directly overlooking the harbour. During the day, pop in for breakfast (daily 8-11.30am), a quiet coffee and a slice of cake, a well-kept pint or a larger meal (daily noon-9pm). The kitchen specialises in fresh, handmade pizzas (daily noon-10pm; £12-14), but they also have classic dishes with a twist such as Penang prawn curry (£14), or Wherry battered cod (£12), and claim to cook the best roast on the coast (Sun only). You can eat in the atmospheric bar or the upstairs restaurant, which really makes the most of the views.

The elegant Dutch clipper *Albatros* (see Where to stay), moored on the quayside offers visitors Dutch pancakes (sweet and savoury; £4.75-8.95) and dressed crab from £13.95 (food daily noon-4pm & 5-8.30pm, winter Thur-Mon) and has a rough and ready bar (daily noon to late) below deck adorned with nautical memorabilia that sells a range of real ales. However, it can also be hired for events so may be closed to the public.

Ollie's Restaurant at The Edinburgh Inn (see Where to stay; food daily noon-2pm & summer 5-8.30pm, winter 5.45-8pm) serves good pub grub around its open fireplace or in the courtyard out the back. They are also open for breakfast (9-11am).

The menu at *The Globe Inn* (see Where to stay; food served daily 8-10am, noon-2.30pm & 6-8.30pm) changes seasonally and depending on the time of year may include venison and beef burger (£14.95), or a Globe curry using their own blended spices (from £13.95) to be enjoyed in its spacious, well-presented bar. There's also a courtyard with a wood-fired pizza oven (from £12.50) and tables out front overlooking The Buttlands on which to enjoy a pint of Nelson's Revenge (See box p24).

You can eat casually in the bar of *The Crown Hotel* (see Where to stay; food noon-2.30pm & 6.30-9.30pm, Sun noon-9pm), or more formally in their restaurant. The restored beams and open fires in the bar provide a relaxed, rustic atmosphere, whilst the upstairs dining area is a smarter venue and the orangery provides a peaceful conservatory. The menu varies but you could start with half-a-dozen quail eggs & curried mayonnaise (£4.95), or venison & black pudding scotch egg (£7.70), then gorge on roast venison & braised red cabbage (£21.95), or char-grilled sirloin steak with hand-cut chips (£24.95). Good-value menus are also available on Sunday with two/three courses for £20.95/26.95. Breakfast (daily 8-10am) and afternoon tea (daily 3-5pm) comprising finger sandwiches, cakes, brownie and a pot of tea (£15pp) are also served.

The Coast Path continues along Wells's waterfront, past the old Granary that dominates this stretch, to the far end of East Quay. The road then gives way to a grassy embankment to climb away from the town. Passing between grassy fields and salt-marshes, the path edges past **Warham** (Map 35), after which it broadens and gives glimpses of the sea way off in the distance. Stick to the clearly defined path, ignoring trails that head into the marshes as these can be dangerous, particularly as the tide changes. Local legend has it that a giant dog, Black Shuck, haunts the marshes at night, attacking anyone who ventures out there. Put about by smugglers looking to keep people out of the marshes, Black Shuck became the inspiration for Conan Doyle's *Hound of the Baskervilles*.

At **Green Way** (Map 36) there is a car park and **campsite**, *High Sand Creek* (see p164).

ROUTE GUIDE AND MAPS

45–60 MINS BETWEEN WELLS-NEXT-THE-SEA (MAP 34) AND STIFFKEY TURNING (MAP 36)

36

TO STIFFKEY

A149

AVOID TAKING SEAWARD PATHS AS CAN BE DANGEROUS & YOU RISK DAMAGING ECOSYSTEMS

COCKLESTRAND DROVE

WARHAM SALT MARSHES

GARDEN DROVE

HOLKHAM NATIONAL NATURE RESERVE

STONEMEAL CREEK

WARHAM

MAP 35

0
0
APPROX SCALE
¼ mile
500m

PATCH OF SCRUBBY TREES

A149

34

STIFFKEY [MAP 36]

Pronounced '**Stookey**', this picturesque hamlet full of houses with knapped flint walls and painted woodwork, has stood since Roman times but has always remained small. Local residents included the Reverend Harold Davidson who became embroiled in a scandal involving London prostitutes in the 1930s as part of a newspaper sting. Having been defrocked, the 'prostitutes' parson' joined a circus and was later mauled to death by a lion. The author Henry Williamson, who wrote *Tarka the Otter*, used to live by the river here too and documented his daily life in *The Story of a Norfolk Farm*.

Stiffkey Salt Marshes (see p63) are a nature reserve, a continuation of Morston Salt Marshes (Map 37). They contain some of the oldest salt-marsh on this section of coastline.

There is a superb local store, **Stiffkey Stores** (☎ 01328-830489; daily 8.30am-5pm; Jan-Mar Wed & Sun till 1pm) on the main road, which doubles as a general shop, **post office** (Mon-Sat but half days on Wed & Sat), *café*, gift shop and studio. Stop by to browse the kitchen wares, local organic produce and pick up one of the homemade cakes or sandwiches to snack on in their attractive outdoor terrace.

The village is on Sanders No 4 **bus** service which calls at the bus stops opposite and adjacent to Stiffkey Stores. For details see box p54.

High Sand Creek (☎ 01328-830235; 🐕 on lead; Easter-mid Oct) **campsite** has 80 tent pitches spread over five acres. The rate for a pitch and up to two people is £15-25 (£12-17.50 for solo campers). Hot showers (inc in rate), washing-up facilities and a small laundry are available. Booking is recommended in the summer school holidays. The site overlooks the slightly melancholic, but romantic, salt-marsh and is wonderfully quiet at night.

Stiffkey Red Lion (☎ 01328-830552; 🖳 stiffkey.com; 7D/2T/2Tr/1Qd, all en suite; 🛉; wi-fi bar area only; Ⓛ; 🐕), on Wells Rd, is an atmospheric, traditional pub; it began life as an inn during the 1600s but has also been a private house and doctor's surgery before reverting to its original purpose. The rooms on the first floor have balconies and south-facing views of the Stiffkey Valley. **B&B** costs £54.50-74.50pp (sgl occ room rate). The pub (**food** Mon-Fri noon-2.30pm & 6-9pm, Sat & Sun noon-9pm) has bare tiled floors, exposed beams and several big open fires. There's an ever-changing menu based on seasonal ingredients. As a starter you might find a pot of local cockles and freshly baked tomato bread (£4.75), or crispy breaded whitebait (£6.50), and then a main of local lobster (half £18, whole £24), or crab (£12.95) baked in garlic butter. Puddings cost £6.95. Sandwiches (Mon-Fri noon-2.30pm, Sat-Sun till 3pm) cost £7.

STIFFKEY TO WEYBOURNE   MAPS 36-41

This is one of the most spectacular parts of the entire trek, with the **12-mile (19km; 5-5¼hrs) path** hugging the shoreline, skirting the marshes and connecting some of the region's most attractive, charming and reputed small towns, where you can pick up some of the freshest seafood. The coast's rich mosaic of habitats, sandy islands backed by salt-marshes, mean that it is excellent for a wide variety of birds and animals. Look out too for specialist plants such as the shrubby sea-blite, sea aster and carpets of purple sea lavender. There's access to some of the country's best birdwatching sites here so keep an eye peeled for noisy red shanks nesting in the summer and hen harriers or short-eared owls quartering over the marshes in winter. Then there's Blakeney Point, home to a permanent colony of seals, which you can sidle up to on organised boat tours from Morston and Blakeney, or walk to from Cley.

← 45–60 MINS FROM/TO WELLS-NEXT-THE-SEA (MAP 34) →   STIFFKEY TURNING ▶   ← 90 MINS TO/FROM MORSTON QUAY (MAP 37) →

37

TO MORSTON

MAP 36

APPROX SCALE
¼ mile   500m

STIFFKEY SALT MARSHES

BANGAY GREEN WAY

ST JOHN &
ST MARY'S

GARBOROUGH CREEK

HOLLOW LANE

PHONE

BUS STOPS

STIFFKEY Red Lion

STIFFKEY STORES
& POST OFFICE

△ High Sand Creek

STIFFKEY

CAR PARK

GREEN WAY

A149

WARBOROUGH HILL

TO WELLS-NEXT-THE-SEA

A149

35

Beyond Green Way follow a path between more fields and marshes, home to the celebrated **'Stewkey Blue' cockles**, so called for the blueish tinge they acquire living in the mud. Look out for other lanes leading inland to Stiffkey.

Blakeney Point (see box p170) begins to dominate the horizon as you approach **Freshes Creek**, after which you suddenly come across **Morston**.

MORSTON [MAP 37]

Set back from the coast slightly, Morston lies either side of Blakeney Rd (the A149). A small, traditional place that's still home to working fishermen, it has a quiet charm. Look out for bags of mussels being sold outside the cottages along the road.

Sanders No 4 **bus** service stops here; see box p54 for details.

The National Trust **information centre** (☎ 01263-740241; opening times are season and weather dependent but it's usually open daily two hours either side of high tide in the main season and weekends only in the winter) in the car park next to Morston Quay has a small number of leaflets and local information but the staff are very friendly and helpful. Adjacent are public toilets and a small *café* (hours variable but generally 11am-3pm) selling sandwiches, soup and emergency rain capes for people caught unprepared.

Boat trips to see the seals and birds on and around Blakeney Point (see box p170) depart from Morston Quay throughout the year. **Bean's Boat Trips** (☎ 01263-740038 or ☎ 01263-740505, ⌨ beansboattrips.co .uk) run up to three times per day in the summer months, less frequently at other times, on their orange and white boats. Timings are varied as they can only operate at high tide. Seal viewings last about an hour while trips that include landing on Blakeney Point last up to two hours. The crews are knowledgeable and there are plenty of opportunities to watch the seals and take photographs. Tickets (£12/6 adult/child 14 and under) should be reserved in advance and collected half-an-hour before departure.

Temple's Seal Trips (☎ 01263-740791, ⌨ sealtrips.co.uk) also offers a seal-spotting service from its red and white ferry boats. The trip duration, operating conditions and cost are the same; tickets can be booked over the phone or in The Anchor Inn (see p168).

In the village itself, there is **B&B** at *Scaldbeck Cottage* (☎ 01263-740188, ⌨ bluejacketworkshop.co.uk/bbcampsite; 1T/1D private facilities but shared if people who know each other book both rooms; ☞; WI-FI; Feb-Nov), a traditional flint and brick family home. The smart but slightly old-fashioned rooms cost from £35pp (sgl occ from £60). There's space for up to 12 people to **camp** (🐾; Easter-Oct or earlier/later if weather permits; from £6pp) in the field behind the house. Campers have access to a shower and toilet separate to the cottage. Cooked breakfasts (from £8) are available if booked by the night before.

More upmarket accommodation and fabulous food can be found at the Michelin-starred *Morston Hall* (☎ 01263-741041, ⌨ morstonhall.com; 10D or T/3D, all en suite; ☞; WI-FI; (L); 🐾), which is owned and run by sometime TV chef, cookery book writer and Michelin-starred culinary Galton Blackiston. A cosy country house, the flint-built hall has spacious, tastefully decorated rooms boasting all mod cons; some rooms include a spa bath and TV in the bathroom. Simple and elegant, it is familiar rather than formal and enjoys an intimate atmosphere. Standard rates are £180-205pp (sgl occ £245-310) and they include a seven-course set dinner in addition to breakfast the following day. Residents can enjoy a light lunch in their room or in the hotel lounge; on Sunday (12.15 for 1pm) a spectacular set menu roast including coffee and canapés (£40pp) is put on for those who book in advance. Reservations are also taken for afternoon tea (£25pp) served 3-5pm. In the evening, non-residents can join guests for supper, which is served daily in a single sitting: 7.15 for 8pm. Booking in advance is essential and the seven-course

MAP 37

← 90 MINS FROM/TO STIFFKEY TURNING (MAP 36) →

▶ MORSTON QUAY

38

TO BLAKENEY

MORSTON SALT MARSHES

MORSTON QUAY-
WHERE BOAT TRIPS
TO BLAKENEY
POINT LAUNCH

046

PATH
FOLLOWS THE
SEA WALL

A149 BLAKENEY RD

MORSTON CREEK

CAR PARK &
NATIONAL TRUST
INFO CENTRE &
CAFÉ & TOILETS

Scaldbeck
Cottage

BUS STOP

Morston
Hall

PHONE

MORSTON

The Anchor
Inn

GOOD VIEWS OF
BLAKENEY POINT

FRESHES
CREEK

GARRET
HILL

A149

★ trailblazer

36

TO STIFFKEY

¼ mile

0   500m

APPROX SCALE

0

ROUTE GUIDE AND MAPS

set menu costs £80pp. The menu changes nightly but is drawn from fresh local produce. Dishes might include North Sea Dover Sole with salsify purée and Holkham Hall venison accompanied by salt-baked beetroot & white pepper jus. To finish look out for hazelnut Bavarois and chocolate sorbet and the outstanding cheeseboards (£10 supplement). The restaurant also has an exemplary wine cellar and offers a 'Wine Flight' to complement the tasting menu, with a wine paired with each course (£55pp).

Alternatively, for something a little more affordable, drop into **The Anchor Inn**

(☎ 01263-741392, 🖵 morstonanchor.co.uk; food daily 9am-11am, Mon-Sat noon-3pm & 6-9pm, Sun noon-8.30pm, winter Sun to 3.30pm; WI-FI; 🐾 bar area), a bustling pub filled with bric a brac and photographs of the area, dedicated to providing locally sourced, home-cooked food and the finest ales in the area. The menu offers starters such as smoked haddock chowder (£7.50) and pan-fried scallops with crispy pork belly (£9.50), with mains that might include homemade beefburger & bacon jam (£15), and local sirloin steak (£22). Sandwiches (served noon-3pm) cost £7.50.

Pressing on east from Morston Quay, the path hugs the edge of Morston Salt Marshes, meandering along a sea wall and following a succession of creeks and rivulets for 1½ miles until it arrives at **Blakeney**.

BLAKENEY [MAP 38]

Blakeney is an attractive, traditional town comprising fishermen's houses built with flint and narrow-winding lanes stretching back from the sea. Once an important port for goods and trade, the town thrived on its connections to the sea.

A commercial seaport until the early 20th century, the harbour is now silted up so only small boats can nose their way gently out along a narrow channel, past **Blakeney Point** (see box p170), to reach the sea. Nonetheless there is a sense of activity and bustle about the place, with children often to be seen **crabbing** (see box below) on the quayside (they're guaranteed

to catch plenty) and people strolling along the front. Look out for the **flood high-tide markers** on the quayside showing where the waters reached in 1897, 1953, 1978 and 2013 – you'll have to crane your eyes upwards to spot the 1953 plaque, the highest recorded water mark, some 8ft above the quay; see also box p171.

Increasingly dependent on tourism, the town is full of covetable second homes and is popular with visitors who are drawn to the picturesque surroundings to explore its history and revel in its atmospheric buildings.

The 14th-century **Guildhall** (open daily at 'any reasonable time'; free), an

❏ Crabbing

CRABBERS
PLEASE DO NOT
USE HOOKS ON YOUR LINES.
BARBED HOOKS CAN INJURE WILDLIFE, DOGS AND CHILDREN
TIE YOUR BAIT ON THE LINE:- IT'S BETTER!
And PLEASE....... TAKE YOUR LITTER HOME!
MANY THANKS

It's a coastal tradition to hang a bit of line over the edge of a quay, strung with bait aimed at enticing crabs to grab hold.

To get started, equip yourself with a bucket, crabbing line and a bag of bacon bits for bait. Set yourself up on the quay in Wells or Blakeney, watching out for boats and other traffic on the water. Fill the bucket with water, tie the bait to the line (don't use a hook as they pose a serious threat to other wildlife), then lower the line into the sea for a couple of minutes. Give it a moment and then check to see who has grabbed your bait. Pull up the line and pop your catch in the bucket. After an hour tot up the number of crabs you've caught, then put the lot back into the sea and begin again!

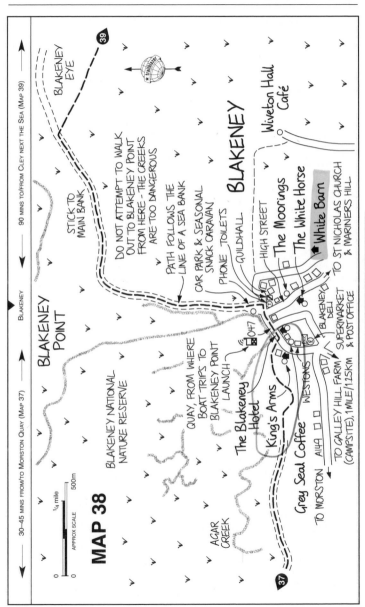

MAP 38

0 ¼ mile
APPROX SCALE
0 500m

BLAKENEY POINT

BLAKENEY NATIONAL NATURE RESERVE

AGAR CREEK

37

BLAKENEY EYE

39

STICK TO MAIN BANK

DO NOT ATTEMPT TO WALK OUT TO BLAKENEY POINT FROM HERE – THE CREEKS ARE TOO DANGEROUS

PATH FOLLOWS THE LINE OF A SEA BANK

CAR PARK & SEASONAL SNACK CARAVAN

PHONE TOILETS

GUILDHALL

HIGH STREET

The Moorings

The White Horse

White Barn

BLAKENEY

Wiveton Hall Café

TO ST NICHOLAS CHURCH & MARINERS HILL

QUAY, FROM WHERE BOAT TRIPS TO BLAKENEY POINT LAUNCH

The Blakeney Hotel

King's Arms

WESTONS

Grey Seal Coffee

A149

TO MORSTON

TO GALLEY HILL FARM (CAMPSITE), 1 MILE/1.25KM

BLAKENEY DELI

SUPERMARKET & POST OFFICE

intricate brick undercroft, or vault, that was probably the basement of a merchant's house, overlooks the quayside.

Just inland is **Mariners Hill**, a man-made vantage point thought to have acted as a look out for the harbour. On the inland edge of the village, on the hill, stands the double-towered **church of St Nicholas**. The church is incongruously large for its location; the 100ft main tower acted as a local landmark. The main chancel dates

from 1296 and includes a rare stepped seven-lancet window. The church's chief feature though is its smaller octagonal tower thought to have been a lighthouse or a beacon for boats accessing the harbour even though the main tower is taller. The graveyard is filled with sailors' headstones and is also worth a visit.

Boat trips, run by local families to explore Blakeney Point and see the seals and birds resident there, depart from the

ROUTE GUIDE AND MAPS

❏ Blakeney Point

The horizon beyond Blakeney is dominated by the shingle ridge of Blakeney Point: a thousand acres of marram grass dunes and empty creeks. The spit runs east to west and is roughly 9½ miles (15.5km) long although this varies all the time. The shingle can be up to 65ft/20m wide and 33ft/10m high. Formed by the process of longshore drift, the shingle protects a network of creeks and salt-marshes. Gifted to the National Trust in 1912, it became the first **national nature reserve** in Norfolk (see box p63) and is now one of the most important breeding sites for many species of seabird.

The Point can be accessed on foot or by boat, although you shouldn't attempt to cross the marshes from Blakeney itself. Instead, it is possible to walk westwards from the car park at the end of the lane running from Cley to Cley Eye (see Map 39) along the spit to Blakeney Point. The invigorating walk is three miles long and it can comfortably take you half a day to do the return journey. Alternatively, to get to the head of the spit catch one of the boats operating from Morston (see p166), or Blakeney (see above). Bear in mind that entry to the sensitive nesting grounds on the point is restricted during the breeding season.

The Point is an internationally important breeding site for four species of tern (arctic, common, little and sandwich), which nest here between April and July. During this time you'll also be able to spot oystercatchers and ringed plovers. In the winter months look out for brent geese, wigeon, dunlin and curlew. As well as birds, the Point is an excellent spot from which to spot seals; you can't fail to see them. They are incredibly inquisitive and will often pop up alongside the boats whilst the terns, also unfazed by the boats, fuss over their chicks or dive for fish. The resident colony is made up of grey and common seals and numbers around 500, although this fluctuates during the year. The seals usually bask on the sandy banks at the far end of the spit. They are distinguishable by their size: the grey are larger and have longer pointed heads, the common seals are smaller and have a more rounded face. The common seals have their pups between June and August whilst the grey seals, which are confusingly more common, have their young between November and January. Both suckle their pups for about three weeks during which time they grow very quickly.

As you walk west along the point, you'll pass **Halfway House**, a hut marking the mid-point of the walk. At the far end of the curved spit is a distinctive blue-painted building that operates as a **visitor centre**, open to coincide with people arriving on the various boat trips. There are toilets next to the centre (closed Oct-Apr). Operating from Morston and Blakeney, boat trips to see the seals sometimes land about 300m to the east of the visitor centre. The building used to be a lifeboat station right on the edge of the sand, but it now stands marooned amidst a sea of dunes as a result of the sand and silt collecting on the end of the point. Inside are some historic black and white photographs and general information on the Point, its flora and fauna.

❏ **High waters**
They know all about flood tides in Blakeney. Periodically high spring tides combined with low pressure and strong winds cause the waters to rise up and over the quayside. In 2013 the village was hit with the worst tidal surge in 60 years. Those waters deposited half a dozen boats onto the quayside, floating some clear over its 3ft-high railings, along with tonnes of weeds and mud from the inlet. Houses and business were flooded when sandbags and boards failed to prevent the water from getting inside. Elsewhere, sea defences were breached or washed away, allowing salt-water to flood the fresh-water marshes, badly affecting the fragile eco-systems. Slowly though, once the waters had receded, work was carried out to repair the sea defences, bolstering them and making them taller, while sluices ensured the flooded marshes were able to drain and the fresh-water return, restoring these delicate environments to their original status.

quay. **Bean's Boat Trips** (see p166) and **Bishop's Boats** (☎ 01263-740753, 🖳 bish opsboats.com; trips daily early Feb-early Nov) run regular outings to the Point. Trips simply to see the seals last an hour, while landing on Blakeney Point adds up to an extra hour to the journey time; trips cost £12/6 (adult/child aged 14 and under) and reservations should be made in advance; you collect the tickets from the quayside. Departure times are chalked on blackboards on the quay, but are generally in the morning. However, they are dependent on the higher tides, so times vary – check the websites or call ahead for up-to-date details. The craft used are traditional clinker-build boats which offer little protection from the elements so take warm and waterproof clothing to be safe. The skippers have in-depth knowledge of the coast and its inhabitants.

Services and transport
There is a small but well-equipped Spar **supermarket** (daily 7am-10pm) on Westgate St. Within the shop is a **post office** counter (Mon, Tue, Thur, Fri 9am-1pm & 2-5pm, Wed 9am-1pm, Sat 9am-12.30pm) and a Link **ATM**.

Also on Westgate St is **Westons** (☎ 01263-741112; summer Mon-Fri 9.30am-4pm, Sat to 5pm, Sun 10am-4pm, winter Mon-Sat 9.30am-2.30pm, Sun 10am-2.30pm); it sells fabulous fresh fish as well as potted shrimps, fishcakes, fish pies and pre-prepared sandwiches.

Blakeney Deli (☎ 01263-740939; Easter to end Oct Mon-Thur 8.30am-5pm,

Fri-Sat till 5.30pm, Sun till 2.30pm, Nov to Easter Mon-Fri from 9am), on the High St, is a perfect pit-stop for upmarket treats. The family-owned establishment sources seasonal and local produce, often organic, as well as a selection of wines, but is best known for the tarts, breads and pastries produced on-site; the sausage rolls (£2.50) alone are worth the visit.

Sanders No 4 **bus** service stops on New Rd; see box p54 for details.

Where to stay
A mile inland from the quay is **Galley Hill Farm** (☎ 01263-741201, 🖳 sal.savory @tiscali.co.uk; late March to end Oct), which has 20 **tent pitches** (£7.50pp) and rather basic shower and toilet facilities. There's also a '**camping pod**' – bring everything you would normally for camping, except the tent. The wooden structure sleeps up to five people (£35 for up to two sharing, additional adults £7.50pp); it is fully insulated and has a heater.

On the quayside, **The Blakeney Hotel** (☎ 01263-740797, 🖳 blakeney-hotel.co.uk; 8S/20D/34D or T/1T, all en suite; ☛; WI-FI; ①; 🐾) is a traditional hotel, with pebble-covered walls and high gables.

Some of the rooms have balconies or south-facing garden views whilst others have patios leading onto the gardens. B&B in mid-season starts at £126.50pp but can climb to £183pp (sgl from £129, sgl occ rates on request) for a top-end room with four-poster bed and antique furnishings in the high season. The hotel also has a heated

ROUTE GUIDE AND MAPS

swimming pool, steam room, sauna and spa.

In town, there is also B&B at *White Barn* (☎ 01263-741359, 🖳 raymillard @btinternet.com; 2D/1D or T, all en suite; WI-FI; (Ⓛ), on Back Lane, for £40pp (sgl occ from £45). Each room has its own private entrance. They generally require bookings of two nights or more but will accept single-night bookings for walkers if they can, particularly during the week. They do not take children though.

King's Arms (☎ 01263-740341, 🖳 blakeneykingsarms.co.uk; 4D/2T/1Tr, all en suite; WI-FI; (Ⓛ); 🐾), on Westgate St, is easily identifiable by the legend 'FH+1760' tiled into its red roof although it's unclear what the initials refer to; the date was when the roof of the much older building was replaced. Most rooms have views of the marshes and put up beds can be put in some rooms for additional people. There is a minimum two-night stay policy at weekends (Feb-end Oct). They charge £50-55pp (sgl occ £60-65).

The White Horse (☎ 01263-740574, 🖳 blakeneywhitehorse.co.uk; 1S/6D/1T/a suite which can sleep up to six people, all en suite; 🖛; WI-FI; (Ⓛ); 🐾), a former coaching inn on the High St, is a high-quality, good-value accommodation option. Each room is individually furnished with a mix of contemporary and traditional styles and there are great additional touches. Three rooms (Nos 1, 8 and 9) enjoy views of the coastal marshes and sea beyond. Room 10, the suite, has a separate living room and its own on-street entrance. Rooms cost £49.50-80pp (sgl £84-99, sgl occ rates on request). They'll lend you wellies or binoculars if you've forgotten yours and are going out onto the marshes.

Where to eat and drink

The **seasonal caravan** in the car park next to the quay sells delicious snacks such as fresh crab sandwiches and oysters at remarkably cheap prices. If you have more time, drop into *Grey Seal Coffee* (🖳 grey sealcoffee.co.uk/blakeney; daily 9am-4pm), tucked in one of the oldest buildings in Blakeney. They serve their own speciality

coffee and teas and there's always a selection of cakes and pastries.

Alternatively, visit *The Moorings* (☎ 01263-740054, 🖳 blakeney-moorings.co .uk; summer Tue-Sat 10.30am-5pm & 6-9pm, Sun 10.30am-5pm, winter Fri-Sun only), just up from the quay on the High St. It is an unpretentious bistro with a buzz about it. During the day drop in for a coffee and one of the tantalising home-cooked cakes or, over lunch enjoy great salads, daily fish specials and a renowned chowder. In the evenings the menu, which changes regularly, is biased towards local seafood, often bought straight from the boats that catch it, but also includes local meats and game as well as home-grown fruit and veg. Try the local crab, brown shrimp & fennel risotto (£8.95), or grilled scallops & black pudding (£11), followed by roast hake fillet with squid, chorizo & cannellini bean casserole (£18.95), or pan-fried Norfolk venison, roast squash & wildberry jus (£19.95). Puddings include a lemon tart to die for and a rhubarb honey & saffron tart, all for £6.25.

King's Arms (see Where to stay; food daily noon-9pm) serves hearty home cooking throughout the day. Dishes such as cod, prawn & bacon chowder (£11.50), homemade steak & Adnams ale suet pudding (£14.25), or tempura halloumi cheese in a brioche bun with chips (£12.50) are all well-prepared and portions are ample. They also serve breakfasts (9.30-10.30am). Look out for the plaque halfway up the wall showing the levels of the flood that hit the area in 1953. There is also a large, child-friendly beer garden.

The White Horse (see Where to stay; food Mon-Sat noon-2.30pm & 6-9pm, till 8.30 on Sun) has a large informal bar serving local real ales and a number of well-chosen wines. However, most people are here for the delicious food served either in its light and airy conservatory or more formal dining room. The bread is all home baked and ingredients are sourced from local suppliers. The menu changes daily but often includes a homemade scotch egg with Adnams brown sauce (£7) and Cley Smokehouse fish pie (£14). Leave room for the sumptuous desserts (£7); look out for the apple & fig crumble, or the white chocolate & orange cheesecake.

The Blakeney Hotel (see Where to stay; food daily noon-2pm & 6.30-8.45pm) has a restaurant overlooking the quay that offers a range of breakfasts, light lunches, afternoon tea (3-5.30pm; £15pp) and seasonal à la carte evening menus for guests and non-residents alike. If you can, pause here to drink in the views across the marshes and estuary before moving on. Roasted sirloin of local beef, horseradish & watercress slaw sandwiches cost £7.75 (noon-4.30pm) while fish pie will set you back £12.50 and a twice-baked Norfolk dapple cheese soufflé costs £12. The three-course supper using regional and seasonal produce costs £32.

If you walk out of the eastern end of the village and pick up a footpath heading east, you will wind your way to **Wiveton Hall**, a flint-faced, Dutch-gabled, Jacobean manor house built in the 17th century. Alongside the Grade II-listed Hall is a working farm and a vibrant *restaurant-café* (☎ 01263-740515, 🖳 wivetonhall.co.uk; late Mar-mid Nov daily 9am-4.30pm). During the day there are great cakes and wholesome meals based around food grown on the farm or locally sourced, including Weybourne crab salad (£13.50) and guinea fowl with braised radicchio (£16.50). During the summer, the restaurant also opens in the evenings (5.30pm till 8pm), with pizzas or theme nights such as tapas or Beef and Reef. Booking is advisable.

From the quayside in Blakeney cross the car park and step onto the sea bank curving north towards Blakeney Eye. The path affords excellent views of the vast expanse of marsh and sky before bending south again and aiming inland towards the distinctive **windmill** of Cley next the Sea. Although drawn towards the mill you can't access it from this side of the marshes and must circle around to reach the village and its centrepiece.

When the path finally joins the Blakeney to Cley road (A149) turn left, cross a sluice (Cley Channel) and climb down from the bank. Follow the road as it bends round to the left and walk through **Cley**.

CLEY NEXT THE SEA
[see map p174]

During medieval times Cley (rhymes with 'sky') was a prosperous port, one of East Anglia's principal export points. In the early 17th century the River Glaven began to silt up and access to the sea became impossible for large boats. These days the village is little more than a row of Georgian houses and flint cottages alongside a marshy inlet that just about offers access to the sea.

Further inland, at the site of the original village green (Newgate Green), stands the medieval church of **St Margaret**. The arrival of the Black Death meant construction of the church ceased suddenly, which is why the unassuming chancel and spectacular nave are so wildly different in design and detail. Look out for the fine figures of

musicians, a lion and St George facing down a dragon depicted here.

To the north of the village is a mile-long track (see Map 39, p175) that leads to the sea, a car park and **Cley Beach**. This is the start point for the 4-mile walk west to Blakeney Point (see box p170). Make sure you stick to the low-water mark for the firmest track and to avoid nesting birds.

Cley Marshes Nature Reserve (see box p63) hugs the coast here. Established in 1926 it is one of the oldest nature reserves in England; more than 300 species of bird have been spotted here. Half a mile east of Cley on the A149 coast road is the **Norfolk Wildlife Trust information centre** (see p61 and Map 39, p175; ☎ 01263-740008; daily Apr-Oct 10am-5pm, Nov-Mar 10am-4pm) associated with the reserve. In the exhibition building is a remote-controlled wildlife camera and audio-visual presentations about the coastline. The centre has fabulous views over the bird reserve.

There is also a *café* (daily 10am-4.30pm, to 3.30pm in winter, lunch noon-2.30pm) serving delicious food and a gift shop on site. Admission to the nature reserve costs £4.50 for adults (children go free) and allows you access to a series of hides dotted amidst the marshes; trails for children are also available at various times in the year.

Made in Cley (☎ 01263-740134, ☐ madeincley.co.uk; Mon-Sat 10am-5pm, Sun 11am-4pm) occupies the old general store and many of the old Regency fittings and wooden features are still present, creating a charming space to display the hand-thrown pottery, prints and jewellery on sale.

Services and transport

Picnic Fayre (☎ 01263-740587, ☐ picnic-fayre.co.uk; school summer holidays daily 9am-6pm, rest of year Mon-Sat 9am-5pm, Sun 10am-4pm) set in an old forge on the T-junction as you enter the village; it sells a wide variety of fruit and veg from the local area as well as take-away hot drinks, ice-creams, homemade lavender bread and cakes, venison pies, local chutneys and preserves.

Cley Smokehouse (☎ 01263-740282, ☐ cleysmokehouse.com; Mon-Fri 9am-5pm, Sat 8.30am-5pm, Sun 9.30am-4.30pm), a little further up the road, has been working for more than 30 years, producing traditionally cured and smoked fish, shellfish and meats as well as homemade patés. If nothing else, buy some of the traditional North Norfolk kippers – herring, slit in two, gutted, cleaned, brined and then smoked over oak. Simply delicious, though remember they need to be cooked.

Crabpot Books (daily 10am-5pm) is a second-hand bookshop specialising in anti-quarian and natural history books; it also carries a number of local history titles.

Sanders No 4 **bus service** (see box p54) stops in the village near Picnic Fayre and again by Norfolk Wildlife Trust centre.

Where to stay, eat & drink

The smartest accommodation option is *Cley Windmill* (☎ 01263-740209, ☐ cleymill.co .uk; 8D, all en suite, cottage with 2D; ✆; WI-FI; Ⓛ; 🐾), a stylish converted windmill dating from the 18th century. With its restored sails, cap and wooden galleries the mill has become a well-known local landmark, easily identifiable across the marshes and commanding breathtaking views of the surroundings. Converted into a guesthouse with masses of character, the mill boasts antique furniture, comfortable sofas and, in winter, a large open fire. The rooms are spotless and **B&B** costs £79.50-122.50pp (sgl occ £129-225). The cottage is usually let on a self-catering basis (for weekly lets) but can also be booked as B&B accommodation. A three-course evening meal (£32.50) is available most nights (to non-residents as well) and is served at 7.30pm but it must be booked in advance. The menu features seasonal and local produce.

The George (☎ 01263-740652, ☐ the georgehotelatcley.co.uk; 8D and two suites, all en suite; ✆; WI-FI; ⓁL; 🐾) is a good-sized inn with a cosy public bar and two larger dining rooms. Dark wood and green-painted furniture provide an attractive backdrop to the photographs of local scenes and a large stained-glass window depicting St George fighting the dragon. **Food** (Mon-Fri noon-9pm, Sat 11.30am-9.30pm, Sun till 8.30pm) served includes good sandwiches, ploughman's and soup (available as

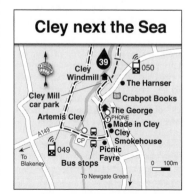

Cley next the Sea

CLEY NEXT THE SEA ← 15 MINS → BLAKENEY POINT

BEACH CAR PARK

45 MINS TO/FROM SALTHOUSE CAR PARK (MAP 40) →

MAP 39

⬤ 38

⬤ 40

CLEY NEXT THE SEA

PATH LIES ON THE LANDWARD SIDE OF A SUBSTANTIAL SHINGLE RIDGE - CAN BE TOUGH-GOING, AS EXPOSED BUT SUPERB VIEWS & SENSE OF ISOLATION

TO SALTHOUSE

ARNOLD'S MARSH

WALSEY HILLS

A149

SNIPES MARSH

NORTH POOL

CLEY MARSHES NATURE RESERVE

NORFOLK WILDLIFE TRUST INFO CENTRE

SOUTH POOL

OLD WOMAN'S LANE

TO HOLT

CLEY BEACH

CLEY EYE

WAR-TIME GUN PLACEMENT

CAR PARK & START OF TREK TO BLAKENEY POINT

CLEY WINDMILL

SEE VILLAGE PLAN

📷 051

📷 050

GATE

CLEY CHANNEL

📷 048

PATH RUNS ALONG THE TOP OF SEA WALL

TANTALISING VIEWS OF CLEY WINDMILL

📷 049

CLEY MILL A149 CAR PARK

TO NEWGATE GREEN

trailblazer

¼ mile

APPROX SCALE

500m

ROUTE GUIDE AND MAPS

light snacks) alongside a Cley Smokehouse platter of prawns & salmon (£7.95), half a dozen Blakeney oysters (£7.25) as well as pub grub such as sausages & mash (£9.95) and fish & chips (£10.95); they also offer takeaway fish & chips. There is a grassy beer garden on the opposite side of the road that backs onto the marshes. The rooms above the pub are modern and well-furnished, and **B&B** costs £60-92.50pp (sgl occ room rates) depending on the size, view, season and day of the week required. A suite will set you back £107.50-195pp (sgl occ room rate).

At the entrance to the village is *Artemis Cley* (☎ 01263-741674, 🖳 artemis coffeeshop.co.uk; Easter to end Oct daily 9am-5pm, Nov-end Dec & mid Feb to Easter Mon-Tue & Thur-Sun 9/9.30am-4pm, breakfast till 11.30am, lunch noon-3pm; WI-FI; 🐾), a café with spectacular views and a nice side line in homeware and antiques. Locally roasted coffee, home-made food and a selection of cakes, scones

and sausage rolls baked freshly that morning make this a good pit stop. They're fully licensed (but not for takeaway) and have a range of beers and wines.

At the entrance to Cley, where the road bends left, if you go right on the junction and follow the road for half a mile you will come to **Newgate Green** and *The Three Swallows* (☎ 01263-740526, 🖳 thethree swallows.co.uk; 4D, all en suite; WI-FI bar only; Ⓛ; 🐾). This rustic pub's rooms are in converted outbuildings and cost £37.50-42.50pp for **B&B** (sgl occ from £50). The pub has pine tables and log fires at which to relax, and black and white photographs of Cley over the years. The **food** (Mon-Sat noon-2pm & 6-8.30pm, Sun noon-8pm; in the winter the pub closes Mon-Fri 2.30pm-5.30pm) – from sandwiches up – is reasonably priced, with local seafood a speciality.

At the time of writing **The Harnser** was changing ownership but it is possible when it reopens it will provide accommodation and/or food.

The onward path enters Cley Mill car park and goes through a gate before climbing onto a sea bank. Head north towards the sea, passing alongside **Cley Marshes Nature Reserve**, one of the foremost bird-spotting grounds in the country. At the end of this stretch is another car park. Here sand gives way to a shingle beach. Turn right past a **war-time gun placement** and begin an enervating 4-mile walk along the landward side of a substantial shingle ridge, stumbling up and over **Cley Eye**, **Little Eye** (Map 40) and **Gramborough Hill** in turn. There is a path just before Little Eye where you can turn right for **Salthouse**.

SALTHOUSE [MAP 40]

There is a **bus** stop (Sanders No 4; see box p54) on Cross St and a couple of good food options on the village green; *Cookies Crab Shop* (☎ 01263-740352, 🖳 salthouse .org.uk; daily summer 9am-6pm, winter 9am-3.30pm) sells delicious shellfish, seafood platters piled high with dressed crab, smoked mackerel, chunky hot-smoked salmon, anchovy fillets, cockles and prawns along with pickled beetroot and cucumber salad, sandwiches and hot & cold drinks, which can be taken away or eaten in

the rather rudimentary shed that comprises their dining room.

If you want a glass of wine or well-kept beer though you'll need to pop over the green to *Dun Cow* (☎ 01263-740467, 🖳 salthouseduncow.com; food served daily noon-9pm; WI-FI; 🐾 on lead), an inviting pub with views across the marshes. The Red Poll beef on the menu is reared right in Salthouse, while there's also fish of the day and local crab linguine (both about £15) to tempt you to stay. There are sandwiches (from £7) until 5pm as well.

In places, the shingle ridge will have been flattened and knocked across the path by the storms that occasionally lash this stretch of coast. High tides and bad

MAP 40

45 MINS FROM/TO BEACH CAR PARK (MAP 39) — 15 MINS — SALTHOUSE CAR PARK

RADIO MAST

PATH CONTINUES ON SHINGLE RIDGE, CLIMBING & FALLING AS IT CROSSES A SERIES OF HILLOCKS WHICH MAY ONCE HAVE BEEN USED AS WATCHTOWERS & SIGNAL POINTS

STRONG UNDERTOW OFF THE COAST – DON'T SWIM HERE

GRAMBOROUGH HILL

LITTLE EYE

CAR PARK

SALTHOUSE MARSHES

Cookies Crab Shop

A149

SALTHOUSE

CROSS ST

Dun Cow

TO CLEY NEXT THE SEA

MEADOW LANE

A149

TO WEYBOURNE

WIRE FENCES, RADIO MAST & WIRELESS STATION OF A MINISTRY OF DEFENCE INSTALLATION

052 A

0   ¼ mile
0   APPROX SCALE   500m

weather can mean that the path becomes flooded. The trade-off for the tiring walk and the exposure to the elements is stunning views across the marshes and along the coast.

Wire fences and sturdy faceless buildings beneath a **radio mast** signal are a sign you are approaching a Ministry of Defence installation. Beyond this is the approach to **Weybourne Hope**, where sea-anglers can often be spotted casting from the beach. Inland a little under half a mile from here lies Weybourne.

WEYBOURNE   [MAP 41]

Weybourne is mentioned in the *Domesday Book* as 'Wabrunna'. An old **Augustinian priory** dating from around 1200 stands on the site of an earlier, simpler Saxon church, whilst well-preserved 17th-century brick and flint cottages line its streets. The town has a history of military defence and has been a base for repelling invasion from the time of the Spanish Armada in 1588. The old rhyme 'He who would old England win, must at Weybourne Hoop (Hope) begin' recognises that, because of the deep sea-water, access to Weybourne Hope was simple and invading armies could put ashore.

In 1914 the area became a front-line defence with the construction of pillboxes and other armaments and the billeting of large numbers of troops. An anti-aircraft artillery base and training station from 1936 it finally ceased action in 1958. Thirty years later many of the buildings were demolished and the town turned over to tourism. The memory of its past lives on though in the **Muckleburgh Military Collection** (☎ 01263-588210, 🖳 muckleburgh.co.uk; Feb half-term week & Easter-Oct daily 10am-4pm; adult/child £11/7) which is housed in the site's original NAAFI building. The Collection is the UK's largest privately owned military museum; it includes more than 120 tanks, guns and military vehicles from all around the world as well as a large number of operational radios. Some of the attractions, such as tank demonstrations and rides in vehicles round the old Royal Artillery Camp (£3pp) are available only in the summer months; contact them for details. There's also a small *café* and gift shop on site.

Weybourne station (a mile inland from the town centre) is also one of the four stopping points for **North Norfolk Railway**

(The Poppy Line; ☎ 01263-820800, 🖳 nn railway.co.uk; daily Feb half-term & Mar to end of Oct, Nov weekends only, Dec Santa trains 4-11/day) connecting Sheringham to Holt. Services operate with steam locomotives and occasionally diesel. A Rover ticket allowing unlimited travel for a day costs £13/9.50 adult/children.

Weybourne hosts North Norfolk Country Fair (see p15).

Services and transport

On Beach Lane there is a small village **shop** (☎ 01263-588219; Mar-end Dec Mon-Sat 8am-5pm, Sun 8.30am-4pm, Jan-Feb to 2pm) selling basic provisions and household items as well as local produce, sandwiches and coffee/tea either to eat in or takeaway.

There is a **post office** (Tue & Thur 9.30-11.30am) in the village hall.

Sanders No 4 **bus service** (see box p54) stop just outside Foxhills (see Where to stay) gate as well as near the church.

Where to stay, eat & drink

Campers can head to *Foxhills* (☎ 01263-588253, 🖳 foxhillscamping.co.uk; WI-FI; 🐾), adjacent to Muckleburgh Military Collection, a small **campsite** charging £9pp for walkers (note they only accept adults). Hot and cold water and toilet/shower facilities are available.

The Maltings Hotel (☎ 01263-588731, 🖳 maltingshotel.co.uk; 9D/2T, all en suite; 🖤; WI-FI public areas only; 🐾; Mar-mid Dec), on The Street, has slightly old-fashioned-looking rooms from £46pp (sgl from £64, sgl occ rates on request). They require a minimum two-night stay on Friday and Saturday nights between March and September.

MAP 41

← 15 MINS FROM/TO RADIO MAST (MAP 40) WEYBOURNE CAR PARK 60 MINS TO/FROM LOOKOUT STATION (MAP 42) →

¼ mile

500m

APPROX SCALE

SHINGLE GIVES WAY TO CLIFFS

WEYBOURNE HOPE

PATH CUTS INLAND TO ROUND HOUSE, NOW PERCHED PRECARIOUSLY ON CLIFF EDGE

HEAVILY ERODED CLIFFS – TAKE CARE CLOSE TO EDGE

BUNKERS

42

CRUMBLING CLIFFS GAIN HEIGHT

GOOD VIEWS INLAND OF ROLLING FIELDS AND WEYBOURNE WOOD

GATE

TO SHERINGHAM

NORTH NORFOLK RAILWAY

WATER HILL

GATE

The Ship Inn

CAR PARK

053

CHURCH

REMAINS OF AUGUSTINIAN PRIORY

A149

WINDMILL

WEYBOURNE

TO WEYBOURNE STATION FOR THE NORTH NORFOLK RAILWAY

STATION ROAD

BUS STOP

BEACH LANE

POST OFFICE IN VILLAGE HALL

VILLAGE SHOP

The Maltings Hotel

BUS STOP

HOLT ROAD

Foxhills

THE STREET

MUCKLEBURGH MILITARY COLLECTION

MUCKLEBURGH HILL

A149

TO SALTHOUSE, ¼ MILE

40

ROUTE GUIDE AND MAPS

The Ship Inn (☎ 01263-588721, 🖳 theshipinnweybourne.com; food served Mon-Fri noon-2.30pm & 6-8.30pm, Sat noon-2.30pm & 5.30-9pm, Sun noon-7pm, winter to 5pm; WI-FI; 🐾) is a cheerful pub on The Street, identifiable by the attractive hanging baskets at the front. The large bar is comfortable and accommodating and has a wood-burning stove for those chilly evenings. A changing selection of real ales is on offer as are decent wines by the glass. The menu varies but as much as possible is locally sourced. Their seafood chowder costs £6.75, while 'curry of the day' is £12 and a 'Weybourne surf and turf' is £25.

WEYBOURNE TO CROMER   MAPS 41-45

This short (**7½-mile (12km; 2-3hr) stretch** sees you explore the sea cliffs before Sheringham, the largest town encountered so far along the trek, after which you follow the cliffs and coast to the pier at Cromer.

Beyond Weybourne Hope the shingle gives way to crumbling **sea cliffs**. Although not especially substantial they are cliffs nonetheless and the most impressive so far seen along the coast! These fragile defences are constantly eroding and in places the path has had to be re-routed as the edge crumbles away; a good example is at **Water Hill** where the path now has to pass to the landward side of a house precariously perched on the edge of the fast-eroding cliff and destined to slip into the sea.

The path undulates as it gains height above the beach. Passing a golf course it climbs steeply to the summit of **Skelding Hill** and the old coastguard lookout station from where there are spectacular views out to sea, along the beaches and over the town below. Descending the easterly shoulder of the hill, the path passes a boating pond and descends to the promenade below **Sheringham**.

SHERINGHAM   [see map p183]

Sheringham is an appealing, traditional place. Historically the upper part of the town, set further inland, was for farming families whilst fishermen lived in the lower section. However, these days it's mostly full of tourists, drawn by the safe swimming and huge expanse of sand exposed at low tide. You'll still see a handful of crabbing boats dragged high and dry on the sand and pebble beach though and the slipway by the quay is often festooned with nets and buoys. The town centre is busy and packed with independently owned specialist shops selling second-hand books, antiques and bric-a-brac as well as arts and crafts.

The unusual red-brick church of **St Joseph** on Cromer Rd was designed by Sir Giles Gilbert Scott, the man responsible for Battersea Power Station and Liverpool Cathedral amongst many other buildings. It towers over its neighbours and has a high rose window set in the east wall.

The **Fisherman's Heritage Centre** (Wed-Fri noon-4pm, during high summer Tue-Sat noon-4pm provided volunteers are available to man it; free) is housed in part of the historic Fishing Sheds on West Cliff and is dedicated to demonstrating the history of the town's lifeboats. There is also information about, and a photographic record of, some of the fishermen who crewed the rescue boats.

Some of the original lifeboats are preserved at **Sheringham Museum** (☎ 01263-824482, 🖳 sheringhammuseum.co.uk; Mar-Oct Tue-Sat 10am-4.30pm, Sun & bank hol Mon noon-4pm; £4/2 adult/child), affectionately known as **The Mo** and set above the promenade. It tells the story of Sheringham and its people, looking at the past, present and future for the town to

MAP 42

← 60 MINS FROM/TO WEYBOURNE CAR PARK (MAP 41) —— LOOKOUT STATION —— 15 MINS TO/FROM SHERINGHAM (MAP 43) →

DEAD MAN'S HILL

A STEADY CLIMB TO A GREAT VANTAGE POINT WITH SUPERB VIEWS

ROBIN FRIEND

SKELDING HILL

THE ESPLANADE

GROYNES

LIFEBOAT STATION

DESCEND TO SHERINGHAM

CLUB HOUSE

SHERINGHAM
SEE TOWN PLAN

HOLT RD

B1157

TO UPPER SHERINGHAM

LOOKOUT STATION

054

TO UPPER SHERINGHAM

OLD HITHE RD

GOLF CLUB

NORTH NORFOLK RAILWAY

A149

SHERINGHAM PARK

OAK WOOD

TO WEYBOURNE

TO WEYBOURNE NNR STATION

¼ mile
500m
APPROX SCALE
0
0

show how it has evolved from fishing village to tourist destination. Stroll through the galleries and walk amongst an historic fleet of lifeboats and fishing vessels. There are good views across the seafront from an elevated viewpoint and a small shop on site. The Mo is also home to **Sheringham Shoal Windfarm Visitor Centre** (🖥 sher inghamshoal.co.uk; same hours as museum; free), which contains interactive displays, films, a model and educational panels so people can learn about climate change and renewable energy in general as well as the construction and operation of the Sheringham Shoal in particular. See also box below.

A couple of miles south-west of the town is **Sheringham Park** (see Map 42; daily dawn to dusk, visitor centre Mar-Oct daily 10am-5pm; free), a large tract of woodland covering 770 acres that erupts into colour in May-June when hordes of azaleas and rhododendrons flower. There is a series of walks through the park, including a path that connects to the North Norfolk railway station at Weybourne, and some specially constructed towers to scale for dramatic views.

For entertainment try **Little Theatre** (☎ 01263-822347, 🖥 sheringhamlittletheatre .com), on Station Rd; it presents an eclectic programme of drama, comedy, films and pantomimes and has a small coffee bar.

The North Norfolk Railway (The Poppy Line, see p178 and box p49) to Holt departs from a restored 1950s station on Station Approach; stepping onto the platform here is like being transported back in time. The steam and diesel trains chug along five miles of track allowing you to soak up the views.

Sheringham hosts both the Crab & Lobster Festival and the Potty Morris & Folk Festival (see p14), which celebrate crustacea and traditional dancing respectively.

Transport
Sanders' Nos 4 & X40/X44 **buses** services stop on Station Approach. See box p54 for details.

Sheringham Station, on the eastern side of Station Approach, is the terminus for **train** services on Greater Anglia's Bittern Line (see box p48) to Norwich: from Norwich there are frequent services to other destinations.

Services
Sheringham Tourist Information Centre (TIC; ☎ 01263-824329, 🖥 visitsheringham .co.uk; Jun-Aug Mon-Sat 10am-5pm, Sun 10am-4pm, Sep-Nov & Mar/Apr-May daily 10am-2pm), on Station Approach, is a mine of information with pleasant and helpful staff.

There are several **banks** and **ATMs** on High St and Station Rd. The local **library** (Mon, Tue & Fri 10am-5pm, Wed 10am-1pm, Thur 10am-7pm, Sat 9.30am-1pm) is on New Rd, and has free **internet access**. There is a **post office** counter (Mon & Thur 8.30am-5.30pm, Tue, Wed & Fri 9am-5.30pm, Sat 9am-1pm) in Starlings Newsagent on High St. Lloyd's **pharmacy** is at 31 Station Rd.

❏ Sheringham Shoal offshore wind farm
Sheringham Shoal offshore wind farm features 88 turbines; each stands from nine nautical miles (17km) up to 13 nautical miles (23km) offshore, where the waters are comparatively shallow (at 17-22m), wind speeds are high and consistent, and access is good. The turbines are 80m (262ft) high and each blade is 52m long; they stand on foundations fixed to the seabed.

Although this massive farm, which covers a total area of approximately 14 sq miles, generates power for around 220,000 average UK homes and is helping to meet government targets of producing 15% of the UK's energy needs from renewable sources by 2020, it has undoubtedly affected the view and natural appearance of the North Norfolk coastline.

Sheringham

Where to eat and drink

1 The Two Lifeboats
2 Grey Seal Coffee
3 The Lobster
4 The Windham Arms

5 The Funky Mackerel
6 Dave's
7 Pungleperry's
8 Poppyfields
9 Rallentando

10 Number 10
11 Marmalades Bistro
12 The Robin Hood

There are two **supermarkets** (Sainsbury's and Tesco), one at the southern end of High St and the other on Cromer Rd. Additionally, there is a **butcher** and a **greengrocer** on Station Rd. The **market** takes place in the car park by the North Norfolk railway station every Saturday throughout the year and on Wednesdays between March and the end of October.

For **cycle hire**, see box pp38-9.

Where to stay

YHA Sheringham (☎ 0345-371 9040, 🖳 yha.org.uk/hostel/sheringham; 10 x 2-bed rooms and 3-/4-/5-/6-/7-bed dorms, shared facilities; WI-FI communal areas only; Ⓛ; mid Feb to end Oct), at 1 Cremer's Drift, is in a large rambling Victorian building in a quiet residential area. It has a common room, games room, TV lounge, dining room and small self-catering kitchen that still has everything you might need. However, meals are available. A bed costs from £13pp, though expect to pay £25pp in the summer months. A private room for two costs from £19 but up to £49 in summer.

Note that many of the places offering B&B here require a minimum two-night stay at least for advance bookings.

The friendly, family-run *Holway House* (☎ 01263-823299, 🖳 holwayhouse .co.uk; 4S/6D, all en suite; WI-FI), at 9 Holway Rd, is centrally located and charges from £40pp (sgl from £50) for B&B.

The smart *Bayleaf Guest House* (☎ 01263-823779, 🖳 bayleafbandb.co.uk; 3D /2T/2D or T, all en suite; WI-FI intermittent; Ⓛ; Mar-end Oct), at 10 St Peter's Rd, charges from £39.50pp (sgl occ from £55) on a B&B basis.

A short stroll from the centre but almost on the route of the Coast Path is *Camberley House* (☎ 01263-823101, 🖳 camberleyhouse.co.uk; 2S/3D/2D or T, most en suite; ➥; WI-FI; Ⓛ), perched precariously at 62 Cliff Rd. B&B costs £38.50-51pp (sgl occ from £60, sgl occ rates on request).

Pirate House B&B (☎ 01263-825943, 🖳 piratehousebandb.co.uk; 1D, en suite; WI-FI; Ⓛ), at 16 Priory Rd, has a good-sized, south-facing stylish room in a smartly renovated Edwardian property. They charge

from £42.50pp (sgl occ from £60). There's a spacious shower and sole use of a smart lounge area as well. Breakfasts are taken in the kitchen, or al fresco in the pretty garden.

Myrtle House (Map 43; ☎ 01263-823889, 🖳 myrtlehouse-sheringham.co.uk; Mar-Nov), at 27-29 Nelson Rd, some five minutes' walk from the town centre, has two self-contained self-catering cottages (➥; WI-FI). One cottage sleeps up to three (1D plus extra bed) and the other up to five people (1D or T plus extra bed/1T). They require payment for a minimum of three nights (cottages from £250 for up to two sharing for three nights) although of course you can stay for less.

The Two Lifeboats (☎ 01263-823144, 🖳 thetwolifeboatssheringham.com; 1S/4D/ 1T, all en suite; ➥; WI-FI), at the northern end of High St, is a small, unpretentious place. Many of the rooms (B&B from £50pp, sgl from £65, sgl occ room rate) have sea views. The building dates from 1728 and the hotel is named after the *Augusta* and *Duncan* lifeboats, which saved the crew of the Norwegian brig *Caroline* when it was wrecked offshore in December 1882.

The Lobster (☎ 01263-822716, 🖳 the lobsterinn.co.uk; 2D/16D or T, all en suite; WI-FI; 🐾), at 13 High St, is a traditional family pub (see Where to eat) which also offers B&B (£40-50pp, sgl occ from £80).

Where to eat and drink

For good coffee head to *Grey Seal Coffee* (🖳 greysealcoffee.co.uk/sheringham; daily 9am-4pm), at 11 High St, which serves their own blend espresso based drinks and pastries made at their base in Glandford and delivered fresh.

For the chance to sit and look out over the beach while you enjoy your cuppa joe, try *The Funky Mackerel* (🖳 funkymacker el.com; daily 9.30am-5pm; 🐾), at 54 Cliff Rd, which is best accessed from the promenade and sits proudly looking out over the shingle and sand in front. They claim to make the best bacon sandwiches in Sheringham and are famous for their gooey flapjack.

Pungleperry's (☎ 01263-822078; Mar to end Oct/early Nov daily 9am-5pm; WI-FI;

🐾), on High St, is a funky espresso bar serving freshly made pancakes, homemade pasties and quiche as well as smoothies and good coffee.

Opposite on the High St, *Poppyfields* cooks up burgers (£6.50), lasagne (£7.25) and three-bean chilli (£7.50). For a light meal try *Rallentando* (☎ 01263-820011; Mon-Sat 8am-4pm, Sun 10.30am-4pm; WI-FI; 🐾), by the clocktower on the High St; they serve authentic stone-baked thin-crust pizza and a simple range of tasty Italian dishes.

For good-quality fresh fish & chips there's *Dave's Fish Bar* (☎ 01263-823830; summer daily 11.30am-8pm, winter hours variable; WI-FI), on Co-operative St. As well as a large eat-in restaurant they also offer a full takeaway menu.

Marmalades Bistro (☎ 01263-822830, 🖥 marmaladesbistro.co.uk; summer Tue-Thur 6-8.30pm, Fri & Sat to 9pm, Sun to 8pm, winter Tue-Thur 6-8.30pm, Fri to 8.30pm, Sat till 9pm), on Church St, is a venerable wood-beamed cottage serving a variety of English and European dishes depending on seasonal produce. Start with honey-roasted figs & Binham blue (£6.50) before ordering pan-roasted cod with bacon & hazelnut crust (£15.95). Booking is recommended, particularly for the evening; the latest time quoted is when last orders are accepted.

Number 10 (☎ 01263-824400; summer Wed-Sat 10am-2pm & 6.30-9.30pm, Sun lunch noon-2pm, winter hours variable), at 10 Augusta St, is the pick of the local eateries. Guests dine in an intimate room decorated with candles, mirrors and chapel chairs, and select from a menu that changes every four weeks. Dishes might include Morston mussels or local asparagus to start, while main courses could range from cod fillet with spring onion risotto to sea bass with roasted fennel. The chef also brings his native Moroccan influence to bear on dishes such as mackerel fillet with couscous and harissa dressing, or authentic tagine. Booking in advance is recommended.

The Two Lifeboats (see Where to stay; food daily noon-3pm & 6-9pm; WI-FI; 🐾) serves meals from an extensive menu in both their bars and in their cosy restaurant; it's the location that's the main draw here though, as the big bay windows have good sea views.

The Robin Hood pub (☎ 01263-820291, 🖥 robinhoodsheringham.co.uk; food summer daily noon-2.45pm & 6-8.45pm, winter same but no food Sun evening; WI-FI; 🐾) offers everything from sandwiches and snacks through to pizzas (from £9.50) and mixed grills for £19.95.

The Lobster (see Where to stay; food daily noon-3pm & 6-9pm) serves sandwiches, jacket potatoes, light bites, great seafood and steaks in smart, contemporary surroundings. They have 3-6 real ales as well as an extensive wine list.

Overlooking the promenade and with views of the sea, *The Windham Arms* (☎ 01263-826003; WI-FI; 🐾; bar daily 11am-11pm), on Wyndham St, just behind the High St, serves excellent ales in a friendly and welcoming atmosphere that is full of vintage character. However, at the time of research they were not serving food.

Follow the promenade above the beach, past the town and towards a line of beach huts. When you come to a set of concrete steps adjacent to a compact two-storey building called The Wee Retreat (once a Victorian toilet block but now converted into a compact self-catering cottage), turn right and begin to climb. Continue up a concrete incline and turn left adjacent to a putting green before winding your way to the top of **Beeston Hill** (see box p186), affectionately known as **Beeston Bump**, marked by an old Ordnance Survey triangulation point. The panoramic views from this 63m/207ft vantage point are spectacular and you can readily see the impact of coastal erosion on the cliffs below the summit.

❑ **Beeston Bump 'Y-Station'**
The dominant landmark of **Beeston Hill** has a secret history. During WWII this innocuous mound, little more than a giant rounded molehill, was the site of a top-secret military listening post, known as a '**Y-station**', that was vital to Britain's success in the fight against Germany. Nazi ships would patrol the coast off Sheringham, and the British command would spy on them from a series of listening posts such as Beeston Hill, which required height in order to maximise the distance they could listen. Today there is little physical evidence of the site but, when in use, the listening posts would have consisted of wooden towers almost 4m/12ft wide, and around 10m/30ft high, set on large concrete bases. The structures would have been double-skinned, with the cavity filled with shingle in an attempt to make it bullet, or at least splinter, proof.

The outline of the concrete octagonal base is actually all that remains on the summit of Beeston Hill. Radio signals and code intercepted at Beeston would have been passed on to military command and the codebreakers at Bletchley Park. In this sense, the listening stations provided the raw material for the codebreakers and played an essential role. The nine listening stations along the Norfolk coast would also relay the co-ordinates of the signals intercepted to one another in order to triangulate the location of the ship or plane sending them and thereby pinpoint the position of the craft.

After the war the listening stations were deliberately dismantled to maintain their secrecy and their location and role has since become a forgotten piece of history.

Descend the eastern side of Beeston Hill towards Beeston Regis Caravan Park. Historically the Coast Path cut inland at this point to climb Beacon Hill before descending again to enter Cromer but these days the path has been re-routed to stay closer to the cliff tops because of the England Coast Path. Where some older maps and guides might show you to turn right alongside the edge of Beeston Regis Caravan Park, continue instead in front of the caravans, adjacent to the cliff edge. If you fancy a climb and a break from the coast though, follow the signposted route inland, cross the railway line and climb to Roman Camp before descending the forested hill via Manor Farm to join the road that approaches Cromer from the south west.

WEST RUNTON   [MAP 43]

West Runton is a small and friendly village within easy walking distance of both Sheringham and Cromer. There is a **post office** (Mon-Fri 9am-1pm & 2-5pm, Sat 9am-1pm) on Cromer Rd.

Beeston Regis Caravan Park (☎ 01263-823614, 🖳 beestonregis.co.uk; WI-FI; 🐾; Mar-Oct) has 43 tent pitches overlooking the sea as well as shower blocks with hot water and laundry rooms. A pitch with up to two people costs £20-35; booking is advised.

In the centre of this unspoilt village **B&B** is available at *Homefield Guesthouse*

(☎ 01263-837337, 🖳 homefieldguesthouse.co.uk; 4D/2T, all en suite; 🛏; WI-FI; ⓛ), a refurbished Victorian house on Cromer Rd. The rate for two sharing is £32.50-42.50pp (sgl occ £50-70).

Clementine's (☎ 01263-838770, 🖳 clementinesofrunton.co.uk; late May to end Oct Wed-Mon 9.30am-4pm, rest of year Thur-Sun 9.30am-4pm; WI-FI; 🐾), a café bistro on Cromer Rd that sells simple tasty food. The restaurant isn't licensed but you can bring your own wine. In the summer they are sometimes open in the evening (Thur-Sat till 8.30pm).

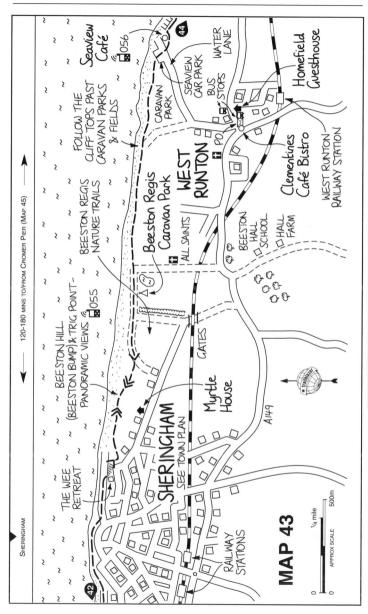

SHERINGHAM

← 120-180 MINS TO/FROM CROMER PIER (MAP 45) →

THE WEE RETREAT

BEESTON HILL (BEESTON BUMP) & TRIG POINT– PANORAMIC VIEWS 📷055

FOLLOW THE CLIFF-TOPS PAST CARAVAN PARKS & FIELDS

Seaview Café 📷056

BEESTON REGIS NATURE TRAILS

Beeston Regis Caravan Park

Seaview Car Park

BUS STOPS

WATER LANE

Homefield Guesthouse

CARAVAN PARK

West Runton

All Saints

PO

Clementines Café Bistro

WEST RUNTON RAILWAY STATION

Beeston Hall School

HALL FARM

SHERINGHAM (SEE TOWN PLAN)

GATES

Myrtle House

A149

RAILWAY STATIONS

MAP 43

¼ mile

500m

APPROX SCALE

ROUTE GUIDE AND MAPS

Seaview Café (🖳 seaviewbeachcafe.co
.uk; mid Mar to end Oct daily 9am-5pm)
has a small deck above a slipway and sells
drinks and snacks.

West Runton is served by **trains** on
Greater Anglia's Bittern Line (see box
p48). Sanders Nos 4 & X40/X44 **bus** services stop here; see box p54 for details.

Stick to the cliff top for the next section. The rock beds that form the cliffs
along this stretch of coast are almost two million years old in parts, making
them a haven for fossil hunters, who have unearthed evidence of rhinos, hyenas
and, most famously, a 16ft-tall mammoth. Skirt a series of caravan and static
sites with occasional steps down to the beach on the seaward side. Respect the
residents of these holiday homes and keep to the cliff edge while staying safe.
Having crossed a grassy field, descend to Seaview Car Park at the end of Water
Lane. There's a simple ***beach café*** here (see Seaview Café above).

Pick up the path as it passes through a fence and continues along the cliff tops.
If you look inland from here you can see the Cromer Ridge, which boasts some
of the highest land in East Anglia, reaching a dizzying 102m/335ft in places.

The path climbs slowly and you gain your first glimpse of Cromer pier.
Having crossed a patch of wild flowers and scrub you'll reach the edge of
Woodhill Caravan Park. The path turns inland along a hedge and having stepped
onto a gravel access road briefly, turns left into the caravan park grounds just in
front of the reception block. Round the building, bearing right then left, following the tarmac between caravans to the far corner of the site. Here, a gate
lets you out onto the pavement of Cromer Rd. Turn left and walk down the road,
which becomes High St as you enter **East Runton**.

EAST RUNTON   [MAP 44]

On the High St you can grab a drink and
something to eat at the traditional ***Fishing
Boat Pub*** (☎ 01263-519070; food Mon-Sat
noon-2.30pm & 6-8pm, Sun noon-4pm; WI-
FI; 🐾), a friendly locals' pub that has a
sunny garden out back. Alternatively pick up
good quality fish & chips from ***Will's Plaice***
(☎ 01263-519222, 🖳 chipshopeastrunton
.co.uk; Easter to end Sep daily 12.30-2pm &
5-8.30pm, rest of year Fri 5-7pm, Sat 12.30-
2pm & 5.30-7pm), or pause for decent
Greek food – accompanied by live Greek
music, of course – at ***Constantia Cottage
Restaurant*** (☎ 01263-512017, 🖳 constantia
restaurant.co.uk), although it's only open in
the evening (Mon-Sat from 7pm).

Most of the accommodation in East
Runton is rental cottages or caravan parks
but **camping** is available at ***Manor Farm***
(☎ 01263-512858, 🖳 manorfarmcampsite
.co.uk; 🐾 on lead; Easter to end Oct), a
large, gently rolling, inland site with good
views to the coast, set in 18 acres of working farmland. A standard pitch costs
£15.50-19.50 for up to two people; there
may be a discount for solo campers in the
low season. There are six amenity blocks
with power showers and laundry rooms
shared across the three fields.

Sanders Nos 4 & X40/X44 **bus** services stop here; see box p54.

At the far end of the High St, where the road bends right, turn left off the
road and into another caravan park, Leakes Caravan Park, following the path
straight ahead. As the tarmac turns left to access more caravans, take a footpath
to the right and climb slightly to arrive back on the main A149 road. Turn left
and follow the pavement until you reach the town sign for Cromer, just after
Wyndham Caravan Park, where a path leads left across a grassy space towards

120–180 MINS BETWEEN SHERINGHAM (MAP 43) AND CROMER PIER (MAP 45)

43

057 ~ Will's Plaice ~ Constantia ~
~ Cottage Restaurant
Fishing   BEACH RD   PATH GOES
Boat   ~   THROUGH
WOODHILL   TOILETS   LEAKES
CARAVAN PARK   ~   CARAVAN
PARK

GRAVEL
ACCESS ROAD
BUS STOPS
RECEPTION
BLOCK
HIGH ST   BUS   PARK
STOP
CROMER RD   45
A149   EAST   058
CROMER   RUNTON
ROAD
trailblazer   MAP 44   Manor Farm
Caravan &
Camping Site
0   ¼ mile
0   APPROX SCALE   500m
LONG HILL

the cliff tops once more. Cross a large common area adjacent to the cliff edge, pass through a surfaced car park. To the right of The Lookout is a paved path which winds its way to the clifftop path that descends above West Cliffs and the Esplanade to the pier. As you approach, the path runs parallel with the main road until, with a petrol station on your right, you edge left around *No 1 Cromer* (see Where to Eat, p193), a fish & chip restaurant, to walk in front of a row of smart terraced houses overlooking the sea. At the end of the row you arrive at steps leading down to Cromer Pier, with the waves breaking onto the beach below.

CROMER   [see map p191]

The gentrification of North Norfolk has meant that Cromer, once a fairly trashy, workaday seaside town full of amusement arcades and novelty shops is now more closely associated with local art, independent shops and, of course, Cromer crab. Nonetheless, there's a certain shabbiness to the place, what Paul Theroux described as an 'atrophied charm' (*Kingdom by the Sea*).

The **Church of St Peter and St Paul** dominates the centre of Cromer and recalls the town's prestige and wealth. During the summer months the 160ft/49m steeple, the tallest in the county, can be climbed via 172 steps to enjoy excellent views of the town and surrounding area. The interior is mostly Victorian, having been rebuilt in the late 1880s, but the sheer scale of the arches and aisles make it impressive. Lofty windows depicting some of Cromer's seafaring characters line the walls.

Tourists have been drawn to the town for more than a century to stroll on the blustery cliff tops and relax on the beach, a long stretch of sand and shingle interrupted by groynes, which is popular with all sorts, particularly with a growing number of surfers. There has been a jetty or **pier** in Cromer since 1391. The 70ft wooden jetty was so badly damaged by storms that it had to be replaced by a new pier in 1901. Yet more storms wrecked this in 1953, destroying the pavilion. Two years later **Pavilion Theatre** (☎ 01263-512495, 🖳 cromerpier.co.uk/whats-on) reopened though; it hosts comedy, music, dance, opera and community performances throughout the year as well as the Seaside Special, an end-of-the-pier variety show that runs through the summer and at Christmas.

There are two museums in town: **Cromer Museum** (☎ 01263-513543; Mar to end Oct Mon-Fri 10am-4pm, Sat & Sun noon-4pm; £4.15/3.30 adult/child) displays local history, geology and archaeology and is housed in a row of fishermen's cottages adjacent to the church. The **RNLI Henry Blogg Museum** (☎ 01263-511294; Tue-Sun Apr-Sep 10am-5pm, Feb-Mar & Oct-Nov to 4pm, Dec weekends only 10am-4pm; admission free) dedicated to the life of Henry Blogg, who served as a lifeboatman for 53 years, launching 387 times and saving 873 lives around the Cromer coast, is in the old lifeboat house at the foot of The Gangway.

The current lifeboat, which launches from the new **Lifeboat station** at the end of the pier, can also be visited. **Cromer Lighthouse** (Map 46) stands half a mile from the cliff edge at Foulness to the east. The present structure dates from 1833 and

Cromer

Where to stay
1 The Cliftonville Hotel
2 Sandcliff Guest House
3 Beachcomber Guesthouse
8 Cambridge House
9 The Red Lion
12 Virginia Court Hotel

Where to eat and drink
1 Bolton's Bistro,
  The Westcliff & The
  Buttery Bar & Coffee
  Shop
4 No 1 Cromer &
  Upstairs at No 1
5 Pavilion Bar
6 The Old Rock Shop
  Bistro
7 Mary Jane's Fish Bar
9 The Red Lion
10 Huckleberries
11 Bond St Bakery

Car park

The Lookout

Esplanade

Car park

Lifeboat station

Pavilion Theatre

Pier

Co-op Supermarket & Post Office

The Gangway

RNLI Henry Blogg Museum

9 Cromer Museum

High St

Jetty St

Tucker St

Brook St

Church St

HSBC

Bond St

Mount St

St Peter & St Paul

Boots

NatWest

Lloyds

Pharmacy 10

11

Regal Moviplex

Louden Rd

Chapel St

North Norfolk Information Centre

Car park

The Croft

Meadow Rd

West St

Canada Rd

Central Rd

Library & internet

Bus stop

Petrol station

Richard & Julie Davies's fishmongers

New St

Garden St

Prince of Wales Rd

Hamilton Rd

West Cliff

A149 Runton Rd

Beach Rd

Cabell Rd

Cadogan Rd

Alfred Rd

Bernard Rd

Macdonald Rd

Morrisons Supermarket

Railway station

Police station

Hall Road

Holt Rd

Norwich Rd

A149

Overstrand Rd

Cliff Ave

12

Vicarage Rd

Bond St

0 50 100m

44

46

the light can be seen for 23 nautical miles (26½ miles).

Regal Movieplex (☎ 01263-510151, 🖳 cromer.merlincinemas.co.uk), on Hans Place, shows the latest film releases.

Cromer hosts an annual Crab & Lobster Festival and a Carnival (see pp14-15).

Services

The large, well-equipped, eco-friendly **North Norfolk Information Centre** (☎ 01263-512497, 🖳 cromerinfo@north-norfolk.gov.uk; June-Aug Mon-Sat 10am-5pm, Sun 10am-4pm, rest of year daily 10am-4pm; WI-FI) is on Louden Rd; the staff can answer questions and provide a list of accommodation as well as inspiration for things to do in the area. There is also free **internet access** in the centre.

Cromer **Library** (Mon & Fri 9.30am-7pm, Tue & Thur 9.30am-5pm, Wed 9.30am-1pm, Sat 10am-1pm), on Canada Rd, also offers free **internet access**.

There are **banks** and **ATMs** on Church St and Chapel St. Both a Boots **chemist** (daily 8.45am-6pm) and Lloyds **Pharmacy** can be found on Church St.

There is a **post office** counter (Mon-Fri 9am-5.30pm, Sat 9am-noon) within the Co-op **supermarket** on High St. There is also a large Morrisons **supermarket** (Mon-Sat 7am-10pm, Sun 10am-4pm) adjacent to the railway station.

For dressed crab, lobsters, cockles, whelks, and fish of all description head to Richard and Julie Davies's (☎ 01263-512727; summer daily 8.30am-5pm, winter Tue-Sat 8.30am-4pm) **fishmonger** on Garden St.

Cromer **Hospital** is to the east of town, off Mill Rd (see Map 46). The **police station** is opposite the railway station on Holt Rd.

Transport

Sanders Nos 4, 5, 6A & X40/X44 **buses** stop on Cadogan Rd (see Services). See p54 for details.

Cromer is one of only a few points on the north coast accessible by **rail**. The railway station is on Holt Rd, a short walk west of the centre, with a regular service operating on Greater Anglia's Bittern Line to Norwich (see box p48). From Norwich there are rail connections to London and other destinations in the UK.

Where to stay

There's a wide range of relatively inexpensive accommodation.

For **B&B** head to *Beachcomber Guesthouse* (☎ 01263-513398, 🖳 cromer-beachcomber.co.uk; 3D/1D or T/1Tr, all en suite; WI-FI; ⒧), at 17 Macdonald Rd; it is a charming Victorian house and charges from £36.50pp (sgl occ £40-50). In July and August they generally only accept bookings for a two-night stay.

Slightly more expensive, *Cambridge House* (☎ 01263-512085, 🖳 cambridge cromer.co.uk; 2D/4D or T, most en suite; ☞; WI-FI), on East Cliff, Tucker St, was built in 1887 and retains much of its original character. Ideally located overlooking the beach and pier, there are steps to the promenade opposite the front door. B&B costs £41-45pp (sgl occ £41-45pp).

The Red Lion (☎ 01263-514964, 🖳 redlion-cromer.co.uk; 11D/4T, all en suite; ☞; WI-FI; ⒧; 🐾), on Brook St, charges from £57.50pp (sgl occ from £62.50) for B&B; many of the warm, comfortable rooms have sea views.

Sandcliff Guest House (☎ 01263-512888, 🖳 sandcliffcromer.co.uk; 4S/10D/4T/5Tr, most en suite, rest shared facilities; ☞; WI-FI; 🐾) overlooking the sea on Runton Rd. The room rate (£24-46pp, sgl £42-47, sgl occ £48-90) depends in part on whether rooms have a sea view; it also doesn't include breakfast but that is available (light/full English £5.95/7.95). Check their website for special deals and discounts.

The Cliftonville Hotel (☎ 01263-512543, 🖳 cliftonvillehotel.co.uk; 9S/7D/13D or T/1T, all en suite; ☞; WI-FI; ⒧; 🐾), also on the seafront, has rooms with spectacular sea views. Many of the hotel's Edwardian features are intact including attractive stained-glass windows and doors. B&B costs £65-80pp (sgl £65-100, sgl occ room rate).

Edwardian grandeur is also on offer at *Virginia Court Hotel* (☎ 01263-512398, 🖳 virginiacourt.co.uk; 3S/16D/4D or T, all en suite; 🛏; WI-FI), a grand gentleman's club reputedly built to tempt Edward VII to stay. The wide sweeping staircase leads to a range of rooms (from standard double to king-size and suites), which have been carefully restored and refurbished, with clean lines, tasteful décor and modern amenities. B&B costs £55-97.50pp (sgl £70-80, sgl occ £110-160).

Where to eat and drink

With some of the best views in Cromer, the *Pavilion Bar* (daily all day) on the pier is a good place to pop in to for a coffee, smoothie or snack.

On the seafront, at The Cliftonville Hotel (see Where to stay) is *Bolton's Bistro* (daily noon-2pm & 6-9.30pm), a popular eatery offering freshly prepared dishes including Cromer crab, locally caught lobster and a range of changing specials such as slow-cooked lamb shank (£15.95) and sauté king prawns & crayfish tails with noodles (£15.95). The hotel's restaurant, *The Westcliff* (summer daily 6-9pm) is a grand Edwardian affair with a Minstrel's gallery, marble fireplace and a stained-glass windows. The à la carte menu provides a more formal and consequently pricey experience. *The Buttery Bar and Coffee shop* (daily 10am-6pm) serves snacks and lighter meals.

For fantastic fish & chips to eat on the seafront, look no further than *No 1 Cromer* (☎ 01263-515983, 🖥 no1cromer.com; school summer holidays Mon-Thur noon-8.30pm, Fri-Sat noon-9pm, rest of year Mon-Thur noon-8pm, Fri-Sat noon-8.30pm, Sun noon-7pm; WI-FI; 🐾), the restaurant and takeaway owned by Galton Blackiston, the Michelin-starred chef of Morston Hall fame. The thriving takeaway set up sells cod & chips for £7.50 but you can also pick up breaded scampi, breaded brie and a local battered sausage. In the restaurant, as well as classic cod & chips (£12) cooked expertly look out for cockle popcorn (£7.25) and dressed Cromer crab (£8.50). As well as the fish & chips

offering, there is a more upmarket restaurant *Upstairs at No 1* (contact via No 1 Cromer; school summer holidays Mon-Thur noon-3pm & 5-8.30pm, Fri noon-3pm & 5-9pm, Sat noon-9pm, Sun noon-8pm, out of season till half an hour earlier each day) that serves a range of smaller bites that might include cockle popcorn, fish tacos, Tandoori mackerel and a Spanish squid bun with tomato & chorizo jam (£6.50 each, three for £18), or a varied and unique menu featuring British staples such as their No 1 fish stew (£16.50) and braised beef short rib (£14.95) along with internationally influenced dishes such as chicken katsu bun (£13.95) and green-curried spiced hake with lentils & onion bhaji (£13.95). If you've room, desserts are £6.50.

You can also pick up fish & chips at *Mary Jane's Fish Bar* (☎ 01263-511208; daily summer 11.30am-9pm, winter hours vary), on Garden St.

Bond St Bakery makes good cakes, filled rolls and fresh bread if you just want a snack. Close by, on Church St, is *Huckleberries* (☎ 01263-510899; summer Mon-Sat 8.30am-6pm, Sun 9.30am-4pm, winter Mon-Sat to 5pm, Sun from 10am; WI-FI), which serves good coffee, cakes, sweet and savoury snacks, thick shakes and ice-cream as well.

On Hamilton Rd you'll find *The Old Rock Shop Bistro* (☎ 01263-511926, 🖥 theoldrockshopbistro.co.uk; daily 8am-6pm; 🐾), a café-cum-bistro that does decent homemade cakes and savouries as well as reasonably priced light lunches.

The Red Lion (see Where to stay; food daily noon-2.30pm & 6-9.30pm) is an Edwardian-era pub that still has most of its rich mahogany fittings. The pub serves a wide range of real ales, an ideal way (though clearly only for those who like real ale!) to toast completing the trek as far as Cromer. During the day you can graze on sandwiches (from £6.95), salads, shared platters and pub staples, while the evening menu might feature sea bass fillets (£15.95), or venison loin (£18.95).

ROUTE GUIDE AND MAPS

❑ **Onwards, ever onwards**
Cromer Pier used to represent the end of the Norfolk Coast Path and the point at which you could reward yourself with a pint after a walk well trekked. However, these days, where a plaque once stood there's an onward pointing finger sign arrowing down the beach, initially towards Overstrand, Sidestrand, Mundesley, Happisburgh and Sea Palling.

From Cromer, the onward route leans to the right as it rounds the long shoulder of Norfolk and heads towards Suffolk, now finishing beyond Great Yarmouth at Hopton-on-Sea, just shy of the county border. Owing to the lack of tourist pamphlets, accommodation guides and literature on this even quieter corner of Norfolk you'd be forgiven for thinking that there was nothing here. The truth though is that this is a secret corner of the country. The coast path shuttles between the back of beaches and the low tops of crumbling cliffs on a stretch of impressively wild hinterland. Here the sea and the land have been fighting it out forever, with the land in slow retreat, beaten back by the relentless waves. It's not just cliffs that are being washed away by the waves though; whole communities, especially around embattled Happisburgh are in danger from **coastal erosion**. Between the towns and villages along this stretch the beleaguered land has a strong sense of being empty, making it an interesting and unusual stretch of England to walk through. Standout attractions on this new extension include vast sandy beaches at Waxham, Horsey and Winterton-on-Sea that are a match for the beautiful beaches on the north coast, a seal colony right on the shore and a number of once fashionable, upmarket seaside destinations that act as a counterpoint to the pleasure beaches and kiss-me-quick charm of the larger towns such as Great Yarmouth at the southern end of the sweep towards Suffolk.

CROMER TO MUNDESLEY [MAPS 46-49]

This **8-mile (12.5km; 3hr) route** gives you a first sense of what lies ahead on this section of coast, leaving the bustle of Cromer quite quickly and beginning the easterly trek along the beaches before you reach Mundesley, a one-time holiday retreat popular with Victorians.

Having descended the promenade beyond the pier the path passes in front of the Henry Blogg Museum to come to a clutch of beach huts. Although you can continue along the sand, the Coast Path turns right and ascends the cliff on long zigzags. At the top, turn left and follow the cliff top into an open area of grass, where the path abruptly descends a section of steps to return you to the beach below. Turn right and head east along the sand below the scrubby cliffs until a series of sea defences appear. At the end of these structures is a concrete slipway and path that leads up to **Overstrand**.

OVERSTRAND [see map p196]
Overstrand is an appealing, albeit small, village that was once a modest fishing station and later a fashionable, well-to-do holiday destination. It was dubbed '**Poppyland**' due to the profusion of the flowers in the area and had an underrated allure. These days its attraction is that its beach is much quieter than the bustling sands in nearby Cromer. Be aware though that at high tide you're not left with much more than a slither of sand and a promenade. There are three **Edwin Lutyens' buildings** (Overstrand Hall on Map 46, the Methodist Church and The Pleasaunce) for fans of architecture.

MAP 46

OVERSTRAND
SEE VILLAGE PLAN

← 45 MINS FROM/TO CROMER PIER (MAP 45) →

OVERSTRAND

CLIFF FALL HAS MADE
THE BEACH PATH ONLY
ACCESSIBLE AT LOW TIDE

GROYNES & SEA DEFENCES
ALONG THE BEACH HERE

BEACH HUTS

COASTGUARD LOOKOUT

WARREN WOODS

CLIFF ROUTE

CROMER LIGHTHOUSE

CROMER HOSPITAL

ROYAL CROMER GOLF CLUB

OVERSTRAND ROAD

OVERSTRAND HALL

The Sea Marge

¼ mile
500m
0
0
APPROX SCALE

061

060

45

47

ROUTE GUIDE AND MAPS

Your first impression of the village itself will be of the small **Fisherman's Green** at the top of the cliff, which has an anchor set in its midst. On one side is a shack, *Crab Shed* (daily 9am-5pm in the main season) selling fresh boiled crab and lobster. On the far side is the well-appointed *Cliff Top Café* (☎ 01263-579319; Feb-Dec daily 8am-4pm, till 5pm in high season; WI-FI; 🐾). This has been a café in some form since 1925. These days it is bright and fresh, offering breakfasts, sandwiches, jacket potatoes and afternoon tea with spectacular views from the outside seating.

In the heart of the village there's a **General Store** (☎ 01263-579233; summer Mon-Fri 7.30am-6pm, Sat 8.30am-6pm, Sun 8am-1pm, winter Mon-Sat to 5pm) selling groceries and fresh vegetables, meat and frozen foods. The store includes a **post office** (Mon-Fri 9.30am-5pm, Sat 9.30am-1pm) and has a free **ATM**.

Sanders Coaches' No 4 bus service calls here; see box p54.

Sadly at the time of research camping was no longer available at **Overstrand Campsite**.

White Horse (☎ 01263-579237, 🖥 whitehorseoverstrand.co.uk; 6D/3T/1Qd, all en suite; ▼; WI-FI; Ⓛ; 🐾) is a traditional pub a couple of minutes from the beach. Rooms are individually designed and decorated. **B&B** costs £25-44.50pp (sgl occ £50-74). The **food** (daily noon-3pm & 6-9pm) in the pub has a heavy emphasis on being home-made; breads are baked, fish is smoked, and ice-cream is churned all on site, while local produce such as Overstrand lobsters, Cromer crab and marsh samphire features prominently. Breakfast is also available (8-11am) for non-residents.

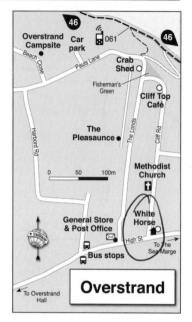

Alternative accommodation is available at *The Sea Marge* (Map 46; ☎ 01263-579579, 🖥 seamargehotel.co.uk; 25D or T, all en suite; ▼; WI-FI; Ⓛ; 🐾), a luxury Grade II-listed house with a commanding position on the High St and the coast at the end of its garden. B&B starts from £85pp (sgl occ from £105), while suites with feature bathrooms and a comfortable seating area cost from £115pp (sgl occ room rate). From October to May there's a two-night minimum stay policy. There are two **restaurants** (food available all day) and a bar on site; non-residents are welcome.

The Coast Path returns to the cliff tops after Overstrand, beginning by briefly joining the Cromer Road and heading towards **Sidestrand** before turning left off the main road into a cul de sac (Tower Lane) that gives way to a grassy path that traverses the field edges above the crumbling cliffs. Follow the unstable and eroding cliffs, keeping away from the unfenced edge as the slopes are very sensitive to further erosion.

The path curves left and enters a **small copse** where it divides; take the left-hand fork and bend back towards the cliffs, exiting the trees. Contour along the

ROUTE GUIDE AND MAPS

ROUTE GUIDE AND MAPS

CLIFTONVILLE

45 MINS

TRIMINGHAM

MAP 48

¼ mile

500m

APPROX SCALE

PATH GOES INLAND TO ANOTHER CARAVAN PARK

GROYNES ALL ALONG BEACH

ALBION RD

49

066

MARL POINT

TRIMINGHAM HOUSE CARAVAN PARK

CROMER RD

CLIFTONVILLE

AIR DEFENCE RADAR STATION

BEACON HILL

065

064

47

CHURCH OF ST JOHN THE BAPTIST'S HEAD

TRIMINGHAM

exposed cliffs and then strike inland again, through a stand of trees to wind your way onto a track that emerges in the small village of **Trimingham**. Once a centre for pilgrimage, the village is now a quiet place. The spireless church of St John the Baptist's Head stands at the heart of it and was the focal point for people coming to the village; the strange dedication dates from the medieval period when a life-size alabaster head of the saint was kept at the church and attracted people unable to make the journey to Amiens Cathedral in France where a relic said to be of the real head was kept.

Turn left on the main road opposite the church and follow it alternately on the pavement and on the field-side of a hedge. Coming out of a short section of trees, the path crosses the road and strikes across a field towards the cliffs again, aiming at what looks like a giant golf ball. This is in fact a remote **air defence radar station** (RAF Trimingham). Cross the road and enter the grounds of Trimingham House Caravan Park, perched on the cliff tops. Walk through the site and at the top of the crags bear right to head east along them, first dropping down to cross a beach access road before passing through another caravan site in **Cliftonville** to join the main road. Then, having returned to the wide sandy beach defended by a series of dilapidated groynes and passed in front of a line of gaily coloured beach huts, you ease into **Mundesley**.

MUNDESLEY [see map p201]

The sizeable village used to be a popular Victorian holiday resort and there are several faded larger buildings that date from this era. North Norfolk Railway used to serve the village, ferrying holidaymakers to the coast and the excellent beach here but the branch line was axed in 1964. The lack of public transport has meant that Mundesley's star has waned, although it has not lost its old-world charm, with well-maintained thatched roofs, stone walls and quaint cottages. Because the village is set in a slight dip in the hills, you can gain good views across the whole of it and right the way to Happisburgh lighthouse just by climbing a little way out of town.

On the seafront stands **Mundesley Maritime Museum** (🖳 mundesleymaritimemuseum.co.uk; June-mid Sep Sun-Fri 11am-1pm & 2-4pm), a (very) small museum housed in what was a coastguard lookout but these days is manned by local volunteers. It has displays of village history as well as information on the coastguards, lifeboats, shipwrecks and fishing industry in the area.

The **cinema** in Coronation Hall, on Cromer Rd, has occasional screenings and is also home to the Mundesley Players, who stage regular productions.

Services and transport

The **village store** (Mon-Fri 6am-5.30pm, Sat 6am-1pm, Sun 6am-noon), at 15 High St, also contains a **post office** and offers **cashback**. There's a Spar **supermarket** (daily 7am-10pm) with an **ATM** in the wall as well. Coastal **Pharmacy** (☎ 01263-720585; Mon-Fri 8.30am-1pm & 2-6pm, Sat 8.30am-1pm) is on the High St.

You can get tourist information and leaflets on the area from the volunteer-staffed **Visitor Advice Centre** (☎ 01263-721070, 🖳 mundesley-visitor-advice-centre.norfolkparishes.gov.uk; Mar/Apr-end Oct Mon-Sat 10am-4pm, Sun till 3pm) in the Station Rd car park.

Sanders Coaches Nos 4 & 34 **bus** services call here; see box p54 for details.

Where to stay

The majority of accommodation is holiday homes but **B&B** is available at *The Durdans* (Map 49; ☎ 01263-722225, 🖳 the durdans.co.uk; 1S/4D/1T, mostly en suite, 1D private bathroom; ☕; WI-FI) to the south of the village, is a family run B&B in an imposing Edwardian house with grounds of over two acres. The rooms are tastefully and thoughtfully furnished; they charge £37.50-60pp (sgl £50-60, sgl occ from £65).

There are also **hotel** options including *Manor Hotel* (☎ 01263-720309, 🖳 manor hotelmundesley.co.uk; 3S/14D/2D or T/3T, all en suite; ☞; WI-FI; (Ⓛ); 🐾), on Beach Rd, a Victorian hotel whose traditionally styled rooms start from £55pp (sgl/sgl occ from £65/70-75) for B&B, and, on Paston Rd, *The Royal Hotel* (☎ 01263-720096, 🖳

royal-hotel-mundesley.co.uk; 1S/3D/1T, six suites sleeping up to two and one suite with a single bed, all en suite; ☞; WI-FI; 🐾), whose claim to fame is that Lord Nelson frequented its 16th-century bar. The rooms are simple but comfortable, with B&B for £50-67.50pp (sgl from £65, sgl occ £70-135).

Where to eat and drink

On the stretch of sand by the beach huts there's a *Beach Café* (generally May to mid Sep Mon-Sat 10am-5pm, Sun 9am-5pm, but check on their Facebook page) selling snacks, sandwiches, cold drinks and ice-creams.

If you're after a seafood snack try *Lobster Pot*, a seasonal seafood van in the central car park selling mussels, whelks, prawns, crab, lobster, cockles and jellied eels.

On the main Beach Rd drag, try *Jonet Bakery & Café* (daily during the summer for breakfast 9-11am and lunch noon-3pm), or pop into the bright *Corner House Café* (Mon-Sat 9.30am-4.30pm, Sun 10am-3pm), at 2-4 Cromer Rd, for snacks, sandwiches and Cromer crab followed by pancakes and waffles.

For something more substantial head into the relaxed *Ship Inn* (☎ 01263-722671, 🖥 mundesley-ship.co.uk; WI-FI, 🐾), which overlooks the sea and has been in operation for round 300 years. Meals (Mon-Sat noon-3pm & 6-9pm, Sun noon-8pm) consists of fresh seaside cuisine cooked simply. Along with fish & chips (£11.95) and the ubiquitous burger (£10.95), dishes might include pan-seared haddock with mustard rarebit sauce (£13.50).

The Manor Hotel has a restaurant (Mon-Sat noon-2pm & 6-9pm, Sun noon-3pm & 6-9pm) serving pub grub, steaks and offering a carvery on Sunday lunch.

ROUTE GUIDE AND MAPS

MUNDESLEY TO SEA PALLING   [MAPS 49-55]

This **10-mile (16km; 4hr) stretch** sees you return to the beach for an extended trek along the shoreline. It can be readily combined with the previous section of path to make for a longer walk. Be aware though that unlike on the previous stage, parts of this section of path can't be fully traversed at high tide. With this in mind, check the **high-tide timings** (see p84) before you start.

Beyond Beach Café (see map p201) you follow the sand below a series of crumbling cliffs. The reason there's no inland route here is that above you

45 MINS FROM/TO MUNDESLEY (MAP 49)

BACTON

49

PATH FOLLOWS THE BEACH BELOW A SERIES OF CRUMBLING CLIFFS

MAP 50

0   1/4 mile
0   APPROX SCALE   500m

GROYNES ALL ALONG BEACH

068

BACTON GAS TERMINALS

B1159

ALTERNATIVE HIGH TIDE ROUTE

069

SEA WALL

51

BACTON

trailblazer

stands a 200-acre expanse of gas pipeline terminals (Bacton Gas Terminals) that are fenced off and inaccessible. After this obstacle, there is the potential to duck inland if the tide is high or you can stay on the beach, climbing onto a raised path that sits at the back of the beach, above the sand and sea defences.

Follow this as you approach **Bacton**, a slightly uninspiring seaside village fronted by a ramshackle array of tired looking houses and caravan stays, where a sea wall develops. At the start of this stands the friendly, accommodating *Poacher's Pocket* (☎ 01692-650467, 🖳 bacton-norfolk.co.uk; 2D/3T, all en suite; WI-FI bar only; 🐾), a pub-restaurant that also has five comfortable chalets (£34pp, sgl occ £48), situated at the rear of the pub, which have panoramic views overlooking the coast. The pub serves good **pub grub** (daily noon-2.30pm & 6-9pm; mains from £12.95) daily in its upstairs restaurant.

Just outside Bacton on the inland side of the village are the partial **remains of Broomholm Priory**, which was established by William de Glanvill for the Cluniac order (see box p89) in 1113; it achieved an enormous amount of popularity with pilgrims when the monks claimed to have a piece of the True Cross. Much of it is now in ruins, though a medieval gateway and arch survives.

Beyond here, follow the coast road as it passes out of Bacton and straight into **Walcott**.

WALCOTT   [MAP 51, p204]

On this fairly unappealing stretch of road lined with caravan parks you'll find *Kingfisher Fish Bar* (☎ 01692-652999; summer Tue-Thur noon-2pm & 5-7.30pm, Fri-Sat till 8pm, Sun noon-7pm, winter hours variable) offering up traditional fish & chips to eat overlooking the sea.

Next door is the basic *Kingfisher Café* (☎ 01692-651431; Jun-Sep Mon-Fri 10am-6pm, Sat & Sun 9am-6pm, rest of year Tue-Fri 10am-3pm, Sat & Sun 9am-3pm; WI-FI; 🐾) where you can pick up coffee, cakes, sandwiches and lunchtime snacks.

On the same stretch is a toilet block and **Mace Convenience Store** (Mon-Sat 8.30am-8pm, Sun 9am-8pm), which has a **post office** (Mon-Tue & Thur-Fri 9am-1pm & 2-5pm, Wed 9am-1pm, Sat 9am-12.30pm); there's also an **ATM** inside the store.

Sanders Coaches' No 34 **bus** service calls here; see box p54 for details.

Step off the road at **Walcott Gap**, a point where there's beach access for vehicles, and start to hug the beach once more, either trekking along the sands or sticking to the raised walkway at the back of the beach. At **Ostend Gap** turn inland up a dirt track, walking adjacent to a field full of static caravans. Briefly join Ostend Rd on a bend and quickly turn right into Coastline Village, another caravan holiday park. Walk through the statics, following a tarmac path to the clifftops, then strike out along them, watching out for the fact that here they are exposed and at risk from erosion after severe weather, making them potentially unstable.

As you approach the lovely village of **Happisburgh** (see p204) you'll see a large church, St Mary The Virgin, ahead and beyond that the town's famous red-and-white ringed lighthouse (see p205). After another caravan park, cliff damage forces you to cut inland on a trail that goes past a pub and a coffee shop.

At a junction turn left onto The Street and walk through the village, which is a pretty place, with traditional flint and thatch cottages lining the narrow

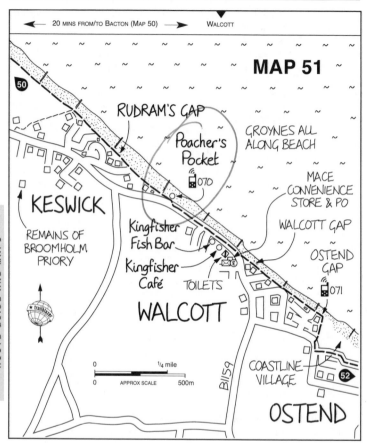

MAP 51

20 MINS FROM/TO BACTON (MAP 50) ⟶   WALCOTT

50

RUDRAM'S GAP

GROYNES ALL ALONG BEACH

Poacher's Pocket

📱070

MACE CONVENIENCE STORE & PO

KESWICK

REMAINS OF BROOMHOLM PRIORY

WALCOTT GAP

OSTEND GAP

📱071

Kingfisher Fish Bar

Kingfisher Café

TOILETS

WALCOTT

0   ¼ mile
0   APPROX SCALE   500m

B1159

COASTLINE VILLAGE

52

OSTEND

ROUTE GUIDE AND MAPS

lanes. Turn left onto Beach Rd and walk to the car park at its end, where you'll find a modern toilet block.

From the car park, you'll have more superb views of the lighthouse nearby.

HAPPISBURGH   [MAP 52]

Happisburgh is pronounced in typical Norfolk fashion as '**Haisbro**'.

At the commanding 15th-century **St Mary's the Virgin church** you can ascend the 133 steps of the tower (Apr-Sep assorted dates Sun, Mon and Wed usually 1-4pm; £2/1 adult/child) to look out over the area;

they claim that on a clear day, from the top you can see 30 churches, 2 lighthouses, 7 water towers, 5 corn mills, 3 wind farms, a radar installation, gas terminal and even the Cathedral spire in Norwich some 16 miles away. The other St Mary church here is an historic property.

MAP 52

PATH ALONG CLIFF TOPS

GROYNES ALL ALONG BEACH

Happisburgh Halt Coffee Shop

CARAVAN PARK

The Hill House Inn

ST MARY THE VIRGIN

072

BEACH RD

ALTERNATIVE ROUTE THROUGH VILLAGE AS CLIFF IS DAMAGED

ST MARY'S

THE STREET

073

HAPPISBURGH

0   ¼ mile
0   APPROX SCALE   500m

CAR PARK, TOILETS & PLAYGROUND

HAPPISBURGH LIGHTHOUSE

ROUTE GUIDE AND MAPS

Happisburgh Lighthouse, dating from 1791, is the oldest working lighthouse on the Norfolk Coast and the only independently operated lighthouse in the UK having been declared redundant in 1987. It's well worth taking the time to pick up the little worn path to the lighthouse and wander around it. The building itself is open to the public on occasional Sundays and Bank Holidays throughout the summer.

The vertiginous climb to the top of 96 stone steps (£3/1 adult/child) reveals stunning panoramic views of the coast and surrounding countryside. You can also see the working lamp, which emits 500 watts of light that are visible for about 18 miles.

The Hill House Inn (☎ 01692-650004, 🖳 hillhouseinn.co.uk; 2D, both en suite; WI-FI bar only; ⓛ; 🐾) is a traditional Grade II-listed 16th-century country inn.

There's a double room in the **Coach House** and the **converted 1901 signal box**, which sleeps up to four people, has a 21ft panoramic window overlooking the coast. Both have their own entrance and **B&B** costs from £37.50pp (sgl occ from £45). On tap are well-kept ales, some that have travelled only as far as from the Dancing Men Brewery on site. The brewery name derives from the Sherlock Holmes' story *The Adventure of the Dancing Men*, which legend has it was conceived by Sir Arthur Conan Doyle here in 1905 while he took a sabbatical at The Hill House. Sample a drop of Cliffhanger or Soggy Seagull as you pause out front of the pub or in the leafy beer gardens to the rear. If the weather is against you, take refuge by the open fire. The pub kitchen (**food** daily noon-2.30pm,

Mon-Sat 7-9.30pm, Sun 7-9pm) serves up seasonal ingredients, locally sourced meats and freshly caught fish alongside typical bar snacks.

Adjoining the pub and accessed via the courtyard to the beer garden is *Happisburgh Halt Coffee Shop* (☎ 01692-651374; Easter-end Oct Fri 8am-4pm, Sat to 5pm, Sun 8am-7pm, Mon 8am-noon, winter Sat 8am-noon, Sun 8am-7pm; WI-FI), a modern, bright café with a breakfast menu and popular Sunday Carvery (2-7pm). There's a range of tasty homemade cakes to choose from along with a variety of teas and coffee and a small bar. At the weekend the menu features locally sourced meats as well as a vegetarian option.

Sanders Coaches' No 34 **bus** service calls here; see box p54 for details.

Once you've marvelled at the lighthouse, drop down from the car park to the beach on a sandy ramp, where you'll find a beautiful and unspoilt bay. Happisburgh has always had serious problems with coastal erosion as the soft clay and gravel cliffs are very vulnerable. Beneath the sea nearby are in fact the remains of a second lighthouse, centuries of lost fields and possibly the entire medieval village of Whimpwell, which was mentioned in the Domesday Book of 1086 but which, by the 18th century, had been deserted and today its location is unknown, believed to have long since surrendered to the sea.

Over more recent years, the village has lost two dozen houses to the erosion – but it has meant the creation of this attractive stretch of sand. Steel and wood defences stretching the length of the beach have slowed the rate of erosion and cut down land loss. Although frangible, the cliffs are ideal for sand martins who, in the summer every year fly thousands of miles from their winter homes in Africa to nest.

❏ **In the footsteps of our ancestors**
Initial erosion and then archaeological excavations on Happisburgh Beach in 2013 have revealed human footprints held fast in the estuarine mud. Analysis of these footprints, the oldest left by humans outside of Africa, showed that ancient humans lived in Britain more than 800,000 years ago, making them the earliest northern Europeans. Evidence uncovered of these early people and their settlement included more than 70 flint tools that have been crafted by hand, with carefully filed sharp edges, possibly for skinning or butchering animals.

The British Museum funded the dig, the results of which pre-date previous discoveries by at least 100,000 years. Fossil plants, pollen and beetles uncovered at the site show that there was a large river, thought to be the Thames at that stage, flowing slowly, with freshwater pools and marshes nearby. Nonetheless life for early residents of the area would doubtless have been tough.

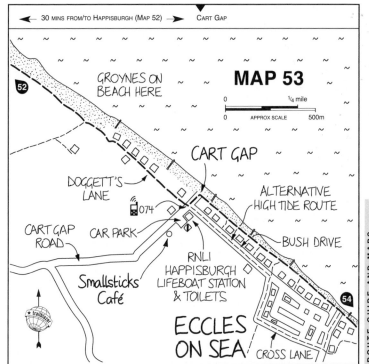

As you walk away from Happisburgh along the beach you come to **Cart Gap**, (Map 53) which is used by the RNLI lifeboats stationed here. About 50m along the road leading to Cart Gap you will find *Smallsticks Café* (☎ 01692-583368, 🖥 smallstickscafe.co.uk; school summer holidays daily 9.30am-5pm, low season closed Tue & Wed, winter Mon & Fri 10am-3.30pm, Sat & Sun 9.30am-4pm; WI-FI), a tea room in a converted barn serving a good selection of drinks, snacks, sandwiches from £5.50, and more substantial meals including steak & ale pie (£9.95), and spinach & mushroom lasagne (£9.25). There's a takeaway service as well. In the car park at Cart Gap there are toilets.

Beyond here there are two onward paths; the **official path** for the next 2½ miles uses the beach but it is impassable during severe weather and for two hours either side of some high tides. During these times use the signed **alternative route** that passes slightly inland, behind a sea defence wall. There are various exit routes from the beach through the dunes to this alternative path but you shouldn't rely on escaping this way; check the tide times (see p84) and height before you set off.

Continue along the beach, towards **North Gap** (Map 54). After here a series of man-made offshore reefs, that have been set up to try and combat coastal erosion, are visible. Behind these are small lagoons that create wonderful swimming pools although they are tidal so can have strong currents. From late spring and through the summer months this area of beach is also home to a colony of little terns who nest here – if you encounter a section fenced off please respect the wildlife and walk around the nesting sites.

In the middle of the line of reefs is another access point, Cart Gap, backed by the compact resort village of **Sea Palling** (Map 55; see opposite), equidistant between Cromer and Great Yarmouth. Above the beach here stands an independent lifeboat station and a large ramp. The Coast Path climbs this ramp, which can be secured with a large flood gate in the threat of a tidal surge, and

ROUTE GUIDE AND MAPS

60 MINS BETWEEN CART GAP (MAP 53) AND SEA PALLING (MAP 55)

53

NORTH GAP

075

MAP 54

0   1/4 mile

0   APPROX SCALE   500m

ALTERNATIVE
HIGH TIDE ROUTE

ARTIFICIAL REEFS WITH
MASTS AT EITHER END
OF ROCK REEF LINE

DUNES (LOOK OUT FOR
FENCED-OFF NESTING
SITES)

HEATH
RD

HEMPSTEAD
MARSHES

THE
EYRIE

55

★ trailblazer

descends into the lively little knot of eateries and entertainment buildings here.
There are toilets at the foot of the ramp as well.

SEA PALLING [see map p210]

Sea Palling is a small community in a designated Area of Outstanding Natural Beauty. On account of the nine off-shore reefs built as part of flood prevention, there's an excellent sandy beach, while the town has everything you need for a really good break.

Reefs Bar (☎ 01692-598177, 🖳 reefs bar.com; food Mon-Sat noon-10pm, Sun

noon-9pm; WI-FI; 🐕) serves pub grub such as chilli, chicken curry and a rack of ribs. They host a carvery on Sunday (noon-4pm), featuring a choice of roast meats and a dessert (1/2 courses £6.50/8.95). You'll find live sports showing on the screens and live music most weekends.

Alternatively, pick up classic fish & chips from *Beach Rock Fish & Chip Shop* (daily noon-3pm & 6-11pm), or stop in the adjacent *Beach Rock Café* (summer Mon-Fri 9.30am-5pm, Sat-Sun 9am-6pm), which serves pastries, milkshakes, all-day breakfast, baguettes and jacket potatoes.

Over the road, *Sandy Hills Café* (☎ 01692-598391; summer daily 10am-9pm, winter Mon-Fri 10am-5pm, Sat & Sun 9.30am-6pm) serves all kinds of hot and cold snacks and drinks as well as donuts and ice-creams. There's an **amusement arcade** (summer daily 10am-10pm, winter Mon-Fri to 6pm, Sat & Sun 10am-10pm) next door that has an **ATM** inside.

Inland a little is **Premier Post Office & Stores** (☎ 01692-598235; summer shop Mon-Sat 7.30am-7pm, Sun 8am-6pm, winter Sat to 6pm & Sun to 4pm; post office Mon-Tue & Thur-Fri 9am-1pm & 2-5.30pm, Wed to 1pm and Sat to 12.30pm).

Sanders Coaches' No 34 **bus** service to Stalham picks up from the main road here and from there services operate to Norwich; see box p54 for details.

Although the majority of accommodation here is holiday lets, **B&B** is available at *Rowan Tree House* (☎ 01692-598418, 🖳 rowan-tree-house.co.uk; 1D private facilities; WI-FI; ✂), on Beach Rd, right across from the village post office and store. It has a smart self-contained apartment room (from £35pp, sgl occ room rate) including a light continental breakfast as well as self-catering facilities.

Alternatively try *The Old Vicarage* (☎ 01692-598015, 🖳 theoldvicarage-norfolk.co.uk; 4D/1T, most en suite; WI-FI; ✂), on Church Rd; they charge £32.50-35pp (sgl occ rates on request), including a full English breakfast.

SEA PALLING TO CAISTER-ON-SEA [MAPS 55-60]

Ahead is a **10½-mile (17km; 4½hrs) hike** through some of this area's wildest and most empty coastline, where you'll encounter glorious expanses of sand, big skies and seemingly endless sea. The stretch between Waxham and Winterton-on-Sea is especially good for birdwatching, with twitchers hunkered down amid the dunes to glimpse chiff-chaff, stonechat, cranes and red-throated divers, while Horsey is home to a seal colony right on the shore.

Begin by walking away from the sea up **Beach Rd**. Look for a narrow alley on the left and duck between two houses to emerge on a path that follows the landward side of a dune ridge through a landscape that is typical of this stretch of coast. Wind along the edges of fields, through grassy and scrubby patches and in and out of small thickets of trees.

After a mile briefly join a beach access road before continuing along the coast; if you continue 300m up the road you'll come to **Waxham Great Barn** (☎ 01692-598824; Easter-Oct Mon-Tue & Thur-Sun 10.30am-5pm), a magnificent, fully restored Elizabethan barn that was a dilapidated wreck before a careful restoration project. Built in the last quarter of the 16th century from the remains of several dissolved monasteries, this Grade I-listed barn is the longest in the county, measuring 180ft. Visit when the barn is open during the summer months to take in the exhibition on local life, agriculture, the people who built the barn and the smugglers who operated along the coast. There's also a *café* in a converted cow shed, selling snacks and light lunches.

Return to walking behind the ridge of dunes until you climb up onto them and follow the path as it weaves through the tussocky grasses. There are far-ranging views from this vantage point. You will then pass in front of *Waxham Sands Holiday Park* (Map 56; ☎ 01692-598325, 🖳 waxhamsandsholidaypark .com; 🐾; mid May-end Sep), which has camping pitches adjacent to the dunes and above a half-mile stretch of sandy beach. Rates for a pitch are £14-18 based on up to three adults sharing a tent. There are shower blocks, toilets, a small supermarket, off-licence, launderette and hot food takeaway.

After the campsite, the next five miles passes through a nationally and internationally sensitive wildlife area noted for its unusual acid soils that support a number of rare plants and animals including natterjack toads, breeding and wintering birds, dragonflies and large numbers of fragile mosses, lichens, heather and dune grass.

Arrive at **Horsey Gap**, where there is a car park with a *seasonal snack van*, beach access and a signpost indicating which way to the seal colony found here. The beach itself is very quiet, often populated only by birdwatchers, dog-walkers and the seals who come to bask and breed.

The old smugglers' village of **Horsey** lies about a mile inland but is worth a look for the unusual round-towered, thatched All Saints Church and a chance to grab a pint of Woodforde's and a pie at the welcoming, tucked away *Nelson Head* (☎ 01493-393378, 🖳 thenelsonhead.com; food served summer daily noon-8.30pm, winter Sun-Fri noon-2.30pm & 6-8.30pm, Sat noon-8.30pm; WI-FI; 🐾).

Follow the well-trodden path behind a tall set of sand dunes and alongside a grazing marsh. At various points clamber onto the dunes to check where the **seals** are. The first viewing area is on your left about 10 minutes from the car park having climbed up past an old WWII pillbox; there's a second, bigger and better positioned viewing area about another 15 minutes further on. The colony of grey seals congregates on the beach, affording excellent opportunities to get close (but not too close) to these animals. Although visitors are drawn here in winter (late Oct-Feb, at its busiest in Dec/Jan when the pups are born and the beach is off-limits) when the seals mass at this rookery to breed, more often than not the site is relatively free from crowds and you can observe the seals while you sit quietly on the sand or the sea defence wall. Unlike Blakeney Point or Morston, there are no limits on how long you can stay, how far you can walk and how you can spend your time, making this a special close-up encounter; remember though to stay at least 10m from the seals and don't get between them and the water.

ROUTE GUIDE AND MAPS

45 MINS FROM/TO WAXHAM (MAP 55)

HORSEY GAP

DELPH HILLS

MAP 56

0   ¼ mile
0   APPROX SCALE   500m

DELVE BANK

55

MARRAM HILLS

Waxham Sands Holiday Park

WARREN FARM

GROYNES ON BEACH HERE

WWII PILLBOX

HORSEY GAP CAR PARK & SEASONAL SNACK VAN

☎078

FIRST SEAL COLONY VIEWING POINT

57

HORSEY CORNER

TO HORSEY & NELSON HEAD PUB, 1KM

After you've torn yourself away from the seals, pick up the path as it enters **Winterton Dunes** (Map 58), another important landscape and a National Nature Reserve that is home to little terns, skylarks, night jars and stonechats, as well as adders and natterjack toads. Head towards **Somerton Gap** and climb

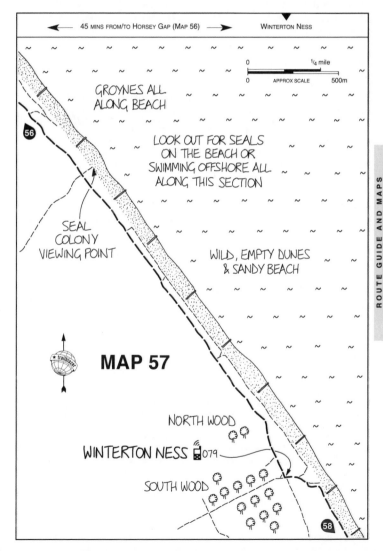

← 45 MINS FROM/TO HORSEY GAP (MAP 56) →

WINTERTON NESS

0   ¼ mile
0   APPROX SCALE   500m

GROYNES ALL ALONG BEACH

LOOK OUT FOR SEALS ON THE BEACH OR SWIMMING OFFSHORE ALL ALONG THIS SECTION

56

SEAL COLONY VIEWING POINT

WILD, EMPTY DUNES & SANDY BEACH

MAP 57

NORTH WOOD

WINTERTON NESS 079

SOUTH WOOD

58

ROUTE GUIDE AND MAPS

again onto the dunes to walk along the ridge, with great opportunities to revel in the perfect interface between sea and sky as you pass through what is a wild and empty section of coast. Onward views reveal the village of **Winterton-on-Sea** (see below), where you are headed. Just before you reach the village, the path drops down to the landward side of the dunes and meanders towards and through a car park, in the corner of which is ***Dunes Café*** (see below). The beach here is vast and you're likely to see seals basking in the waves too. One of the country's biggest populations of little terns nests nearby as well.

WINTERTON-ON-SEA   [MAP 58]

The pretty village is reached by following the road inland, has a post office & store by the name of **Poppy's** (☎ 01493-393238; shop Mon-Sat 6.30am-5.30pm, Sun 7am-1pm; post office Mon-Fri 7am-5pm, Sat 8am-2pm, Sun 9am-noon) on Market Place. **Loomes** (daily 7am-8.30pm) is a handy convenience shop with an **ATM**. For general information visit 🖳 wintertononsea.co.uk.

First Norfolk & Suffolk's No 1/1A **bus** service calls here; see box p54 for details.

The excellent ***Dunes Café*** (☎ 01493-394931; Feb-end Oct daily 9am-5pm, rest of year Thur-Sun only) is right on the Path. Breakfast is available 9-11.30am while lunch is served 11.30am-3pm.

There's also a decent chip shop, ***Winterton Fish Bar*** (☎ 01493-393302; end May-Sep Mon-Sat noon-1.30pm, Mon-Thur 5-8pm, Fri & Sat from 4.30pm, Sun 5-7pm, winter Tue & Thur noon-1.30pm & 5-7pm, Wed 5-7pm, Fri noon-1.30pm & 4.30-8pm, Sat noon-1.30pm & 5-7.30pm).

You can also eat well at the picturesque village pub, ***Fisherman's Return*** (☎ 01493-393305, 🖳 fishermansreturn.com; 5D/1T, all en suite; ▼; WI-FI; 🐾), a 330-year-old brick-and-flint freehouse, which specialises in real ales and fish dishes and has a handful of rooms upstairs if you're particularly taken with the place. **B&B** including a full English breakfast costs from £50pp (sgl occ from £70). **Food** (summer generally daily noon-9pm, winter Mon-Fri noon-2.30pm & 6-9pm, Sat-Sun noon-9pm) features fish fresh from Lowestoft; look out for home-prepared meals such as fish pie (£11.50), honey roast ham (£10.95) and sirloin steak (£18.95). The log fires in winter make for a cosy atmosphere but note that during the week in the winter the pub is closed in the afternoon.

Although most accommodation is again holiday lets, there is also B&B at ***Burleigh House*** (☎ 01493-393669, 🖳 burleighbandb.co.uk; 3D, all en suite; ▼; WI-FI), where rates are from £31-34.50pp (sgl occ £57-64). They have a self-catering option as well that sleeps up to four (£100-114 for two nights minimum).

From the car park, follow the road inland very briefly before bearing left below a row of pastel-painted roundhouses overlooking the beach. This is ***Hermanus*** (☎ 01493-393216, 🖳 hermanusholidays.com; WI-FI main building only; 🐾) and the unusual buildings here were inspired by a trip to the namesake town in South Africa. Each roundhouse comprises a bedroom, lounge/kitchen and bathroom with shower. Single roundhouses have a double bed and the double ones a twin room and double-bed room. They're a bit basic but are fully furnished and the kitchens are well equipped; they charge from £40/60pp (sgl occ from £80/120) for the single/double roundhouses. They have a range of chalets and apartments as well but these must be booked for a week at a time. There's a restaurant on site, ***The Highwayman*** (food summer Mon-Sat noon-3pm & 5-9pm, winter Fri-Sat 5-9pm, all year Sun noon-4pm but later in summer), which offers home cooking and favourites from flame-grilled burgers and steaks to pasta and fish dishes, with a view of the waves. On Sundays the menu is replaced with a carvery. Separately, ***The Coach and Horses*** (food hours as for The Highwayman) serves a wide range of drinks along with a full menu of meals with some light lunch options. On site there's also a children's play area, launderette, and heated swimming pool (May-early Sep).

MAP 58

GROYNES ON THE BEACH HERE

SOMERTON GAP

0 — ¼ mile

0 — 500m APPROX SCALE

LOOK OUT FOR SEALS ON THE BEACH OR SWIMMING OFFSHORE

SOUTH WOOD

WINTERTON DUNES (NATIONAL NATURE RESERVE)

COASTGUARD LOOK OUT

CAR PARK & Dunes Café

080

Burleigh House B&B

LOOMES STORES

BEACH RD

WINTERTON-ON-SEA

Winterton Fish Bar

Hermanus

POPPY'S (PO & STORE)

Fisherman's Return

THE VALLEY

HEMSBY RD

DUNES

★ trailblazer

45 MINS FROM/TO WINTERTON NESS (MAP 57)

WINTERTON-ON-SEA

45 MINS TO/FROM HEMSBY (MAP 59)

ROUTE GUIDE AND MAPS

57

59

Enter an attractive grassy expanse known as **The Valley** and walk through pretty meadows edged by ferns. With only low-lying scrub and vegetation, it's a good spot for birdwatching, especially when raptors are on the hunt. Jarringly though, at the far end of The Valley is a car park bordered by a large funfair. **Hemsby**, which is surrounded by holiday parks, is something of a culture shock after the quiet emptiness of the earlier section of coast but a good warm-up for the 'lively' charms of Great Yarmouth to come. The village itself is extremely touristy and has a range of amusements, rides, *beach cafés* and fast-food joints; First Norfolk & Suffolk's Nos 1/1A & 1B **bus** services call here; see pp51-4. This is also another popular East Norfolk beach although out of season it is a different place, with hardly anyone around. The Coast Path continues along this stretch of sand, although there's an alternative inland path as well for when the beach is inaccessible as a result of severe weather, or during some high tides.

Having stepped onto the sand, continue to **Scratby** (First Norfolk & Suffolk's Nos 1/1A & 1B **bus** services also call here; see pp51-4), and then on again to California all the while following the line of the dunes at the back of the beach. The alternative high-tide route tracks behind the dunes, parallel to the beach as far as California as well. On the beach, the soft sand underfoot makes the going relatively slow but gives you time to enjoy the surroundings. By the time you reach California (Map 60; the bus services also call here!), chalk cliffs have started to rise up and replace the dunes, adding an extra sense of separation from the villages above.

Beyond California Gap the path follows the route of a dismantled railway that runs along the top of a sea wall and parallel to the shore for a short distance as you approach the outskirts of **Caister-on-Sea**.

CAISTER-ON-SEA   [MAP 60, p219]

Caister, which is essentially a suburb of Great Yarmouth, has a similar appeal as Hemsby. It's a little more historic though, with the **remains of a Roman fort** hidden rather unglamorously behind some houses. The fort, built around AD200 to see off Saxon raiders, is free to view, but all that's left are some low walls, labelled to help you build up an impression of the site. The name Caister though comes from the Latin *castrum*, meaning 'camp'. There's also a ruined 15th-century moated castle nearby; built between 1432 and 1446, **Caister Castle** (🖳 caistercastle.co.uk; mid May-end Sep Sun-Fri 10am-4.30pm; £15) belonged to Sir John Falstaff, the inspiration for Shakespeare's character, before it was grabbed by the Duke of Norfolk. These days it houses a giant private collection of motor vehicles.

Just after you reach the fringes of the town the tarmac path you've been following ends suddenly, just beyond a toilet block, and you drop back down onto the beach.

The Lifeboat Station at **Caister Point**, at the southern end of Caister, is manned by a proudly independent coastal rescue crew.

The Old Shed has been converted into a **museum** (mid Apr-Oct Wed & Sun 10am-3.30pm; £2 adults) that documents the triumphs and tragedies of the Caister lifeboatmen through the years. Look out for the apt motto of these courageous rescuers above the door of the new building that states, 'Never turn back'.

First Norfolk & Suffolk's No 1/1A & 1B **bus** services call here; see pp51-4.

MAP 59

0   ¼ mile
0   APPROX SCALE   500m

CARAVAN PARK

THE MARRAMS

CAR PARK & FUNFAIR

AMUSEMENT ARCADES & HOLIDAY PARKS

HOLIDAY VILLAGE

FAST FOOD & BEACH CAFÉ OUTLETS & TOILETS

LIFEBOAT STATION 📱081

BEACH RD

HEMSBY

CARAVAN PARKS

PATH ON BEACH

ALTERNATIVE HIGH TIDE ROUTE

SCRATBY RD

SCRATBY

★ trailblazer

📱082

BEACH RD

TOILETS

45 MINS TO/FROM WINTERTON-ON-SEA (MAP 58)

HEMSBY

30 MINS

SCRATBY

ROUTE GUIDE AND MAPS

CAISTER-ON-SEA TO HOPTON-ON-SEA [MAPS 60-64]

This final **10-mile (16km; 4hr) stretch** provides a stark contrast to some of the empty beaches elsewhere as it detours inland and crosses Great Yarmouth, revealing the city's industrial past, before returning to the coast via a hidden gem of a beach and making its way to the end point of the Norfolk Coast Path. It is worth being aware in advance that there are no facilities at Hopton-on-Sea and you will therefore have to return to Gorleston or Great Yarmouth, or make a connection with a local bus.

Beyond Caister lifeboat station wander along the edge of the **Great Yarmouth North Denes SSSI**. Beware the sign at the lifeboat station advising that you are a mile from Great Yarmouth though; this brings you to the furthest edge of the city, which is large and sprawling and doesn't begin in earnest for several miles beyond that point. Follow the path through the dunes, which are an important habitat for little tern colonies, who come here to breed.

As you make your way through the dunes you'll start to see ahead the cranes and working buildings of the port at the mouth of the estuary that bisects Great Yarmouth. North of the town is **Great Yarmouth Racecourse** (Map 61). You'll also pass in front of enormous holiday parks and massed ranks of static caravans. Eventually you will come to the end of a tarmac road adjacent to the entrance for the enormous Seashore Holiday Village; this is North Drive and you will follow it for a little over two miles into Great Yarmouth, tracking alongside the beach until you're almost in the town. However, if staying at *Barnard House* (see p224) it is best to reach it from here.

Once in town you'll step onto a promenade and continue south, past water gardens, car parks and bowling greens until you come to **Britannia Pier**, jutting out into the sea of sand. There are public toilets here along with a fun park and theatre. Pass under the pier and continue onto **Great Yarmouth**'s seafront.

GREAT YARMOUTH [see map p223]

Great Yarmouth stands at odds with many of the towns and villages you will have walked through so far. Brash and boisterous, it's a bit like an East Anglian Blackpool but without the packs of drunken lads and hen parties. Seaside tat stretches from the pier all along the length of Regent Rd to the Pleasure Beach.

Although it's a tacky, neon spectacle for much of the year, people flock here for old-fashioned bucket-and-spade fun and the chance to paddle in the sea, much as holidaymakers have done since the late Victorian era when the town rose to fame as a resort. Prior to that though, the town grew rich on the back of the herring fishing industry. The River Yare, a channel parallel

to the coast, provided a safe harbour and lucrative port over the years, as it led to the network of inland waterways leading to Norwich.

The fishing industry started in the 10th century and expanded through the Middle Ages, making Great Yarmouth one of the wealthiest towns in England. In the early 20th century as many as a thousand fishing boats still sought the 'silver darlings' as the herring were known. Since then though, much like most of the seafaring coast that relied on fishing, the town suffered during the post-war period as the industry faded out, its decline slowed by the North Sea oil industry and rise of tourism as an alternative. *(cont'd on p222)*

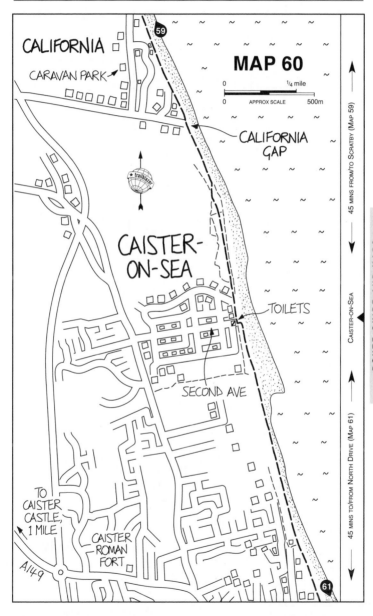

CALIFORNIA

CARAVAN PARK

MAP 60

0   ¼ mile

APPROX SCALE   500m

CALIFORNIA GAP

CAISTER-ON-SEA

TOILETS

SECOND AVE

TO CAISTER CASTLE, 1 MILE

CAISTER ROMAN FORT

A149

59

61

45 MINS FROM/TO SCRATBY (MAP 59)

CAISTER-ON-SEA

45 MINS TO/FROM NORTH DRIVE (MAP 61)

ROUTE GUIDE AND MAPS

MAP 61

MAP 62

0 — 1/4 mile
0 — 500m
APPROX SCALE

RIVER BURE

GREAT YARMOUTH
SEE TOWN PLAN

RAILWAY STATION

BRIDGE RD
📱 086

YARMOUTH WAY

A1243

RIVER YARE

SOUTH QUAY

SOUTHTOWN ROAD

ST GEORGE'S PARK

TRAFALGAR RD

61

NORTH BEACH

CRESCENT GARDENS

NORTH DRIVE

THE WATERWAYS

TOILETS

📱 085

BRITANNIA PIER

MARINE PARADE

THE JETTY

SEA LIFE CENTRE

WELLINGTON PIER

PLEASURE BEACH

63

45 MINS FROM/TO START OF NORTH DRIVE (MAP 61)

BRITANNIA PIER

90 MINS TO/FROM GORLESTON-ON-SEA (MAP 63)

★ trailblazer

ROUTE GUIDE AND MAPS

(cont'd from p218) There are impressive architectural remnants from Great Yarmouth's heyday along with one of the most complete medieval town walls in the country, built between 1261 and 1400, although much of the town was flattened by bombing in 1942.

The **heritage quarter** has merchant houses that are more than 400 years old and a few museums. The best of these are: **Nelson Museum** (☎ 01493-850698, 🖳 nelson-museum.co.uk; Feb-mid Nov Mon-Thur 10am-4pm, Fri & Sun 1-4pm; £4.25), on South Quay, which has an impressive collection of paintings and memorabilia associated with the naval hero; **Elizabethan House Museum** (Apr-end Oct Sun-Fri 10am-4pm; £5.20, free for NT members), also on South Quay, which offers a glimpse into what life in Tudor times would have been like; and **Time & Tide Museum** (☎ 01493-743930; Mon-Fri 10am-4pm, Sat & Sun noon-4pm; £5.70), on Blackfriars Rd, which describes Great Yarmouth's history and looks at the impact of the herring industry. For details of both of these see 🖳 museums.norfolk.gov.uk.

Look out too for the 169ft-high **Nelson Monument** (Map 63), on Ferner Rd/Monument Rd towards the southern end of the peninsula, overlooking the mouth of the river; there's a slim spiral staircase to the top although the monument is open irregularly.

Go to **Scroby Sands Offshore Windfarm Visitor Centre** (May-Oct daily 10am-4pm) for the Scroby Sands offshore wind farm on North Drive if you're interested in learning more about renewable energy and the giant windmills generating enough electricity to power 30,000 homes.

Elsewhere there's quirky shopping along **Market Row** and its neighbouring streets. The main draw though is the front and its great expanse of sand and sea, broken up by three piers. At the northern end is the fun-filled **Britannia Pier** (🖳 britannia-pier .co.uk), which has been rebuilt several times over its 160-year history, twice after being hit by ships and cut in two. The quiet **jetty** is a popular fishing spot, while the 1854 **Wellington Pier** (🖳 wellington-pier.co.uk) in the south is the oldest of the three.

The wide seafront promenade, Marine Parade is stacked with attractions, ranging from **Pleasure Beach** amusement park (🖳 pleasure-beach.co.uk) to the **Sea Life Centre** (🖳 visitsealife.com/great-yarmouth) and **Merrivale Model Village** (🖳 merrivalemodelvillage.co.uk).

Services

To find out about the town's attractions as well as the various historic buildings and their accessibility, visit the **tourist information centre** (☎ 01493-846346, 🖳 great-yarmouth.co.uk; late Mar to end Oct Mon-Sat 9.30am-5.30pm, Sun 10.30am-4pm, rest of year Mon-Fri 9am-1pm & 2-4.30pm) on the seafront. They have information about accommodation and are able to make bookings.

There's a **post office** within WH Smith at 183 King St. **Banks** and **ATMs** for most branches can be found, most often on Market Place or King St. There's a Premier **convenience store** (daily 6.30am-11pm) at 18 St Peter's Rd, and a Lidl **supermarket** (Mon-Sat 8am-9pm, Sun 10am-4pm) on Pasteur Rd. There's a permanent covered **market** (Mon-Sat), in the centre as well, with a large area of pedestrianised space, part cobbled, part paved and surrounded by historical buildings.

Transport

Greater Anglia's Wherry Line connects Great Yarmouth with Norwich; there are regular **train** services (see box p48) and the journey takes about 30 minutes.

National Express (NX375 & 491) **coaches** call here; see box p49.

First Norfolk & Suffolk's operates several **bus** services (1/1A/1B/X1/X11) from here to surrounding towns and villages. Sanders Coaches bus No 6 also calls here. See pp51-4 for details.

Where to stay

There are lots of **B&Bs** just back from the front, particularly clustered on Trafalgar Rd.

Alternatively, *Classic Lodge* (☎ 01493-852851, 🖳 classiclodge.com; 3D, all en suite; WI-FI), at 13 Euston Rd, has original Victorian features and rich fabrics

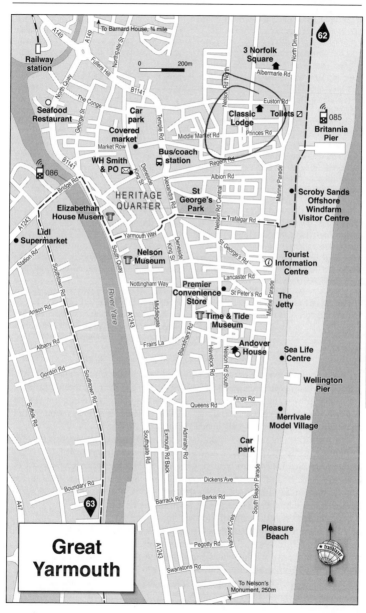

in good-sized rooms with B&B from £27.50pp (sgl occ £45).

Barnard House (Map 61; ☎ 01493-855139, 🖳 barnardhouse.com; 2D/1T, all en suite; WI-FI), at 2 Barnard Crescent, is more modern and a touch more stylish, with well-appointed rooms and they welcome walkers. B&B costs £37.50-40pp (sgl occ £55-60).

Smarter though is *Andover House* (☎ 01493-843490, 🖳 andoverhouse.co.uk; 1S/6D/1T, all en suite; WI-FI), at 28-30 Camperdown, which has a youthful attitude and stylish rooms that stand out from the competition in Great Yarmouth. Rates for B&B are £39.50-54.50pp (sgl from £69, sgl occ room rate).

Alternatively, seek out *3 Norfolk Square* (☎ 01493-843042, 🖳 3norfolk square.co.uk; 1S/1T/6D, all en suite; WI-FI), which has an adults-only policy and a quiet, indulgent atmosphere as a result. The rooms are large and attractive, with B&B for £37.50-55pp (sgl/sgl occ from £60).

Where to eat and drink

The town is full of masses of interchangeable cafés, fast-food outlets and restaurants. Browse the menus and pick one that takes your fancy.

For a more imaginative meal try *Copper Kitchen* (🖳 copperkitchen.co.uk; food Mon-Sat 6.30-9pm) in **Andover House** (see Where to stay). Perhaps start with a ham-hock scotch egg (£6.75), or pork belly with pickled pear (£6.75), followed by woodland mushroom & ale pie (£12.75), or smoked haddock cannelloni (£13.50). Andover House's *bar* (daily 11am-11pm) specialises in gin but serves Adnams ales as well.

Despite the town's heritage, there's a dearth of decent places to eat freshly caught fish. The best bet is the *Seafood Restaurant* (☎ 01493-856009, 🖳 theseafood.co.uk; Mon-Fri noon-1.45pm, Mon-Sat 6-10.30pm; closed on bank hol Mons and for two weeks at the end of May), at 85 North Quay, which offers fish of the day dishes (from £22.50), shellfish such as king scallops (£24) and lobster (from £39).

Or duck into a pub for a drink; *The Mariners* (Sun-Fri noon-midnight, Sat from 11am), on Howard St South, is worth seeking out for its range of decent real ales, while *St John's Head* (☎ 01493-843443, 🖳 stjohnsheadrealalepub.co.uk; WI-FI; 🐾; daily noon-10.30pm), on North Quay, is a long-established and traditional pub.

To carry on down the coast you will need to cross the estuary and the River Yare. To do so involves negotiating your way across Great Yarmouth, no easy feat, especially as the signage for the Coast Path is quite limited here, with the finger boards you've been following replaced by stickers of the National Trail acorn icon stuck on lamp-posts instead.

Beyond Britannia Pier join Marine Parade and head down the broad pavement towards the Marina, where you will turn inland on Trafalgar Rd. If you get as far as the Sea Life Centre you've gone too far. Follow Trafalgar Rd past St George's Park before branching left onto Yarmouth Way and arriving at the edge of the estuary. Turn right on South Quay and head up river until you reach Bridge Rd, which is the first crossing point on the River Yare.

On the far side of the river follow the main road for a short while until you turn left onto Southtown Rd, which runs parallel to the Yare and heads down river. Stay on this route as it passes through residential and industrial neighbourhoods that are a world away from the South Beach pleasure palaces just a stone's throw from here, until you come to the mouth of the estuary, opposite the working port. The scenery on this side of the isthmus is a stark contrast to the wild landscapes elsewhere, with run-down warehouses, rough-looking

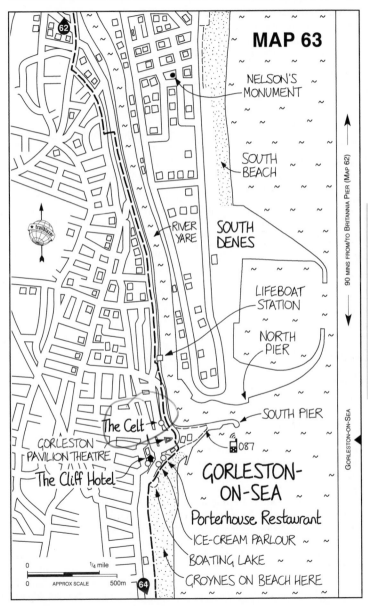

MAP 63

NELSON'S MONUMENT

SOUTH BEACH

RIVER YARE

SOUTH DENES

LIFEBOAT STATION

NORTH PIER

SOUTH PIER

The Celt

GORLESTON PAVILION THEATRE

The Cliff Hotel

087

GORLESTON-ON-SEA

Porterhouse Restaurant

ICE-CREAM PARLOUR

BOATING LAKE

GROYNES ON BEACH HERE

0   1/4 mile

0   APPROX SCALE   500m

90 MINS FROM/TO BRITANNIA PIER (MAP 62)

ROUTE GUIDE AND MAPS

GORLESTON-ON-SEA

working yards and a semi-abandoned air to the streets but they provide an interesting insight into the state of the town.

To the south of the estuary here is **Gorleston-on-Sea**; pause on the quay to look across the estuary at the port and witness a modern example at work.

GORLESTON-ON-SEA
[MAP 63, p225]

Gorleston is the perfect place to decompress after the brashness of Great Yarmouth. It also has far more facilities than Hopton-on-Sea at the end of the Norfolk Coast Path; if you need to stay in the area, this is the best place to base yourself. For information about the village see ▣ lovegorleston.co.uk.

Pass in front of *The Celt* (Sun-Thur 11am-11pm, Fri-Sat to 2am; ✼), freehouse, and round an **amusement arcade** in order to pick up the path south, at which point Gorleston's unexpected 3-mile long beach comes into view. This extensive swathe of soft sand backed by a sea wall with timber groynes is a surprise given the hurly burly of Great Yarmouth and the rust and machinery you've just passed by. Inland you'll find an Edwardian music hall and a traditional seaside theatre.

First Norfolk & Suffolk's 1/1A, X1 and X11 call here as does Sanders Coaches No 6 **bus service** but only in termtime; see pp51-4 for details.

Just back from the beach is *The Cliff Hotel* (☎ 01493-662179, ▣ thecliffhotel.co.uk; 28D/5T/two suites, all en suite; ✿; WI-FI; Ⓛ), a smart property that has rooms from £34pp (sgl occ from £58) without breakfast, and up £62.50pp (sgl occ from £115) if you choose B&B; however, the rates depend on demand and expect to pay much more if you want a suite. If you are feeling peckish you can take advantage of the **bar menu** (daily noon-9.30pm) and eat sandwiches (from £6.50) or pub classics (from £11) on the terrace. The emphasis in the main **restaurant** (food daily noon-2.30pm & 7-9.30pm) is again on trusted staples, cooked well (mains from £16).

Follow the paved promenade past *Porterhouse Restaurant and Rooftop Bar* (☎ 01493-600889; summer daily 9am-9pm, winter Wed-Sun 9am-9pm), an **ice-cream parlour** and a **boating lake**. There's a **beach café**, *Jay Jay's* (Map 64; ☎ 01493-657001; daily 8am-5pm, winter Mon-Fri from 8.30am; WI-FI) along the promenade that is also open later during the summer and fully licensed.

It's then a simple walk down the beach, taking time to embrace the sea air and views out across the North Sea. Although it's just next door to the bustle of Great Yarmouth, this broad expanse offers a much quieter, less crowded alternative to the busy beaches up the coast.

As the final houses of Gorleston fall away, step onto the beach and make your way down it below Corton Cliffs. Just as you approach Hopton-on-Sea there's an alternative high-tide route to the finish point that ducks inland and loops around the giant Holiday Village that sits on the cliff-top overlooking this last length of the route.

Just inland of here is **Hopton-on-Sea** (see p228). If you can, continue on the beach though to see the route to its conclusion. Beyond a ramp that climbs up to the Holiday Village you have the very last leg, a short section of sand that brings you to **League Hole**. Here, at the point that Beach Rd accesses the sand and just before the historic Potters Resort holiday camp, the Norfolk Coast Path concludes.

To the south of Beach Rd the coast curves to a cliff-face that enters Suffolk although the beach can't currently be followed into the neighbouring county

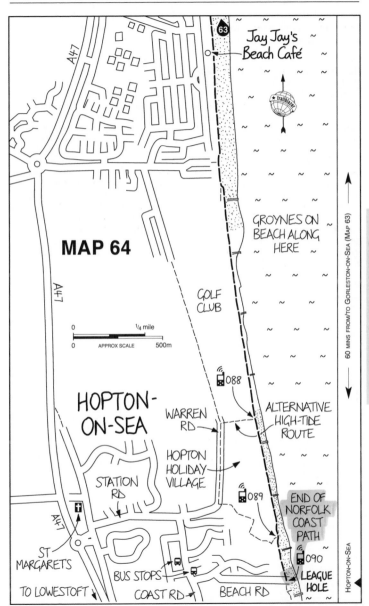

MAP 64

HOPTON-
ON-SEA

Jay Jay's
Beach Café

63

GROYNES ON
BEACH ALONG
HERE

GOLF
CLUB

0   ¼ mile

0   500m
APPROX SCALE

088

WARREN
RD

ALTERNATIVE
HIGH-TIDE
ROUTE

HOPTON
HOLIDAY
VILLAGE

STATION
RD

089

END OF
NORFOLK
COAST
PATH

090

ST
MARGARET'S

BUS STOPS

LEAGUE
HOLE

TO LOWESTOFT

COAST RD

BEACH RD

60 MINS FROM/TO GORLESTON-ON-SEA (MAP 63)

HOPTON-ON-SEA

ROUTE GUIDE AND MAPS

because of storm damage. You will be able to continue on The England Coast path in due course, when a route has been opened as part of the project. But for now, why would you want to leave Norfolk anyway?

HOPTON-ON-SEA   [MAP 64, p227]

Hopton-on-Sea is a small village some five miles south of Great Yarmouth, close to the UK's most easterly point, Lowestoft Ness. The village itself is fairly basic with no real facilities for the walker, meaning that you'll have to backtrack to Gorleston or Great Yarmouth to celebrate the end of the route, stay overnight, or pick up an onward connection. There is a regular if infrequent bus service; First Norfolk & Suffolk's 1/1A, X1 and 922 **bus** services call here as does Simonds No 338; see pp51-4 for details. They provide options for onward travel to Lowestoft, Great Yarmouth and Bury St Edmunds. Hopton once had its own railway station, linking it to Great Yarmouth but this has closed down.

Most visitors come to stay at the giant **Hopton Holiday Village** or historic **Potters Resort**. Potters has an interesting history; in 1914 a solicitor, Herbert Potter, won £500 in a newspaper competition and bought this plot of land with its direct beach access to develop into one of the first ever holiday camps, laying out rows of surplus army Nissan huts as accommodation. Every January though Hopton becomes a focus of attention, at least for some sports fans, as players, spectators and the BBC descend on the village for the World Indoor Bowls Championships. Regarded as the biggest event in the bowls calendar, the Championships are held at Potters Resort.

Hopton's greatest appeal though is the quiet, sandy beach, which is best accessed from the village via Beach Road, a narrow tree-lined route to the beach that's just wide enough for a car. It's a challenging three-point turn at the end so best to park in the village and walk down.

APPENDIX A: GPS WAYPOINTS

Each GPS waypoint was taken on the route at the reference number marked on the map as below. This list of GPS waypoints is also available to download from the Trailblazer website (🖥 trailblazer-guides.com)

MAP	REF	WAYPOINTS (N/E)	DESCRIPTION
1	001	52° 23.433' / 00° 51.318'	Finger-post – start of the Peddars Way
1	002	52° 23.800' / 00° 51.411'	Bridge over Little Ouse River (Suffolk/Norfolk border)
1	003	52° 24.648' / 00° 51.386'	A1066 road crossing
2	004	52° 25.289' / 00° 51.254'	Bridge over River Thet
3	005	52° 26.845' / 00° 50.688'	A11 road crossing
4	006	52° 28.783' / 00° 50.152'	Stonebridge
5	007	52° 30.019' / 00° 49.856'	Junction – take dirt track branching right along edge of Stanford Military Training Zone
5	008	52° 31.066' / 00° 49.099'	Thompson Water
7	009	52° 33.413' / 00° 48.217'	Crossroads – take dirt track left
7	010	52° 33.891' / 00° 47.425'	Dirt track meets B1108 – cross over and turn left
8	011	52° 33.933' / 00° 45.791'	Little Cressingham
8	012	52° 34.804' / 00° 45.647'	Crossroads – go straight over
9	013	52° 36.290' / 00° 44.874'	Crossroads – South Pickenham
10	014	52° 36.719' / 00° 44.886'	Path leaves road and continues behind hedge
10	015	52° 37.522' / 00° 44.869'	Join road and turn right – North Pickenham
11	016	52° 39.122' / 00° 43.532'	A47 crossroads
12	017	52° 39.779' / 00° 42.851'	Sporle Road junction – dog leg right
13	018	52° 41.110' / 00° 41.305'	A1065 crossing – take dirt track heading north-west
13	019	52° 41.904' / 00° 41.140'	Bridge over River Nar
13	020	52° 42.210' / 00° 41.267'	Castle Acre, Stocks Green
14	021	52° 43.547' / 00° 40.456'	The path rejoins the road at the crossroads by Old Wicken Cottages
15	022	52° 44.947' / 00° 39.468'	Trig Point, Shepherd's Bush
16	023	52° 46.293' / 00° 38.517'	Crossroads, dirt track to right goes to Great Massingham
17	024	52° 47.892' / 00° 37.530'	A148 road crossing
18	025	52° 50.000' / 00° 36.182'	B1153 road crossing by Anmer Minque
20	026	52° 51.973' / 00° 34.945'	Snettisham–Great Bircham road crossing
20	027	52° 53.402' / 00° 33.972'	Sedgeford–Fring road crossing
21	028	52° 54.081' / 00° 33.547'	B1454, join road and turn right then immediately left by Magazine Cottage
21	029	52° 54.424' / 00° 33.419'	Cross over disused railway crossing
22	030	52° 56.018' / 00° 32.316'	Turn right by Gin Trap Inn, Ringstead
23	031	52° 56.840' / 00° 32.305'	First view of the sea. Junction, leave road to take dirt track branching left
23	032	52° 57.404' / 00° 31.736'	Holme crossroads
23	033	52° 57.973' / 00° 31.449'	Finger-post on Holme Dunes – end of Peddars Way and point where route joins Norfolk Coast Path

MAP	REF	WAYPOINTS (N/E)		DESCRIPTION
25	034	52° 56.433'	00° 29.250'	Start of Norfolk Coast Path
26	035	52° 58.408'	00° 32.374'	Boardwalk (Gore Point, Holme Dunes)
27	036	52° 57.588'	00° 34.752'	Road curves left in Thornham
28	037	52° 56.646'	00° 35.924'	Junction, leave road to take dirt track branching left
28	038	52° 57.022'	00° 37.949'	Dirt track, turn left towards coast
29	039	52° 57.962'	00° 38.234'	Broad Lane meets dirt track along coast, turn right
29	040	52° 57.964'	00° 39.008'	Gate to Branodunum Roman fort
31	041	52° 57.893'	00° 44.715'	Pass East Harbour Way, Burnham Overy Staithe
32	042	52° 58.706'	00° 46.003'	Holkham Beach entrance
33	043	52° 58.167'	00° 48.838'	Holkham Gap; path doglegs
34	044	52° 58.360'	00° 50.851'	Access to Wells Beach via steps
34	045	52° 57.440'	00° 51.070'	Path joins The Quay in Wells-next-the-Sea
37	046	52° 57.448'	00° 59.158'	Morston Quay – where the boat trips to Blakeney Point launch
38	047	52° 57.345'	01° 00.984'	Blakeney Quay – where boat trips depart
39	048	52° 57.804'	01° 02.545'	Path meets dirt track, turn right
39	049	52° 57.173'	01° 02.369'	A149, join road and turn left – Cley
39	050	52° 57.310'	01° 02.656'	Gate to raised sea defence, bear left
39	051	52° 57.927'	01° 02.870'	Cley (shingle) beach, turn right
40	052	52° 57.087'	01° 07.317'	Ministry of Defence installation
41	053	52° 56.933'	01° 08.395'	Car park at bottom of Beach Lane – Weybourne
42	054	52° 56.732'	01° 11.816'	Lookout station
43	055	52° 56.597'	01° 13.498'	Beeston Hill (Beeston Bump)
43	056	52° 56.480'	01° 15.078'	Seaview Café
44	057	52° 56.309'	01° 15.775'	Turn inland for Woodhill Caravan Park
44	058	52° 56.131'	01° 16.813'	Turn right to join Cromer Rd
45	059	52° 55.955'	01° 18.028'	Entrance to Cromer Pier
46	060	52° 55.479'	01° 18.991'	Cromer Lighthouse
46	061	52° 55.210'	01° 20.536'	Path to Overstrand
47	062	52° 54.661'	01° 21.374'	End of Tower Lane
47	063	52° 54.033'	01° 23.026'	Turn right to exit small copse
48	064	52° 53.893'	01° 23.255'	Cross road by church in Trimingham
48	065	52° 53.573'	01° 23.861'	Leave road
48	066	52° 53.193'	01° 25.226'	Turn right to go inland around caravan park
49	067	52° 52.679'	01° 26.273'	Access beach and continue on sand
50	068	52° 51.513'	01° 28.165'	Alternative high-tide route starts
50	069	52° 51.301'	01° 28.574'	Alternative high-tide route ends
51	070	52° 50.705'	01° 29.685'	Poacher's Pocket
51	071	52° 50.333'	01° 30.546'	Ostend Gap
52	072	52° 49.529'	01° 32.027'	Alternative route starts
52	073	52° 49.365'	01° 32.242'	Alternative route ends
53	074	52° 48.799'	01° 33.367'	Turn left to Cart Gap
54	075	52° 48.214'	01° 34.704'	North Gap
55	076	52° 47.383'	01° 36.140'	Cart Gap
55	077	52° 46.784'	01° 37.140'	Turn right, inland; beach access road
56	078	52° 45.535'	01° 39.031'	Horsey Gap car park
57	079	52° 44.178'	01° 40.751'	Winterton Ness
58	080	52° 43.051'	01° 41.896'	Dunes Café, Winterton-on-Sea
59	081	52° 41.704'	01° 42.541'	Lifeboat station

MAP	REF	WAYPOINTS (N/E)	DESCRIPTION
59	082	52° 40.661' / 01° 43.185'	Link to alternative high-tide route by toilets
61	083	52° 38.765' / 01° 44.144'	Caister Lifeboat station
61	084	52° 37.943' / 01° 44.376'	Coastguard Lookout station
62	085	52° 36.491' / 01° 44.298'	Britannia Pier
62	086	52° 36.404' / 01° 43.370'	Bridge over River Yare
63	087	52° 34.304' / 01° 44.159'	Path to South Pier
64	088	52° 32.645' / 01° 44.121'	Alternative high-tide route starts
64	089	52° 32.222' / 01° 44.254'	Alternative high-tide route ends
64	090	52° 32.173' / 01° 44.266'	End of Norfolk Coast Path

APPENDIX B: TAKING A DOG

Both Norfolk Coast Path and Peddars Way are dog-friendly paths and many are the rewards that await those prepared to make the extra effort required to bring their best friend along the trail. However, you shouldn't underestimate the amount of work involved in bringing your pooch to the path. Indeed, just about every decision you make will be influenced by the fact that you've got a dog: how you plan to travel to the start of the trail, where you're going to stay, how far you're going to walk each day, where you're going to rest and where you're going to eat in the evening.

The decision-making begins well before you've set foot on the trail. For starters, you have to ask – and be honest with – yourself: can your dog really cope with walking day after day? And just as importantly, will he or she actually enjoy it?

If you think the answer is yes to both, you need to start preparing accordingly. For one thing, extra thought needs to go into your itinerary. The best starting point is to study the Village & town facilities table on pp36-9 (and the advice below), and plan where to stop, where to eat, where to buy food for your mutt.

Looking after your dog
To begin with, you need to make sure that your dog is fully **inoculated** against the usual doggy illnesses, and also up-to-date with regard to **worm pills** (eg Drontal) and **flea preventatives** such as Frontline – they are, after all, following in the pawprints of many a dog before them, some of whom may well have left fleas or other parasites on the trail that now lie in wait for their next meal to arrive. **Pet insurance** is also a very good idea; if you've already got insurance do check that it will cover a trip such as this.

On the subject of looking after your dog's health, perhaps the most important implement you can take with you is the **plastic tick remover**, available from vets for a couple of quid. Ticks are a real problem as they hide in the long grass waiting for unsuspecting victims to trot past. These removers, while fiddly, help you to remove the tick safely (ie without leaving its head behind buried under the dog's skin).

Being in unfamiliar territory also makes it more likely that you and your dog could become separated. All dogs now have to be **microchipped** but make sure your dog also has a **tag with your contact details on it** (a mobile phone number would be best if you are carrying one with you).

What to pack

You've probably already got a good idea of what to bring to keep your dog alive and happy, but the following is a checklist:

● **Food/water bowl** Foldable cloth bowls are popular with walkers as they are light and take up little room in the rucksack. It is also possible to get a water-bottle-and-bowl combination, where the bottle folds into a 'trough' from which the dog can drink.

● **Lead and collar** An extendable one is probably preferable for this sort of trip. Make sure both lead and collar are in good condition – you don't want either to snap on the trail, or you may end up carrying your dog through sheep fields until a replacement can be found.

● **Medication** You'll know if you need to bring any lotions or potions.

● **Tick remover** See p231.

● **Bedding** A simple blanket may suffice, or you can opt for something more elaborate if you aren't carrying your own luggage.

● **Poo bags** Essential.

● **Hygiene wipes** For cleaning your dog after it's rolled in stuff.

● **A favourite toy** Helps prevent your dog from pining for the entire walk.

● **Food/water** Remember to bring treats as well as regular food to keep up the mutt's morale.

● **Corkscrew stake** Available from camping or pet shops, this will help you to keep your dog secure in one place while you set up camp/doze.

● **Raingear** It can rain a lot!

● **Old towels** For drying your dog after the deluge.

Dogs on beaches

Bear in mind that during certain times of year dogs are banned from some of the North Norfolk beaches; from 1st May to 30th September inclusive you can not take dogs onto the main beaches at Wells, Sheringham or Cromer and they must be kept on a lead on promenades or stretches of coast adjacent to these areas. For more information visit 💻 www.explorenorfolkuk.co.uk/dog-friendly-beaches.html or check the suggestions in the *Norfolk Beaches Handbook* (see p45).

Where dogs are banned from a beach there will usually be an alternative path that you can take that avoids the sands. If there isn't an alternative, and you have no choice but to cross the beach even though dogs are officially banned, you are permitted to do so as long as you cross the beach as speedily as possible, follow the line of the path (which is usually well above the high-water mark) and keep your dog tightly under control **on a lead**.

Whatever the rules of access are for the beach, remember that your dog shouldn't disturb other beach-users – and you must always **clean up after your dog**.

Finally, remember that you need to bring drinking water with you on the beach as dogs can overheat with the lack of shade.

❏ **Packing for your dog**

When it comes to packing, I always leave an exterior pocket of my rucksack empty so I can put used poo bags in there (for deposit at the first bin I come to). I always like to keep all the dog's kit together and separate from the other luggage (usually inside a plastic bag inside my rucksack). I have also seen several dogs sporting their own 'doggy rucksack, so they can carry their own food, water, poo etc – which certainly reduces the burden on their owner!   **Henry Stedman**

When to keep your dog on a lead

● **When crossing farmland**, particularly in the lambing season (around May) when your dog can scare the sheep, causing them to lose their young. Farmers are allowed by law to shoot at and kill any dogs that they consider are worrying their sheep. During lambing, most farmers would prefer it if you didn't bring your dog at all.

The exception is if your dog is being attacked by cows. There have been deaths in the UK caused by walkers being trampled as they tried to rescue their dogs from the attentions of cattle. The advice in this instance is to let go of the lead, head speedily to a position of safety (usually the other side of the field gate or stile) and call your dog to you.

● **On National Trust land**, where it is compulsory to keep your dog on a lead.

● **In or close to nature reserves** When passing through or close to nature reserves along the Coast Path you should keep the dog on a short lead.

● **Around ground-nesting birds** It's important to keep your dog under control when crossing an area where certain species of birds nest on the ground. Most dogs love foraging around in the woods but make sure you have permission to do so; some woods are used as 'nurseries' for game birds and dogs are only allowed through them if they are on a lead.

● **On cliff tops** It's a sad fact that, every year, a few dogs lose their lives falling over the edge of the cliffs. It usually occurs when they are chasing rabbits (which know where the cliff-edge is and are able, unlike your poor pooch, to stop in time).

Cleaning up after your dog

It is extremely important that dog owners behave in a responsible way when walking the path and all excrement should be cleaned up. In towns, villages and fields where animals graze or which will be cut for silage, hay etc, you need to pick up and bag the excrement. In other places you can possibly get away with merely flicking it with a nearby stick into the undergrowth, thus ensuring there is none left on the path to decorate the boots of others.

If your dog is anything like others, it'll wait until you are 300m past the nearest bin – and about four miles from the next one – before relieving itself. Don't be tempted to leave it, but bag it up; this means you're likely to have to carry it for a couple of miles – just look on it as your own personalised little hand warmer.

Staying and eating with your dog

In this guide we have used the symbol 🐕 to denote where a hotel, pub or B&B welcomes dogs. However, this always needs to be arranged in advance and some places may charge extra. Hostels (both YHA and independent) do not permit them unless they are an assistance (guide) dog; smaller campsites tend to accept them, but some of the larger holiday parks do not. Before you turn up always double check whether the place you would like to stay accepts dogs and whether there is space for them; many places have only one or two rooms suitable for people with dogs. In some cases you may need to pay an additional charge (mostly £10 per dog per night but occasionally more).

When it comes to **eating**, most landlords allow dogs in at least a section of their pubs, though few restaurants do. Make sure you always ask first and ensure your dog doesn't run around the pub but is secured to your table or a radiator.

Map key

♠	Where to stay	📖	Library/bookstore	●	Other
○	Where to eat and drink	@	Internet	CP	Car park
⩑	Campsite	🍷	Museum/gallery	🚌	Bus station/stop
⊠	Post Office	✝	Church/cathedral	▭	Rail line & station
⑧	Bank/ATM	☎	Phone box	▭	Park
①	Tourist Information	☑	Public toilet	📱082	GPS waypoint
		☐	Building		

⟋	Peddars Way/ Norfolk Coast Path	⫽	Gate	∼ ∼ ∼ ∼	Water
⟋	Other Path	✕	Stile	⟋	River
⟋	4 x 4 track	⥿	Boardwalk	⋰	Beach
∥	Tarmac road	⟋	Bridge	↓ ↓	Salt marsh
⫻	Steps	⌇	Hedge	⇞	Conifer trees
↗	Slope	⁚	Fence	♧ ♧	Deciduous trees
⇗	Steep slope	╱	Disused railway line	➋	Map continuation

INDEX

Page references in **bold** type refer to maps

TRAILBLAZER TREKKING GUIDES
Europe
British Walking Guides – 18-title series
Scottish Highlands – The Hillwalking Guide
Tour du Mont Blanc
Walker's Haute Route: Mt Blanc – Matterhorn

South America
Inca Trail, Cusco & Machu Picchu
Peru's Cordilleras Blanca & Huayhuash

Africa
Kilimanjaro
Moroccan Atlas – The Trekking Guide
Asia
Nepal Trekking & The Great Himalaya Trail
Sinai – the trekking guide
Trekking in the Everest Region
Australasia
New Zealand – The Great Walks

Tour du Mont Blanc *Jim Manthorpe,* 2nd edn, £13.99
ISBN 978-1-905864-92-8, 204pp, 60 maps, 30 colour photos
At 4807m (15,771ft), Mont Blanc is the highest mountain in western Europe. The trail (105 miles, 168km) that circumnavigates the massif, passing through France, Italy and Switzerland, is the most popular long-distance walk in Europe. Includes background and history plus town guides to Chamonix, Cormayeur and Argentière.

Peru's Cordilleras Blanca & Huayhuash
The Hiking & Biking Guide
Neil & Harriet Pike, 1st edn, £15.99
ISBN 978-1-905864-63-8, 242pp, 50 maps, 40 colour photos
This region, in northern Peru, boasts some of the most spectacular scenery in the Andes, and most accessible high mountain trekking and biking in the world. This practical guide contains 60 detailed route maps and descriptions covering 20 hiking trails and more than 30 days of paved and dirt road cycling.

Kilimanjaro – the trekking guide
Henry Stedman, 5th edn, £14.99
ISBN 978-1-905864-95-9, 368pp, 40 maps, 50 colour photos
At 5895m (19,340ft) Kilimanjaro is the world's tallest freestanding mountain and one of the most popular destinations for hikers visiting Africa. Route guides & maps – the 6 major routes. City guides – Nairobi, Dar-es-Salaam, Arusha, Moshi & Marangu.

Moroccan Atlas – the trekking guide
Alan Palmer, 2nd edn, £14.99
ISBN 978-1-905864-59-1, 420pp, 86 maps, 40 colour photos
The High Atlas in central Morocco is the most dramatic and beautiful section of the entire Atlas range. Towering peaks, deep gorges and huddled Berber villages enchant all who visit. With 73 detailed trekking maps, 13 town and village guides including Marrakech.

Trekking in the Everest Region
Jamie McGuinness 6th edn, £15.99
ISBN 978-1-905864-81-2, 320pp, 95 maps, 30 colour photos
Sixth edition of this popular guide to the world's most famous trekking region. Covers not only the classic treks but also the wild routes. Written by a Nepal-based trek and mountaineering leader. Includes: 27 detailed route maps and 52 village plans. Plus: Kathmandu city guide

TRAILBLAZER'S LONG-DISTANCE PATH (LDP) WALKING GUIDES

We've applied to destinations which are closer to home Trailblazer's proven formula for publishing definitive practical route guides for adventurous travellers. Britain's network of long-distance trails enables the walker to explore some of the finest landscapes in the country's best walking areas. These are guides that are user-friendly, practical, informative and environmentally sensitive.

'The same attention to detail that distinguishes its other guides has been brought to bear here'.
THE *SUNDAY TIMES*

● **Unique mapping features** In many walking guidebooks the reader has to read a route description then try to relate it to the map. Our guides are much easier to use because walking directions, tricky junctions, places to stay and eat, points of interest and walking times are all written onto the maps themselves in the places to which they apply. With their uncluttered clarity, these are not general-purpose maps but fully edited maps drawn by walkers for walkers.

● **Largest-scale walking maps** At a scale of just under 1:20,000 (8cm or 3¹/₈ inches to one mile) the maps in these guides are bigger than even the most detailed British walking maps currently available in the shops.

● **Not just a trail guide – includes where to stay, where to eat and public transport** Our guidebooks cover the complete walking experience, not just the route. Accommodation options for all budgets are provided (pubs, hotels, B&Bs, campsites, bunkhouses, hostels) as well as places to eat. Detailed public transport information for all access points to each trail means that there are itineraries for all walkers, for hiking the entire route as well as for day or weekend walks.

● **Includes dowloadable GPS waypoints –** Marked on our maps and downloadable from the Trailblazer website.

Cleveland Way *Henry Stedman*, 1st edn, ISBN 978-1-905864-91-1, 208pp, 56 maps

Coast to Coast *Henry Stedman*, 8th edn, ISBN 978-1-905864-96-6, 268pp, 110 maps

Cornwall Coast Path (SW Coast Path Pt 2) *Stedman & Newton*, 5th edn, ISBN 978-1-905864-71-3, 352pp, 142 maps

Cotswold Way *Tricia & Bob Hayne*, 3rd edn, ISBN 978-1-905864-70-6, 204pp, 53 maps,

Dales Way *Henry Stedman,* 1st edn, ISBN 978-1-905864-78-2, 192pp, 50 maps

Dorset & South Devon (SW Coast Path Pt 3) *Stedman & Newton*, 2nd edn, ISBN 978-1-905864-94-2, 336pp, 88 maps

Exmoor & North Devon (SW Coast Path Pt I) *Stedman & Newton*, 2nd edn, ISBN 978-1-905864-86-7, 224pp, 68 maps

Great Glen Way *Jim Manthorpe,* 1st edn, ISBN 978-1-905864-80-5, 192pp, 55 maps

Hadrian's Wall Path *Henry Stedman*, 5th edn, ISBN 978-1-905864-85-0, 224pp, 60 maps

Norfolk Coast Path & Peddars Way *Alexander Stewart*, 1st edn, ISBN 978-1-905864-98-0, 224pp, 75 maps,

North Downs Way *Henry Stedman*, 2nd edn, ISBN 978-1-905864-90-4, 240pp, 98 maps

Offa's Dyke Path *Keith Carter*, 4th edn, ISBN 978-1-905864-65-2, 240pp, 98 maps

Pembrokeshire Coast Path *Jim Manthorpe*, 5th edn, ISBN 978-1-905864-84-3, 236pp, 96 maps,

Pennine Way *Stuart Greig*, 4th edn, ISBN 978-1-905864-61-4, 272pp, 138 maps

The Ridgeway *Nick Hill*, 4th edn, ISBN 978-1-905864-79-9, 208pp, 53 maps

South Downs Way *Jim Manthorpe*, 6th edn, ISBN 978-1-905864-93-5, 204pp, 60 maps

Thames Path *Joel Newton*, 2nd edn, ISBN 978-1-905864-97-3, 256pp, 99 maps

West Highland Way *Charlie Loram*, 6th edn, ISBN 978-1-905864-76-8, 218pp, 60 maps

'The Trailblazer series stands head, shoulders, waist and ankles above the rest.
They are particularly strong on mapping ...'
THE SUNDAY TIMES

TRAILBLAZER
British Walking Guides
SEE OVERLEAF FOR FULL TITLE LIST

Great Glen WAY

Dales Way

THE Ridgeway

South Downs WAY

North Downs WAY

Thames Path

Orkney

Thurso

Stornoway

Scottish Highlands Hillwalking Guide

Inverness

Skye

Great Glen Way

Aberdeen

Fort William

SCOTLAND

Mull

West Highland Way

Edinburgh

Milngavie

Glasgow

Berwick upon Tweed

Arran

Kirk Yetholm

Pennine Way

Hadrian's Wall Path

Bowness-on-Solway

Wallsend

Newcastle upon Tyne

N. IRELAND

Carlisle

Coast to Coast

St Bees

Robin Hood's Bay

Belfast

Bowness-on-Windermere

Filey

Dales Way

Helmsley

Cleveland Way

REP. OF IRELAND

Isle of Man

Ilkley

York

Dublin

Pennine Way

Leeds

Hull

IRISH SEA

Liverpool

Manchester

Edale

Norfolk Coast Path & Peddars Way

Anglesey

Prestatyn

Lincoln

Bangor

Crewe

Cromer

Nottingham

Norwich

Offa's Dyke Path

Birmingham

ENGLAND

Great Yarmouth

Knettishall Heath

Cardigan

Cotswold Way

Cambridge

The Ridgeway

Chipping Campden

WALES

Kemble

Ivinghoe Beacon

Pembrokeshire Coast Path

Amroth

Chepstow

London

Thames Path

Cardiff

Bristol

Canterbury

Bath

Exmoor & N Devon Coast Path

Overton Hill

Farnham

Dover

Minehead

Winchester

Salisbury

Portsmouth

Eastbourne

Brighton

North Downs Way

Bude

Exeter

Poole

Cornwall Coast Path

Plymouth

Isle of Wight

South Downs Way

sles of Scilly

Dorset & S Devon Coast Path

ENGLISH CHANNEL

| 0 | 50 | 100km |
| 0 | 25 | 50 miles |

TRAILBLAZER TITLE LIST

Adventure Cycle-Touring Handbook
Adventure Motorcycling Handbook
Australia by Rail
Cleveland Way (British Walking Guide)
Coast to Coast (British Walking Guide)
Cornwall Coast Path (British Walking Guide)
Cotswold Way (British Walking Guide)
The Cyclist's Anthology
Dales Way (British Walking Guide)
Dorset & Sth Devon Coast Path (British Walking Gde)
Exmoor & Nth Devon Coast Path (British Walking Gde)
Great Glen Way (British Walking Guide)
Hadrian's Wall Path (British Walking Guide)
Himalaya by Bike – a route and planning guide
Inca Trail, Cusco & Machu Picchu
Japan by Rail
Kilimanjaro – the trekking guide (includes Mt Meru)
Madeira Walks – 37 selected day walks
Moroccan Atlas – The Trekking Guide
Morocco Overland (4WD/motorcycle/mountainbike)
Nepal Trekking & The Great Himalaya Trail
New Zealand – The Great Walks
North Downs Way (British Walking Guide)
Offa's Dyke Path (British Walking Guide)
Overlanders' Handbook – worldwide driving guide
Peddars Way & Norfolk Coast Path (British Walking Gde)
Pembrokeshire Coast Path (British Walking Guide)
Pennine Way (British Walking Guide)
Peru's Cordilleras Blanca & Huayhuash – Hiking/Biking
The Railway Anthology
The Ridgeway (British Walking Guide)
Sahara Overland – a route and planning guide
Scottish Highlands – Hillwalking Guide
Siberian BAM Guide – rail, rivers & road
The Silk Roads – a route and planning guide
Sinai – the trekking guide
South Downs Way (British Walking Guide)
Thames Path (British Walking Guide)
Tour du Mont Blanc
Trans-Canada Rail Guide
Trans-Siberian Handbook
Trekking in the Everest Region
The Walker's Anthology
The Walker's Anthology – further tales
The Walker's Haute Route – Mont Blanc to Matterhorn
West Highland Way (British Walking Guide)

For more information about Trailblazer and our
expanding range of guides, for guidebook updates or
for credit card mail order sales visit our website:

www.trailblazer-guides.com

Maps 1-8
Knettishall Heath to Little Cressingham

14½ miles/23km – 5hrs

NOTE: Add 20-30% to these times to allow for stops

East Walton
○ East Walton

B1153

West Lexham

B1145

Litcham
○ Litcham

MAP 14
Castle Acre
○ Castle Acre

West Acre
○ West Acre

East Lexham
○ East Lexham

Beeston
○ Beeston

MAP 13

South Acre
○ South Acre

Great Dunham
○ Great Dunham

Narborough
○ Narborough

A47

A1065

MAP 12

Little Dunham
○ Little Dunham

A47

○ **Sporle**

A1122

A47

MAP 11

Swaffham
○ Swaffham

Necton
○ Necton

0 — 2 miles
0 — 3km

MAP 10

Bradenham
○ Bradenham

North Pickenham
○ North Pickenham

Beachamwell
○ Beachamwell

South Pickenham
○ South Pickenham

MAP 9

Saham Hills
○ Saham Hills

Cockley Cley
○ Cockley Cley

○ **Ashill**

A1075

Gooderstone
○ Gooderstone

Great Cressingham
○ Great Cressingham

MAP 8

Ovington
○ Ovington

Oxborough
○ Oxborough

Hilborough
○ Hilborough

Watton
○ Watton

Carbrooke
○ Carbrooke

Little Cressingham
○ Little Cressingham

B1108

A1075

B1108

Merton
○ Merton

Griston
○ Griston

A1065

Northwold
○ Northwold

MAP 7

100m
75
25

Little Cressingham — **North Pickenham** — *A47 (Turn for Swaffham)* — **South Acre** — **Castle Acre**

A1065

0 miles 2   3   4   5   6   7   8   9   10   11

Holme-next-the-Sea

Hunstanton

Castle Acre

Little Cressingham

Hopton-on-Sea

Knettishall Heath

Maps 8-13

Little Cressingham to

Castle Acre

11½ miles/18.5km

4hrs 10mins-4½hr:

NOTE: Add 20-30% to these times to allow for stop

Maps 13–22

Castle Acre to Ringstead

17 miles/27km – 6-6¼hr

Ringstead to Holme-next-the-Sea (and Hunstanton)

Maps 22-23 (& 23-25)

2½ miles/4km – ¾-1hr

(to Hunstanton add 2½ miles/4km – 1-1½hrs)

NOTE: Add 20-30% to these times to allow for stops

MAP 26

Brancaster Bay

MAP 24

MAP 27

Brancaster
Staithe

MAP 30

Holkham Bay

MAP 31

Old
Hunstanton

A149

Holme-
next-
the-Sea

Titchwell

Thornham

Brancaster

Burnham
Deepdale

MAP 29

Burnham
Norton

Burnham
Overy
Staithe

MAP 23

MAP 25

Hunstanton

MAP 28

Burnham
Market

Burnham
Thorpe

Ringstead

Heacham

MAP 22

North
Creake

MAP 21

B1454

B1153

B1155

B1355

Sedgeford

Docking

Stanhoe

South
Creake

A149

MAP 20

Fring

B1454

Snettisham

B1153

B1155

Syderstone

Ingoldisthorpe

MAP 19

Great
Bircham

Bircham
Tofts

Holme-next-the-Sea

Burnham
Overy Staithe

Hunstanton

Hopton-
on-Sea

Knettishall
Heath

Maps (25-23) & 26-31
Hunstanton to
Burnham Overy Staithe

13½ miles/21.5km – 5¼-6¼hrs

NOTE: Add 20-30% to these times to allow for stops

MAP 30

MAP 31

MAP 32

MAP 33

MAP 34

MAP 36

MAP 37

MAP 35

Holkham Bay

0 ____ 2 miles

0 ____ 3km

Burnham Deepdale

Burnham Norton

Burnham Overy Staithe

Burnham Overy Town

Burnham Market

Burnham Thorpe

Holkham

A149

Wells-next-the-Sea

Stiffkey

Morston

Warham

Westgate

Langham

Wighton

Binham

Field Dalling

B1155

B1355

North Creake

Little Walsingham

Stanhoe

South Creake

Hindringham

Gunthorpe

B1355

West Barsham

Great Snoring

B1105

Thursford

A148

Syderstone

East Barsham

Little Snoring

Barney

Swanton Novers

B1454

Sculthorpe

Kettlestone

B1110

Coxford

Fakenham

A148

A1067

Hempton

100m
75
50
25

Burnham Overy Staithe

Wells-next-the-Sea

Stiffkey

0 miles   2   3   4   5   6   7   8   9   10

---

olme-next-the-Sea

Stiffkey

Burnham Overy Staithe

Hunstanton

Hopton-on-Sea

Knettishall Heath

Maps 31-36
Burnham Overy Staithe to Stiffkey

10 miles/16km – 3½-4hrs

NOTE: Add 20-30% to these times to allow for stops

MAP 35

MAP 36

MAP 37

MAP 38

MAP 39

MAP 40

MAP 41

MAP 42

Morston

Blakeney

Cley next
the Sea

Salthouse

A149

Stiffkey

Kelling

Weybourne

A149

Warham

Upper
Sheringham

Westgate

Langham

B1156

Bodham

A148

Wighton

Binham

Letheringsett

High
Kelling

West
Beckham

Field
Dalling

A148

B1110

Holt

Hindringham

Thornage

Hempstead

Baconsthorpe

Great
Snoring

Gunthorpe

Brinton

Plumstead

A148

Briningham

Edgefield

Matlaske

Thursford

B1354

Little
Barningham

B1149

Barney

Melston
Constable

Briston

Little
Snoring

Swanton
Novers

Saxthorpe

Itteringham

A1067

B1110

Corpusty

Hindolveston

```
100m
75
50          Blakeney
25  Stiffkey  Morston        Cley next
                             the Sea                Weybourne
 0 miles  2   3   4   5   6   7   8   9  10  11  12
```

Holme-next-the-Sea

Weybourne

Stiffkey

Hunstanton

Hopton-
on-Sea

Knettishall
Heath

Maps 36-41

Stiffkey to Weybourne

12 miles/19km – 5-5¼hr

NOTE: Add 20-30% to these times to allow for stop

MAP 40

MAP 41

Sheringham

MAP 42

MAP 43

West Runton

East Runton

MAP 44

Cromer

MAP 45

MAP 46

Overstrand

MAP 47

Salthouse

Kelling

Weybourne

A149

Upper
Sheringham

Beeston
Regis

Felbrigg

Northrepps

Bodham

A148

Crossdale
Street

Trimingham

High
Kelling

West
Beckham

Aylmerton

Gresham

Roughton

A149

Southrepps

Holt

Baconsthorpe

Hempstead

B1436

Lower
Street

Plumstead

Matlaske

A140

Trunch

Edgefield

Little
Barningham

Antingham

B1149

Erpingham

Saxthorpe

Itteringham

A149

B1145

North
Walsham

Corpusty

B1150

Oulton
Street

B1149

B1145

Aylsham

---

0   2 miles

0   3km

Weybourne
100m
75   Sheringham
50
25   Cromer

0 miles   2   3   4   5   6   7

---

olme-next-the-Sea

Cromer

Weybourne

Hunstanton

Hopton-
on-Sea

Knettishall
Heath

Maps 41-45
Weybourne to Cromer

7½ miles/12km – 2¾-3¾hrs

NOTE: Add 20-30% to these times to allow for stops

Cromer
MAP 46
Overstrand
MAP 47
Sidestrand

Crossdale
Street
Trimingham
Roughton **MAP 48**
Cliftonville
MAP 49
Mundesley
Southrepps
Lower
Street **MAP 50**
Trunch
Knapton **MAP 51**
Antingham
Bacton
MAP 52
Walcott
North
Walsham
Witton
Ostend
MAP 53
Happisburgh
East
Ruston
Eccles on Sea
Honing
Lessingham
MAP 54
Sea Palling
Stalham **MAP 55**

Baldersfield
Scottow
Smallburgh
Sutton

0 | 2 miles
0 | 3km

100m
75 Cromer Overstrand Walcott Happisburgh
50
Mundesley Bacton Ostend Eccles Sea
Cliftonville on Sea Palling
0 miles 2 3 4 5 6 7 8 9 10 11 12 13 14 15 16 17 18

Holme-next-the-Sea
Cromer
Mundesley
Hunstanton
Sea Palling
Hopton-
on-Sea
Knettishall
Heath

Maps 45-49, Cromer t
Mundesley 8 miles/12.5km – 3h
Maps 49-55, Mundesley t
Sea Palling 10 miles/16km – 4h
NOTE: Add 20-30% to these times to allow for sto

MAP 54

Sea Palling

0 miles ——— 2 miles
0 ——— 3km

MAP 55

Waxham

MAP 56

Horsey Gap

Horsey

MAP 57

trailblazer

Winterton-on-Sea

MAP 58

Martham

MAP 59

Hemsby

Ormesby

Scratby

Saint Margaret

California

Fleggburgh

Caister-on-Sea

A1064

Thrigby

MAP 60

Runham

Caister-on-Sea

A1064

Thrigby

MAP 60

Runham

Newtown

MAP 61

MAP 62

GREAT YARMOUTH

Gorleston-on-Sea

MAP 63

Belton

MAP 64

A143

Hopton-on-Sea

B1047

Lound

Blundeston

Corton

LOWESTOFT

A47

100m
75
50
25

Sea Palling

Winterton-on-Sea

Newport

Scratby California

Caister-on-Sea

Newtown

Great Yarmouth

Gorleston-on-Sea

Hopton-on-Sea

0 miles 2 3 4 5 6 7 8 9 10 11 12 13 14 15 16 17 18 19 20

Maps 55-60
Sea Palling to Caister-on-Sea
10½ miles/17km – 4½hrs

olme-next-the-Sea

Hunstanton

Sea Palling

Caister-on-Sea

Hopton-on-Sea

Knettishall
Heath

Maps 60-64, Caister-on-Sea to
Hopton-on-Sea
10 miles/16km – 4hrs
NOTE: Add 20-30% to these times to allow for stops

Peddars Way

Norfolk Coast Path